Professional Development of English Teachers

Xianping Yang

Copyright © 2023 Dean & Francis Press

All rights reserved. No part of this publication may be reproduced, distributed, or transmitted in any form or by any means, including photocopying, recording, or other electronic or mechanical methods, without the prior written permission of the publisher, except in the case of brief quotations embodied in critical reviews and certain other noncommercial uses permitted by copyright law.

Title: Professional Development of English Teachers
Author: Xianping Yang
Edition: 1 Edition

ISBN: 979-8-89120-002-9

Published by Dean & Francis Press
201 E Center ST STE
Anatheim, CA, 92805
acceptance@deanfrancispress.com

Printing History: None
First Printing: June, 2023

Legal Disclaimers:

The copyright of this book belongs to Dean & Francis, and no one is allowed to use it without compensation. If you need to use it, please contact the official email address. Only after approval can it be used for academic or commercial purposes.

Trademarks:

Indicate any trademarks included in the book and state the ownership of those trademarks belongs to the author and Dean & Francis Press.

Preface

The improvement of foreign language teachers' professional level has gone through several stages, from initial teacher training to teacher education, to teacher development, and finally to teacher specialization. It reflects the process of people's in-depth understanding of teachers' professional development from elementary to advanced. Educators have come to realize that qualified teachers in the new era should not only master a little knowledge of their major and attend several classes, but also possess a wide range of knowledge and skills. At the same time, they should be not only a teacher, but also an educator and researcher. This book is a reflection of this teaching philosophy.

This book mainly consists of three parts: general education theory part, involving pedagogy, psychology and other related disciplines of theoretical overview; foreign language teaching and research is the theoretical knowledge part of foreign language teaching; case studies are some empirical studies and other relevant cases. These three parts cover the quasi-professional knowledge, professional knowledge and practical knowledge of teachers' professional development. It is a practical reference for language learners and language teachers to learn theoretical knowledge in pre-service and in-service.

The author of this book has accumulated knowledge through years of study and teaching practice, and his writing process has witnessed the professional growth of a foreign language teacher. The author shares what he learns, knows and feels during his professional growth with his peers and readers in order to learn from each other, encourage each other and make progress together. Due to my limited level, I would like to enlighten you about errors and omissions.

Content

Introduction: Professional Development of Language Teachers 1

Chapter 1   Research on Basic Theory 7
   1.1   A review of education and human development 7
   1.2   Summary of foreign educational thoughts and schools 13
   1.3   Historical evolution of the school system 20
   1.4   Summary of teaching theory 30
   1.5   Summary of curriculum theory 46
   1.6   Review of learning theory 57
   1.7   Summary of scientific research methods 70

Chapter 2   Theory and Practice of Foreign Language Teaching 88
   2.1   Summary of the main schools of foreign language teaching methods
         88
   2.2   A review of first language acquisition research 107
   2.3   Summary of the second language acquisition research 114
   2.4   Data analysis method and use of SPSS 134
   2.5   Expression of research results 145

Chapter 3   Culture Teaching 150
   3.1   Language and culture teaching 150
   3.2   Language Teaching and Cross-cultural Communication 155
   3.3   Cultural differences and identity between the West and the East
         170
   3.4   Strategies of Cross-cultural Communication 179

Appendices　Case Study ··· 199
　　Appendix 1　Research on the "Trinity" Teaching Method in College
　　　　　　　　English Teaching ··· 199
　　Appendix 2　Investigation and Teaching Reflection on English Listening
　　　　　　　　and Speaking Ability of Overseas Chinese Students ······ 211
　　Appendix 3　Current Situation and Development Trend of Teachers'
　　　　　　　　Professionalization in Primary and Secondary Schools in
　　　　　　　　China ·· 221
　　Appendix 4　A Contrastive Study on Irish TY Education and Chinese
　　　　　　　　Secondary Education ·· 239
　　Appendix 5　College English Oral Assessment Reform ··················· 248
　　Appendix 6　Analysis of Irish Innovation Education ······················ 257

References ·· 273

Introduction:
Professional Development of Language Teachers

The development of society is increasingly demanding the profession of teachers. With the development of time and the advancement of science, the content and requirements of teaching are constantly changing with the social development. This requires teachers to keep up with the pace of time and constantly update their knowledge structure. The requirements for foreign language teachers are constantly changing. From the professional bookmakers' requirements to the professional researchers, this is not a simple leap, but from the initial teacher training to teacher education, and a series of educational concepts such as teacher development. At present, foreign language teachers should not only pay attention to how to get a good class, but should pay more attention to improving students' creative thinking ability, carrying out comprehensive quality education, and improving students' comprehensive language ability. This requires teachers to pay attention to the "education" of students, observe students' learning behaviors, evaluate teaching effects, encourage teachers to reflect on teaching, and conduct teaching research. It is not enough to master the knowledge of this major. It is necessary to strengthen the education of teachers themselves, and to study psychology, education, anthropology, linguistics, language testing and evaluation, scientific research methods and modernity related to teaching. Multidisciplinary knowledge such as educational technology. At the same time, language teachers should not only focus on the study of theoretical knowledge, but also conduct research on teaching practice, organically combine teaching and practice, and continuously improve teaching skills and scientific research capabilities. Therefore, modern teachers must constantly update their knowledge, apply it to educational teaching theory to study teaching behavior, and cultivate scientific research consciousness and lifelong learning. Therefore, "teachers are researchers" is the requirement of teachers for the development of time. The professionalization of teachers is also put on the historical development agenda and becomes the trend of teacher development.

What is the professional development of teachers? The professional development of teachers is essentially the professionalization of teachers. Teacher professionalization means that teachers have gradually acquired the knowledge and skills of the education profession through specialized training and lifelong learning throughout their careers, and continuously improve their teaching quality in the practice of education, thus becoming a qualified professional education work. **Process of the person**. This definition has two meanings: it means that the individual teachers are trained to become mature teachers with professional knowledge, professional skills and professional attitudes and their sustainable professional development process; it also refers to the professional career of teachers from non-professional, quasi-professional to specialized.

Process of development. In 2001, the Department of Education of the Ministry of Education also clearly stated the connotation of teacher specialization, that is, "teachers through lifelong professional training throughout the professional life, acquire educational professional knowledge and skills, implement pro- fessional autonomy, demonstrate professional ethics, and gradually improve professional quality. It has become a professional growth process for a good educator.

It is not difficult to see from the definition that teacher specialization puts forward specific professional requirements for the teacher profession: 1) The professionalism of teachers, the qualifications of teachers and the institutions of teacher education. The identification system and management system have special content and measures. There are autonomous organizations that monitor individual teachers. The profession of teachers should be the same as that of lawyers. It is not a profession that anyone can change. 2) The teacher's knowledge ability includes not only the subject professional knowledge, but also the foreign language teachers who have the professional language knowledge ability, but also the relevant professional knowledge, such as education, psychology, etc.; not only master the relevant theories of the major, but also have the proficiency teaching and practical skills; not only must have a certain ability to teach and manage, but also have a certain ability to study and teach to guide teaching. Only when the teacher industry becomes an irreplaceable industry has teacher professionalization been realized. 3) The continuity of teacher development. Teacher professional development is not a static concept. Teacher education and training requires specialized learning institutions and training systems. Teacher professional development is also a concept of development. Teacher professional development is also a process of continuous development, both as a state and as a state. In an ongoing process of deepening, teachers should be constantly trained throughout their careers to meet the needs of the times. 4) Lifelong learning awareness. The need to develop self-professional development in teaching practice activities, and the choice of teacher profession means the choice of lifelong learning.

It can be seen that the professional quality of teachers is the key to the professionalization of teachers. Strengthening teacher literacy is nothing more than two aspects. On the one hand, it is a teacher's morality. The new era has more requirements for these two aspects. The so-called teacher morality is also the professional quality of teachers. The traditional "teacher's morality" refers to the noble moral sentiment and the virtue of being a teacher. This is only the tip of the iceberg of the meaning of the teacher. In the new era, teachers are given new professional accomplishment requirements. In addition to noble personality, they also include the professionalism of teachers, such as professionalism, humanistic spirit, and scientific spirit. The humanistic spirit is a universal human self-care, manifested in the maintenance, pursuit and concern of human dignity, value, destiny, the high cherishment of various spiritual and cultural phenomena left over by mankind, and the ideal personality for a comprehensive development. The affirmation and shaping of the humanities are the knowledge education system that focuses on the humanistic spirit. It focuses on human values and spiritual performance. Education in the true sense is actually a cultural process. Once education loses its culture, what remains is the displacement of knowledge, the training of skills, and the preparation for the exam. The scientific spirit refers to the study of teaching and teaching objects, the ability to discover problems in teaching, the continuous reform and practice, and the spirit of research to promote the quality of teaching. There are four points in the professional spirit: self-cultivation, professional responsibility (ie, caring and respecting each student and seeking truth from facts) , the spirit of work and the constant development of self-development. Teachers are still the model of students, leading students to learn in a down-to-earth manner and to be serious. Professional ethics is of great significance to the professionalization of teachers, because ethics is the soul of educational activities. As Goodson said: "Teaching is first and foremost a moral and ethical profession. The new professionalism needs to be reaffirmed as a guiding principle. " In the current field of education, normative ethics replaces moral ethics. It has caused the ethical dilemma of teacher specialization. Virtue ethics is an ethics derived from individual virtues. It is an ethic with individual virtue as its self-determination. It has the characteristics of internality, self-discipline and transcendence. Normative ethics pays attention to moral principles and regulates the actual behavioral effects, but ignores the concern for people themselves, resulting in widespread "personal division" and moral crisis. Modern society is dominated by normative ethics, pursuing the completeness of normative constraints, and virtue ethics is marginalized in modernity. The connotation of educational activities is not only to impart knowledge and training skills, but also to engage in educational exchanges between the subjects around knowledge, emotions and values, and to construct a meaningful world based on such interactions. Therefore, teachers' professional ethics must be based on virtue ethics rather than normative ethics. The core of teachers' professional moral ethics is the understanding and practice of the meaning of life and education. Its form is the realm of freedom rather than obeying norms. Its motivation is the sense of meaning of self-transcendence rather than the fear of punishment. Reflect, experience, comprehend, not restraint, coercion, command, to achieve specialization in the profession of teachers, it is necessary to construct this kind of morality based on meaning experience. However, the moral ethics pursued by teacher specialization is difficult to form. In reality, modernity alienates teachers' professional ethics into management norms formulated according to the norms of teaching methods and bureaucratic power through instrumental rationality and technical rationality, and uses teaching skills to teach knowledge efficiently to ensure the standardized ethics of student exam success. Teachers' professional self-awareness and life attitude are full of instrumental rationality and interest-oriented tendency, which makes it difficult to construct a moral ethic based on individual meaning experience, thus making teacher professionalization fall into ethical dilemma. Therefore, strengthening teachers' ethics and morality is an important part of teacher modernization.

　　The other is the teacher's intellectual ability. People often regard the profession of teachers as "semi-professional", "quasi-professional" or "professional in formation". From such a title, we have to admit that there is still a long way to go before the requirements of the profession of teachers. Therefore, strengthening teachers' knowledge ability is the fundamental requirement of teacher specialization. In general, the teacher's knowledge ability includes three aspects: professional knowledge, quasi-professional knowledge and practical knowledge. The professional knowledge of the teacher is not only the professional knowledge of the taught course, but also the language application ability of the foreign language teacher and the basic skills of the teaching. It is the most basic component of the professional knowledge of the teacher. Furthermore, language and culture literacy is indispensable, understand the culture of the relevant language countries, and have relevant theories such as linguistics, second language acquisition theory, and English teaching method. It should be pointed out that it is also important to have a deep understanding of the native language and culture. It is conducive to teachers' cultural comparative study in teaching. In addition, the curriculum is the core of education. Knowledge must be transformed through the teaching work of teachers. Teachers must not only have the ability to process teaching materials and teach courses, but also have the ability to develop curriculum and textbooks. Quasi-professional knowledge refers to the necessary knowledge about the successful completion of teaching tasks and research. It includes multidisciplinary knowledge such as education, psychology, sociology, and statistics, because foreign language teaching and research involve many problems, not just language knowledge itself. Practical knowledge refers to educational technologies related to education and teaching, such as multimedia application technology and scientific research methods. For example, teachers should be able to use teaching methods and experimental data analysis using questionnaires, interviews, scales, SPSS and other practical research methods.

  To improve the knowledge literacy of these two aspects requires constant efforts. On the one hand, foreign language teachers must strengthen their professional qualities, while strengthening independent learning, and constantly improve their theoretical level and practical ability. Change the teaching concept and use the critical teaching reflection method to participate in, reflect, criticize, improve and improve education and teaching. It is necessary to have the spirit of educational research, use multi-disciplinary research methods to conduct teaching research, research to promote teaching, and promote teaching through teaching; develop awareness and cultivate lifelong learning habits. The profession of a teacher is a profession that needs lifelong development. It needs constant " charging" to meet the needs of social development. On the other hand, education management departments at different levels should continually carry out curriculum reforms, strengthen the training of teachers before and during their work, and continuously improve the overall quality of teachers. Teachers are the implementers of educational activities. Teachers' moral cultivation, healthy psychological quality, broad knowledge horizons and innovative spirit all play an important role in education. Professor Larsen-Freeman talked about his career as a teacher, "In the beginning, I was learning to teach. After a while, with some experience, I was learning teaching. And now I can identify a third Stage in my own development—just learning". Thus, the professional development of teachers is a process from a bookmaker to a researcher, and this process can be achieved after years of study and practice.

Chapter 1
Research on Basic Theory

1.1 A review of education and human development

To understand the relationship between education and human development, we must first define what is meant by "human development". Generally speaking, human development is very complicated. It is a process of life and growth. It is a process of "giving", "self-selection" and "self-construction", interacting and transforming each other. The process of checks and balances and mutual coordination is reflected in the continuous and stable development and change of the physical, psychological, social culture and explicit behaviors within the individual.

1.1.1 Human development concept

Human development mainly refers to the overall process of human beings in the whole process of life, with the increase of age and social life experience, body and mind. That is to say, with the increase of age, the potential of the individual's potential is continuously emancipated and transformed into a realistic personality in social practice activities. This is a constantly changing process involving quantity and quality, content and structure. Simple to complex evolutionary process, human development refers to the continuous process of physical and psychological changes. It includes three aspects. Physiological development, that is, the development of structural morphology and physiological functions. It refers to the development of various organizational systems (neural system, respiratory system, etc.) of the body and the growth of its functions, the continuous enhancement of physical fitness, etc. Cognition development, that is, the development of cognitive ability, psychological characteristics, knowledge and skills, and ideology and morality. It refers to the development of cognition such as feeling, perception, and attention, the formation of intentions, interests, and other intentions, the improvement of individuality such as ability and temperament. Mastery of social experience, it refers to the acquisition of social relations and behavioral norms, and the growth of social individuals into reality. These three aspects are mutually constrained and mutually reinforcing.

1.1.2 Human development theory

1.1.2.1 Recent development zone theory

The recent development zone theory was proposed by the former Soviet educator Vygotsky. Vygotsky's research shows that there are two levels of child development: one is the current level of development, which is formed by the results of the completed development process, which shows that children can solve intellectual tasks independently; The "recent development zone" is still in a state of formation, which is the level of development that children can achieve. It is that children can not complete tasks independently, but with the help of adults, in group activities, they can accomplish these tasks through imitation. Educational activities should be based on children's second level and should be based on continually transforming their most recent development into an existing level of development. The "recent development zone" is mainly about intelligence. There are "recent development zones" in all aspects of students' psychological development. The task of teachers is to grasp the "recent development zone" in teaching and accelerate their physical and mental development.

1.1.2.2 "General development" theory

Zankov is a contemporary Soviet educator, psychologist and teaching theorist. During the 20 years from 1957 to 1977, he conducted research on the subject of "education and development" and achieved great results. He called this development "general development" and refers to the overall development of the individual with intelligence as the core, including emotion, will, personality and collectivism. In the development of intelligence, the development of thinking ability is the core. Zankov has proved that the teaching structure is an external factor that affects the general development of students. It accelerates the development of students by stimulating and promoting the occurrence and development of students' internal incentives for learning. The key to the stimulation and promotion of teaching lies in teachers. The overall grasp of teaching by teachers determines the effect of students' learning and the level of general development to a certain extent. He emphasizes the study of student development by three clues, namely observation, thinking ability and practical ability. These are the three main aspects that enable students to achieve a higher level of intellectual development than they do now. At the same time, five new teaching principles are put forward: the principle of teaching with high difficulty; the principle of teaching at a high speed; the principle of leading role of theoretical knowledge; the principle of understanding the learning process; and the principle that all students are generally developed.

Zankov's educational theory has made people realize that higher-level development is based on lower levels of development, but this process is not spontaneous. It is obtained through the positive influence of educators on the educated.

1.1.2.3 Psycho-occurrence theory

This theory can be divided into three schools:

(a) Personality School: This school emphasizes the focus on the development of the whole personality, trying to derive the development of personality from the depth of the individual motivation. However, it is limited to the description of emotions and experiences, ignores the influence of the objective environment, and lacks certain explanatory power.

(b) Cognitive Generation School: Its representative figure is Piaget. He regards cognitive development as the development process of cognitive structure, and distinguishes the stage of psychological development based on cognitive structure. It is divided into four stages:

- Sensory motor stage Sensorimotor Stage (about 0—2 years old): The main cognitive structure of children at this stage is the perceptual motion pattern. Children can coordinate the perceptual input and action response with this pattern, and rely on the action to adapt to the environment;
- Pre-operational stage Pre-operative stage (2—7 years old): Children internalize the perceptual action into representations, establish symbolic functions, and rely on psychological symbols (mainly representations) to think, thus making the thinking have a qualitative leap;
- Concrete operation stage (6, 7 years old, 11 and 12 years old): In this stage, the cognitive structure of children evolves from the representational schema of the pre-operational phase to the operational schema;

- Formal Operations Stage (1, 12 years old and beyond): During this period, children's thinking developed to the level of abstract logical reasoning.

Piaget emphasizes the biological maturity of intellectual development and believes that development is strictly determined and insurmountable. He believes that external stimuli can cause an individual's active response, or assimilation, or compliance. But the external stimulus itself has nothing to do with the intellectual development of the individual.

(c) Activity Psychology: Also known as the psychodynamics, founder Freud. Its representative is Eriksson. He developed the theory of Freud, abandoned his biologicalism and normative theory, began to notice the conflict between self and cultural life, and noticed the personal and social communication problems and emotional problems. Eriksson attempts to explain the development of personality through the inherent emotions and trends inherent in personality, and has a strong explanatory power.

1.1.3 Human development characteristics

1.1.3.1 Unfinished

(a) The person is an unfinished animal, and the incompleteness of the person is closely related to the non-specificity of the person.

(b) The child is both in an unfinished state and in an immature state.

(c) The unfinished and immature nature of child development, which implies the uncertainty, selectivity, openness and plasticity of human development, potentially huge vitality and development possibilities.

1.1.3.2 Mobility

(a) People are active and autonomously completed and perfected.

(b) Human initiative is embodied in the aspects of human initiative, autonomy, self-determination, self-determination and self-modeling.

(c) Human development is a conscious and active process, which is an important feature that distinguishes human development from animals.

1.1.4 Regularity of human development

1.1.4.1 The order of physical and mental development

It refers to the development of human body and mind is a continuous development process from low to high, from simple to complex, from quantitative to qualitative. Physical development follows the principle of self-centered to marginal and top-down; psychological development includes from specific thinking to abstract thinking, from mechanical memory to meaning memory, from primitive emotions to advanced emotions. To increase the theory of the sequential development of human movement, linguists such as Chomsky further study the order of human language acquisition, which we will specifically mention in the professional knowledge section.

1.1.4.2 The imbalance of physical and mental development

One refers to the development of the same aspect, and the development at different ages is uneven; the second is the imbalance of development in different aspects. This imbalance is the critical period, which refers to the function and ability of a certain aspect of the body or mind. The most appropriate period of formation, during which the educational effects exerted on a particular aspect of the individual can be optimally obtained. By studying the relationship between brain damage and language recovery and the study of language behaviors deprived by children and the study of second language learning, language scientists suggest that the critical period of language development is generally between 2—12, although different scholars It is meaningful for the critical period age segment, but it is agreed that the critical period of language acquisition is affirmative.

1.1.4.3 The stage of physical and mental development

The staged performance of the individual's physical and mental development is that there are regular changes in the two adjacent stages, and the previous stage is ready for the transition to the next stage. Each stage is internally characterized by a change in quantity, which is characterized by a qualitative change.

1.1.4.4 Individual differences in physical and mental development

That is, the individual's interaction between the genetics and the environment during the growth process, so that the individual's physical and mental characteristics show different phenomena.

1.1.4.5 The integrity (complementarity) of physical and mental development

After the loss of function or loss of a certain aspect of the body, it can be compensated for by the extraordinary development of the function on the other hand. Some aspects of an individual's function may be enhanced by special training.

1.1.5 Factors affecting human development

The physical and mental development of a person is governed by a variety of factors, summed up mainly in the four aspects of genetics, environment, education and individual. Genetics refers to the physiological and anatomical features that humans inherit from the previous generation, such as the structure, morphology, sensory and nervous system characteristics, instinct, and natural tendencies. The genetic quality provides the possibility for the development of human body and mind, which determines the development of human beings. The environment is an external world that surrounds people and has an impact on human development. It includes both the natural environment and the social environment. There are two aspects to the more influential views:

(1) Single factor theory, also known as single factor determinism, believes that human development is determined by a certain factor. Commonly, there are internal and external paradoxes. The theory of internalization (genetic determinism) emphasizes that the power of human physical and mental development mainly comes from the inner needs of human beings, and the order of physical and mental development is also determined by the mechanism of physical and mental maturity. Its representative figures are Rousseau, Frobel, Ellen Kay and so on. External public opinion (environmental determinism) believes that human development depends mainly on external forces, such as environmental incentives and demands, the influence of others, and school education. The ancient Chinese scorpion, the British philosopher Locke, and the American behaviorist psychologist Watson are all representative figures. External public opinion regards psychological development as the result of external environmental influence, and denies the internal role of psychological development. Behaviorism emphasizes the influence of the environment, and ignores the subjective initiative of people.

(2) Multi-factor interaction theory is also called multi-factor theory. Multi-factor theory advocates that human development is constrained by the influence of genetics, environment, education, and the individual's existing level of development and subjective initiative. Human development is the result of the interaction of individual internal factors (such as the quality of innate inheritance, the mechanism of body maturity) and the external environment (the intensity of external stimuli, the level of social development, the cultural background of individuals, etc.) in individual activities. The basic idea is: First, the role of genetics and environment in human development is mutually restrictive and interdependent. For example, whether the environment plays a role in the formation of a certain characteristic plays a major role and often depends on the genetic basis of this characteristic. Second, the role of genetics and the environment is mutual penetration and mutual transformation. It includes two

meanings: one is that genetics can affect the environment, the environment can affect heredity; the second is that there is an environment in heredity, and there is heredity in the environment. For example, newborns always come to the world with their different temperament (nerve types), some are good to cry, some are quiet. Third, the interaction between genetics and the environment is not always fixed. They are a dynamic interaction process. Fourth, there is a dynamic relationship between the subject and the object. The representative is American psychologist Wu Weishi and German psychologist Shi Tailun.

The maturity of genetic quality restricts the process and stage of human physical and mental development. The difference in genetic quality has a certain impact on the development of human body and mind, but it is not the determining factor. Genetic quality is malleable and should be opposed to "genetic determinism". Education cannot and should not involve the development of children, but it should not deny the leading role of education in human development. These four factors are interactions, mutual influences, and joint effects on human development. They are a holistic system that cannot analyze the effects of each factor on human development in isolation and unilaterally.

1.2 Summary of foreign educational thoughts and schools

In the West, the word "educate" is derived from Latin, and the original meaning is "extracting" or "exporting", which means to use something to trigger something that is inherently inside the body and mind. It emphasizes that education is a natural activity that aims to bring out the inherent or potential qualities of natural persons from the inside out to become a state of reality. In a broad sense, education is a social phenomenon unique to human society and a social activity for cultivating people. In a narrow sense, education is a purposeful, planned and organized transfer of knowledge and skills to educators based on certain social requirements and the rules of Physical development of the younger generation, cultivating ideology and morality, developing intelligence and physical activity, through which the educated person is trained as a social service person. The field of research education is pedagogy. After the educational practice and theoretical perfection from the 17th to the 19th century, pedagogy has become a specialized discipline, and many educational thinkers and educational schools have emerged, which has promoted the development of world education.

1.2.1 Main educational thought

1.2.1.1 Formal education and substantive education

Formal education, as a kind of educational theory or thought, is formed and developed in the long-term educational theory and practice. It originated in ancient Greece, throughout the Middle Ages, formed in the 17th century, prevailed in the 18th—19th century, and declined in the early 20th century. The main representatives are Locke and Pestalozzi. The first, called classicism, dates back to Plato and Aristotle, which has been formed and developed for centuries. The second form of training theory is called functional psychology, which was founded by the philosopher Wolf. Kravki of West Germany divides the formal education theory into two periods: the theory of functional education believes that the essence is not to accept and master the content, but to use the content as a means to promote the formation of its ability, mind and intelligence. Development and maturity. According to this theory, it is necessary to select the content that has the greatest possibility to develop students' ability as a training method. The methodological education theory believes that the content of teaching that affects students' future life is innumerable. Therefore, it is impossible to determine the essence of education from the content. Methodology focuses on the educational process of students and masters the methods, feelings, and values of thinking. Students master these methods and are able to accept a range of content. Formal education theory includes the following points:

(a) The task of education is to train the mind's faculties. The various organs of the body can only be developed by drilling; the ability of the mind can only be exercised to make them swallow. The main task of education is to discover the mental abilities that are most effective in training students' abilities.

(b) Education should be for the purpose of form. It is considered that instilling knowledge in education is far less important than training. If people's abilities develop due to training, any knowledge can be absorbed at any time. The value of knowledge lies in the training material, and even if the content of learning is forgotten, it still leaves a permanent and more valuable effect. Therefore, it is not necessary to pay attention to the practicality of the curriculum and teaching materials, but to pay attention to their training role.

(c) The migration of learning is the result of the automatic generation of the psychic faculty. It is believed that through certain training, the spiritual function or a certain function of the mind can be developed and migrated to other learning. Students studying Latin, Greek and mathematics will have great benefits in learning other courses and textbooks.

The theory of substantive education originated in ancient Greece and ancient Rome. It was suppressed in the Middle Ages and formed in the 18th century. It flourished in the 19th century and declined in the early 20th century. The main representatives are Herbart and Spencer. The main point is that the purpose of education is to develop students' various abilities or abilities; formal subjects (such as Greek, Latin, mathematics, logic, etc.) or classical humanities courses have the most developmental value; teaching principles and methods are based on student psychology. The internal developmental order of faculties is based. Both formal education and substantive education have their own philosophical, psychological and social foundations, and thus each has its own rationality and bias.

1.2.1.2 Naturalism and nationalism education

The naturalistic educational thought originated from Aristotle in ancient Greece. It was formed during the Renaissance and flourished in the 18th century. It continued into the 19th century and also influenced the 20th century human education thought. The main representatives are Latke, Comenius, Rousseau and so on. They oppose the suppression of children's personality by medieval religious education or feudal education, and advocate that education should follow the natural nature of children. The purpose of education is to cultivate people who meet the needs of capitalist production relations and social relations for harmonious development of mind and body. Schools should make children happy Living and learning. Education according to the physical and mental characteristics of children at different ages. Educational principles and methods should " make nature", oppose corporal punishment, and initially establish modern educational principles and methodologies. The naturalistic educational thought puts forward some basic concepts of modern education, promotes the scientificization of educational theory and practice, and highlights the value of children in educational life. The shortcoming is that abstract humanity is the natural nature of children, ignoring social and cultural factors. The important value in the development of children and the great role of education in social development have a strong idealistic color.

The nationalist educational thought originated from Plato in ancient Greece, which was accompanied by the emergence of modern European and American national countries and reached its climax in the 19th century. Its representative figures are Conduce of France, Aier repair, Fichte of Germany, Jefferson of the United States and others. They believe that the right to education belongs to the nation-state rather than the church. The state should assume the responsibility of educating the people and carry out education legislation; education is the weapon of the nation-state; the purpose of education is to train qualified nationals, such as the French, the British, Germans or Americans; the establishment of a national education system by the state. The nationalist educational thoughts played an important role in the establishment of modern European and American national education systems and the development of universal education. The shortcoming was that education was excessively dependent on the state power of a certain period and became a reactionary regime, such as the hands of the Nazi regime. Naturalism and nationalist educational thoughts have promoted the modernization process of education in Western countries from both internal and external aspects, and established some basic concepts of modern education.

1.2.2 The main genre of education

The 20th century is a century in which pedagogy is active and developing. There have been many schools of thought, criticizing each other, learning from each other, and innovating.

1.2.2.1 Experimental Education

Experimental pedagogy is a theory developed in some countries in Europe and America in the late 19th and early 20th centuries to study the development of children and its relationship with education. His representative works include Mei Yi's *"Experimental Education Program"* (1914) and Rye's *"Experimental Education"* (1908). The main points of experimental education are:

(a) Oppose the speculative education represented by Herbart, arguing that such pedagogy has no use for testing the merits of educational methods;

(b) Promote the application of experimental psychology research results and methods to educational research, so that educational research is truly "scientific";

(c) Divide the educational experiment into three stages: construct a hypothesis on a certain problem; formulate an experimental plan based on the hypothesis, conduct an experiment; apply the experimental results to the actual situation to prove its correctness;

(d) The difference between educational experiments and psychological experiments is that psychological experiments are conducted in the laboratory, while educational experiments are carried out in real school environments and teaching practices;

(e) It is advocated to explore the characteristics of children's psychological development process and the level of intellectual development by means of experiment, statistics and comparison, and use experimental data as the basis for reforming the academic system, curriculum and teaching methods.

The quantitative research emphasized by experimental pedagogy has become a basic paradigm of pedagogical research in the 20th century. It has been widely applied and developed in the past 100 years, which has greatly promoted the development of educational science. The method of experimental pedagogy is also limited, because the problem of value judgment and choice, such as educational purposes, cannot be solved by experimental methods. When experimental pedagogy and its successors exaggerate the quantitative methods of science as education When the only effective method of scientific research, it embarked on the lost path of "scientificism" in pedagogical research, and was criticized by cultural pedagogy.

1.2.2.2 Cultural education

Cultural education, also known as psychiatric education, is a kind of educational theory that has appeared in Germany since the 19th century. Its representative works mainly include Dilthey's " *The possibility of universally appropriate education*" (1888), Sip Lange's "*Education and Culture*" (1919), Litte's "*Professional Cultivation, Professional Education, Human Cultivation*" (1958). The school of cultural education believes that: First, human beings are a kind of cultural existence, so human history is a cultural history. Second, education is aimed at people, and education is carried out in the context of certain social history, so education process is a historical and cultural process. Third, because the process of education is a historical and cultural process, the study of education can neither be carried out using Herbart's pure conceptual speculation nor by the quantitative statistics of experimental pedagogy. The method of psychiatry or cultural science must be adopted, that is, the method of understanding and interpretation. Fourth, the purpose of education is to promote the transformation of social history and culture into individual subjective culture, and to guide the subjective world of the individual to the broad objective. The cultural world, thus cultivating a complete personality; the main way to cultivate a complete personality is to "make up" and "wake up", play an active role in both teachers and students, and construct a teacher-student relationship in dialogue.

Cultural pedagogy exists and develops as the opposite of scientism experimental pedagogy and rationalist Herbart pedagogy, profoundly affecting the development of pedagogy in Germany and the world in the 20th century. In the nature of education, the purpose of education, teacher-student relationship and the nature of education can give people a lot of inspiration. The insufficiency of cultural education is manifested in its strong speculative atmosphere, and it has a strong philosophical color in the discussion of many problems, which determines that it is difficult to give targeted and operational problems in solving real education problems. Sexual advice, which limits its application in practice. In addition, it blindly exaggerates the value relativity of social and cultural phenomena, neglects the existence of its objective laws, and makes many of its theories lack thoroughness.

1.2.2.3 Pragmatic education

Pragmatic pedagogy is an educational trend that emerged in the United States in the late 19th and early 20th centuries. It is a typical "American version" of pedagogy, which has had a great impact on the educational theory research and educational practice development of the entire world in the 20th century. His representative works include Dewey's Democracy and Education (1916), Experience and Education (1938), and Kebo's Design Teaching Method (1918). Pragmatic pedagogy is also put forward on the basis of criticizing the traditional pedagogy represented by Herbart. The basic point is: First, education is life, the process of education and the process of life are one, not preparing for a certain kind of life in the future. Second, education means that the individual experience of the students continues to grow. In addition, education should not have other purposes. Third, the school is a prototype society in which students learn the reality. The basic attitudes, skills and knowledge required in society. Fourth, the curriculum organization is centered on the student's experience, not on the subject knowledge system. Fifth, the teacher-student relationship is child-centered rather than teacher-centered. Teachers are only helpers of student growth, not leaders. Sixth, the teaching process should pay attention to students' independent development, performance and experience, and respect the differences in student development. Based on the American pragmatic culture, pragmatism education is the pedagogical expression of the development of American capitalism. It profoundly criticizes the traditional educational concept represented by Herbart and promotes the development of pedagogy. The shortcoming is that it ignores the learning of system knowledge to a certain extent, neglects the leading role of teachers in the process of education and teaching, neglects the characteristics of the school, and is thus continually being accepted by American society and other society in the 20th century criticism.

1.2.2.4 Marxist education

Marxist pedagogy consists of two parts: one is the discussion of education by Marx and Engels and other classic Marxist writers, that is, their educational thoughts; the other is that educators are modern to the basic principles of Marxism (including educational principles). The results of a series of studies on education. The basic viewpoint of Marxist pedagogy is: First, education is a social historical phenomenon, with distinct class nature in class society, and there is no education that is separated from social influence. Second, education originates from productive labor, labor mode and nature. The change will inevitably lead to changes in the form and content of education. Third, the fundamental purpose of education is to promote the all-round development of students. Fourth, the combination of modern education and modern large-scale labor is not only an important method to develop social productivity, but also to cultivate comprehensive development. The only way for people. Fifth, in the political, economic and cultural relationship between education and society, education is subject to their constraints on the one hand, and relative independence on the other, and counteracts them, promoting industrial social politics. The development of economy and culture has a great role. Sixth, Marxist materialist dialectics and historical materialism are the methodological basis of educational science research. It is necessary to see the complexity of educational phenomena and not to treat education with simplistic attitudes and methods. Research, but also firmly believe that the phenomenon of education is lawful, no it will be caught in the quagmire of agnosticism and relativism go. The emergence of Marxism laid the foundation of scientific methodology for the development of pedagogy. However, for various reasons, in the process of practical pedagogy, people did not understand and apply Marxist theory well, and often made some simplification and mechanization. This is something that we should pay special attention to when studying and developing Marxist educational theory.

1.2.2.5 Critical Education

Critical pedagogy is an educational trend that emerged after the 1970s. It is also an educational trend that is currently dominant in Western educational theories. It has a wide and profound impact on the study of many issues of education. His representative works include Bowers and Kindis's "*Civilism School Education in the United States*" (1976), Buedil's "*Education, Social and Cultural Reproduction*" (1979), and Apple's "*Education and Power*" (1982), Ji Lu's "*Critical Education, National and Cultural Struggle*" (1989). The basic point of critical pedagogy is: First, the school education of contemporary capitalism is not a democratic system of establishment and liberation, as advocated by pragmatism pedagogy, and a powerful force for promoting social equity and achieving social justice. Means and ways, on the contrary, it is a tool to maintain the unfairness and injustice of the real society, and it is the root cause of social differences, social discrimination and social opposition. Second, the reason why this phenomenon occurs is because education is with society. Corresponding, what kind of social politics, economy and culture, what kind of school education institutions, social political ideology, cultural patterns, economic structure strongly restrict the school's purpose, curriculum, teachers and students Relationships, evaluation methods, etc., the function of school education is the social and political ideology, cultural relations and economic structure dominated by regenerative output. Third, people have lost their "consciousness" to this de facto inequality and injustice. Think of it as a natural fact, not as a result of deliberate manufacturing by certain interest groups. Fourth, critical education's purpose is to reveal the interests behind the seemingly natural facts, to help teachers and students to be sensitive to the educational environment in which they are located and the many elements that form the educational environment, that is, to "enlighten" them to achieve the "liberation" of consciousness. Fifth, critical education believes that educational phenomena are not neutral and objective, but full of conflicts of interests. Therefore, educational theory research cannot adopt scientific and scientific attitudes and methods, but adopts practical critique attitudes and methods to reveal the interest relationship in the specific educational life is raised from the unconscious level to the level of consciousness. Critical education inherits some basic ideas and methods of Marxism, and is conducive to a deeper understanding of capitalist education. It has a strong fighting, critical and liberating power.

1.3 Historical evolution of the school system

The education system, that is, the school education system, and the school education system referrs to as the school system, refers to a country's rules system for organizing school education activities and various types of school systems at all levels. The education system is the sum of the various norms, rules or regulations required for the overall composition of the educational institutions and organizational systems at all levels of the country and their normal operation. It specifies the nature, tasks, training objectives, entry conditions, duration of study, management system, and the relationship between schools at all levels. The school system has a close relationship with historical development, and it has evolved with the development of social political economy and cultural education. The school education system is the main part of a national education system. The school system is born after the school. After the birth of the ancient social school, there was an ancient school system. However, there is no strict degree of division and length of teaching. The ancient West did not form a systematic and unified school education system.

1.3.1 The history of Western academic system

The earliest education in the West can be traced back to the ancient Roman period. When the Roman Republic was founded in the Wangzheng period, the agricultural economy was the main factor. In addition to the need for war, education was based on family education and cultivated farmers and soldiers. During the Republican period, the school was divided into three categories. One was a primary school (also known as "Ludas"), which recruited children aged 7—12. The content of education is reading, writing and counting, including the "Twelve Bronze Table Law" and moral maxims, but does not attach importance to sports and music. The second is the grammar school, which is a higher level school for the children of aristocratic families than the primary education. The educational content is Greek and Latin. The third is a rhetorical school that trains the eloquent ("the speaker"). The content of education is rhetoric, logic, law, ethics, mathematics, astronomy, history, and so on. During the Imperial period, the supervision and control of primary education was strengthened, and private grammar schools and rhetorical schools were changed to national; the purpose of education was to cultivate bureaucrats and loyalists who were loyal to the empire; to improve the treatment of teachers and to enjoy some privileges. However, the educational content of Zhongjun has been increased, mainly to cultivate management and follow the people. There is also a form of parish school, which is generally responsible for priests or other church personnel, recruiting young men aged 7—20 to enroll (a few schools also recruit girls), the school's curriculum is based on instilling religious knowledge, but also reading, writing, counting, and teaching of simple worldly knowledge. Compared with the abbey school and the bishop school, the parish school has a larger scope of education and a broader training goal, but the teaching conditions and level are lower.

In the Middle Ages, in addition to the parish schools, there are two forms of education in Western Europe, one is Christian education. With the development of Christianity, early Christian church schools developed. The monastery is the most typical church education institution in the Middle Ages. It was originally accepted only by those who are dedicated to serving God and preparing to serve as clergy. Later, the scope was expanded, and some people who did not make a living in the ministry were accepted. The students of the monastery are usually enrolled at the age of ten, and the study period is about eight years. The early monasteries mainly emphasized the cultivation of religious beliefs. Later, the curriculum gradually deepened and the "seven art" became the main curriculum system. The teacher is completely served by the priest. The teaching method is mainly the combination of teacher dictation and student memorization and copying. Individual teaching, student entry time, learning progress and schedule vary from person to person. The discipline of the school is divided into coastal areas, and corporal punishment is prevalent. The other is feudal secular education, includes court school education and knight education. The court school is an educational institution located in the court of the king or nobles, which mainly cultivates the descendants of the royal family. It is the main form of secular education in Europe. The court school mainly studies the "seven art", and the teaching method mainly adopts the question and answer method prevailing in the church school. The court school mainly cultivates the bureaucracy required by the feudal ruling class. The other is Cavalier Education, which is the product of the feudal social hierarchy of medieval Western Europe. The main goal is to cultivate the knightly spirit and skills of brave and loyalty. Its implementation is divided into three stages: from birth to 7—8 years old for the family education stage; after 7—8 years old is the ceremony education stage, the lower level of the aristocrats sent the son to the senior aristocratic family as a child. 14—21 years old is the attendant education stage, the focus is to learn "Knights seven skills", but also to serve the lord and the lady. At the age of 21, one was officially awarded the title of Knight by the inauguration ceremony.

After the feudal system of Western Europe entered the heyday of development, the kingship became stronger and stronger, the society stabilized, agricultural production rose steadily, and the handicraft industry gradually became a specialized occupation, forming a group of emerging civic classes, proposing new cultural requirements, and pursuing learning to become fashionable. At the same time, the Crusades sent thousands of Christians to the East and strengthened the exchange of different cultures. These two reasons lead to the fact that traditional court schools and knight education can no longer meet this need, and new educational institutions and forms are beginning to emerge. Among them, the medieval university is the most attractive. The original medieval university was a self-made professor and learning center. Generally, prestigious scholars and their followers in a certain field organize themselves to form a group similar to a guild for teaching and knowledge trading. The basic purpose of medieval universities is to conduct vocational training and train the professionals needed for society. It can be divided into two types according to the leadership system: "student" university and "sir" university. The former is taught by the student. The selection of the professor, the amount of tuition, the duration of the semester, and the number of hours of teaching are determined by the student; the latter is governed by the teacher, and the school is determined by the teacher. The course of the university is not fixed at the beginning, and the trend tends to be unified. The social needs are divided into four parts: law, god, and medicine. Medieval universities have a degree system. Students who have completed college courses and passed the examinations can get a Master's degree or a Doctoral degree. The system and characteristics of medieval universities have far-reaching influences, and are the direct source of modern Western universities.

The Western modern school education system was established in the 18th century, and was established in the 19th century, and developed in the 20th century. In modern times, influenced by modern educational thoughts, Britain, the United States, Germany, Russia and other countries have carried out educational reforms. For example, the new university movement in the UK, the Napoleonic education reform in France, the Hundred Castle reform in Germany, and the reform of Peter I in Russia. There were also a large number of educational thinkers during this period. These reforms greatly promoted the economic development at that time and laid the foundation for the modern academic system.

In the 14th century, the United Kingdom set up public schools, and the nature of the schools was private. The schools initially recruited civilian children and later changed to recruit children from the upper class. The study period was 5—6 years, mainly studying academic subjects, and then adding mathematics and natural science. The public school has a close relationship with the medieval university and has become a preparatory school for the university. In the 17th century, some religious and charitable organizations launched the charity school movement and the Sunday school movement, established elementary schools, and recruited children of working people. Their quality of schooling was relatively poor. In 1807, White Bray submitted a bill to the Parliament, recommending the use of public funds to fund the establishment of a national education system. In 1839, the Education Committee of the Government Privy Council was established to manage public education, and the right to primary education was transferred from the hands of the church to the hands of the state. In 1870, Congress passed *the Primary Education Act* to establish a public primary education system. In 1880, compulsory education for 5—10 years of age began. In 1899, compulsory education for 5—12 years old was implemented. The Secondary Education Committee was established in 1894, and a report on the development of secondary education was introduced in 1895. In 1902, the Parliament passed *the Secondary Education Act*, which stipulated that local governments should uniformly manage primary and secondary education. In 1944, the United Kingdom passed *the Butler Education Act*, which had a major impact on the school education system in the UK. The Butler Education Act clearly states: the abolition of the inconsistent and overlapping academic system of primary and secondary schools, and the reclassification of the education system into primary education (5—11 years old), secondary education (11—18 years old) and continuing education (vocational education) three phases.

Before the 16th century, German schools were mainly church schools, and the church controlled the leadership of the school. In the 16th century, Lutheran-led religious reform movement attached importance to primary education, and put forward the idea of universal education, which promoted the development of education. There have been a number of schools with a multi-teaching nature set up for civilian children, and industrial schools and Sunday schools (Sunday schools) founded for tutoring for child labor. A group of classical liberal arts secondary schools, knights colleges and samurai colleges were set up for the aristocratic children to enroll and to cultivate the feudal princes. In 1708, the practice of secondary schools appeared. Since then, such secondary schools have appeared in large numbers, marking the emergence of modern academic systems. In 1763, the Kingdom of Prussia promulgated the "Regulations for Rural Schools", which popularized compulsory education and took back the leadership of primary education from the church. At the beginning of the 19th century, the educational reform led by Hundburger promoted the initial formation of German dual-track education.

The education of the United States before the War of Independence was a replica of the education of the British sovereign state. It was controlled by the church and had a strong colonial color. In 1751, Franklin opened the first pre-university school in the United States in Philadelphia. After the independence of the country, the government proposed policies to popularize primary education and develop secondary and higher education in accordance with the spirit of *the Declaration of Independence*. The states have established many secular schools. In the early 19th century, the United States enacted the compulsory education law, which formed a preliminary public school system managed by the states. In 1821, the first public high school in American history was established in Boston. It was a new type of middle school and formed a public high school movement. After that, public schools developed rapidly. After the Civil War in 1863, the United States formed its first system of school system, namely the "eight-four-four-school system". Schools at all levels were connected to each other and belonged to the monorail system. At the end of the 19th century and the beginning of the 20th century, in order to meet the needs of young people for further studies and employment, the states changed the "eight-four-four-school system" to the "six-three-three-study system". From then on, the "six-three-three-study system" became the basic system of American school education.

The modern academic system consists of two structures, one is the vertical school system, the other is the horizontally divided school system, later on, the branch system is produced. The dual-track system is one of the types of modern Western academic systems, mainly in European countries before the mid-20th century, such as the United Kingdom, Germany and France. It is based on a school system that is produced under specific historical conditions. The school system is divided into two, an academic school with a privilege of hierarchy evolved from a medieval school. It is a top-down structure, from university to middle school. Another mass modern school established for the education of the children of working people is a bottom-up structure, elementary school (later including elementary and junior high schools) —— vocational schools. These two tracks are neither connected nor connected, and initially do not even correspond. In the third industrial technology revolution, the contradiction between the two-track system became more and more acute, which led to the reform of the academic system, eliminated the inequality in the traditional academic system, promoted the integration between the two tracks, and gave everyone more educational opportunities to ensure the distribution of educational opportunities. Fairness. The monorail system first appeared in the United States in the late 19th and early 20th centuries. The monorail system is a historical advancement compared to the dual-track system, at least eliminating formal inequalities. The bottom-up structure of the school system is elementary school → middle school → university. It is characterized by the formation of a series and multiple segmentation modes at all levels of schools, which is conducive to the popularization of education and greater adaptability. Therefore, it is adopted by many countries in the world. The branch school system was born in the former Soviet Union in the first half of the 20th century. It is a new type of school system that has both the characteristics of a monorail and a dual-track system. The front section (primary school, junior high school) is a monorail, and the latter section is a double track. This kind of academic system is conducive to the popularization of education and keeps academics at a high level.

Generally speaking, there are two trends in the development of modern education. One is that the school education system is developed from a two-track system to a branch system to a monorail system, and the other is the modern school education system → modern education system → lifelong education system deve- lopment. In addition, the school stage is always changing. In addition to primary schools, junior high schools, high schools, vocational education, and higher education, many countries have also incorporated early childhood education into the academic system, and have also increased correspondence education, off-campus education, adult education, and old-age university education to return to education and lifelong education.

1.3.2 The history of Chinese academic system

The ancient academic system of our country has a long history, with obvious hierarchy, lacking strict years of study, system and student degree. Schools in the Western Zhou Dynasty began to have a relatively complete system, divided into two categories: Chinese studies and rural studies. There is also a distinction between universities and primary schools in Chinese studies. Local schools are local schools. They are organized according to administrative divisions, prefectures, township schools, party establishments and homes. Western Zhou's admission qualifications are strictly res- tricted. The Chinese studies are designed for the upper-class aristocratic children of the ruling class. The slaves are deprived of the right to education, and the civilians can only enter the hometown. This is the original school education system in China. The establishment of the preliminary outline of the educational system of feudal society in China began in the Han Dynasty, and in the Tang and Song Dynasties became more complete and extended for thousands of years. There are three main types of academies in the school: official school, private school, and "also official and private". Official credits are at the central and local levels. The central government generally has Guozi, Taixue, Simen, etc., as well as primary schools for the Patriarchs; local officials have state studies and county studies. The first level of private school is a primary school or a monastic school that teaches literacy and daily knowledge. It mainly includes township schools, village studies, righteous schools and family members. The first level is a higher degree of young students studying or preparing for the imperial examinations. The academy is a high-level form of private education development, where readers study hard on Confucian classics. Since the Yuan Dynasty, the ancient school education has become increasingly official. The school system is very strict, basically monopolized by the ruling class, and formed an ancient academic system centered on the imperial examination system, including official studies, private schools and academies. Later, gradually becoming a vassal of the imperial examination system, seriously affecting the normal development of school education.

The modern academic system is mainly developed from the single academic system of the United States.

1.3.2.1 Renyin School System

The modern educational system of our country began at the end of Qing Dynasty. In 1902, the Qing government promulgated the "Constitution of the Imperial Schools", also known as the Renyin School System, which was the first modern school system in China. It divides education into three stages: primary education, secondary education and higher education. The whole course lasts for twenty years. There were industrial schools with elementary education, secondary schools with secondary industry schools and normal schools, and higher education with official schools, industrial schools and normal schools. The characteristics of this system were as follows: firstly, it paid attention to national education;

secondly, it paid attention to industrial education; thirdly, it still existed the traditional idea that men are more important than women; fourthly, it retained the traces of the imperial examination system and stipulates that graduates from elementary schools, middle schools, normal schools, higher schools and colleges should be given attachments, tribute students, candidates and entrants respectively. Class titles were still influenced by the imperial examination system. This system had not been implemented in practice at that time.

1.3.2.2　Guimao School System

In 1903, the Qing government promulgated the " Zouding Constitution of the Schools", also known as the " Guimao School System", whose guiding ideology was "middle school as the body, Western learning as the use". Its purpose was "loyalty to the monarch, respect Confucius, respect for justice, advocate martial arts, advocate honesty". It was based on the school system after the Meiji Restoration in Japan, while retaining the characteristics of feudal education such as respecting Confucius and reading classics. The whole school system was divided into three sections and six levels, including a complete system from primary school to university, with a 26-year course, and Industrial Education in parallel with general education. Women's education has no status in this school system. Students are still granted various origins such as "Jinshi" and "Juren" by imitating the imperial examination system. The "Gui Mao school system" had obvious semi-colonial and semi-feudal nature.

1.3.2.3　Renzi School System

In 1912, the Ministry of Education of the Republic of China Government formulated a new school system, called the Renzi school system, which stipulates seven years of primary education (compulsory education for four years in junior high school and three years in senior high school), four years in secondary school, three years in preparatory college and three to four years in undergraduate course, totaling eighteen years. The length of the college was uncertain. The years of normal and industrial education were separated into a system. This educational system was similar to that of France and Germany. There are three kinds of education: general education, vocational education and normal education. Normal education was totally public and students were paid public fees. Compared with the educational system announced by the Qing government, the content of loyalty to the emperor and respect for Confucius was abolished, the training of natural science and production skills was increased, and the length of study was shortened.

1.3.2.4 Renxu School System

In 1922, Renzi's educational system was further reformed, and "Renxu Educational System" was promulgated. This new school system changed the previous seven-four system to the Six-three-three system, stipulating six years of primary education, three years of junior high school, and parallel to secondary schools are normal schools and vocational schools, and four to six years of university. Its basic ideas focused on the popularization of primary education and the improvement of the level of secondary education, abolish the preparatory course of university, so that the University concentrated on professional education and scientific research, implement the system of selecting subjects and subject education, taking into account the preparation of students for further education and employment. This system reflected the bourgeoisie's new requirements for education. It had adopted the single track system of the United States, shortened the length of primary school, and was conducive to the popularization of primary schools and the improvement of the level of secondary education. This system had been in use until 1949.

1.3.2.5 The School System in the Period of the New Democratic Revolution in China

After the founding of the People's Republic of China, the "Decision on Reforming the School System" was promulgated in 1951, which clearly stipulated the school system of our country. Primary and secondary schools implemented the "five-three-three-system". In 1985, the Decision of the Central Committee of the Communist Party of China on the Reform of the Educational System was promulgated to reform the educational system and put forward the idea of implementing nine-year compulsory education step by step. *The Education Law of the People's Republic of China* in 1995 was the first education law since the founding of the People's Republic of China. It consolidated the achievements of the reform of the school system in the form of law, stipulated in special chapters the basic system of education in our country, implements the school education system of preschool education, primary education, secondary education and higher education, and implements the nine-year system. Business education system; Vocational education system and adult education system; National education examination system; Academic certificate system.

The current school structure in China can be viewed from the vertical and horizontal dimensions, namely the horizontal category structure and the vertical level structure. From a vertical per- spective, there are four levels of education in our country.

- Early childhood education, recruiting children aged 3—6, the main task is to according to certain training objectives and the physical and mental characteristics of young children.
- Primary education, for full-time primary education, en- rolling children aged 6 or 7 with a schooling system of 5 or 6 years. The main task is to prepare the educated for a higher level of education.
- Secondary education is a medium general education, and various secondary vocational education based on primary education.
- Higher education refers to full-time universities, specialized colleges, colleges, graduate schools, and various forms of amateur universities. From a horizontal perspective, China's education has established a basic education system, a vocational and technical education system, a higher education system, an adult continuing education system, and a special education school system.

At present, China's academic system is constantly reforming, such as trying to increase the number of college entrance examinations, allowing certain colleges and universities to make individual propositions, enrolling students independently, and encouraging colleges and universities to recruit low-scoring students with a long skill. In the future, China's academic system will inevitably move toward compulsory education to a higher level, and gradually realize the development of higher education popularization and lifelong education.

1.4 Summary of teaching theory

Teaching is an educational activity composed of teachers' teaching and students' learning under the norms of certain teaching purposes. It has two aspects, namely, teaching and learning. It is a bilateral activity process of teacher's teaching and student's academic composition. It is not only a part of the whole educational activity, but also a process of imparting knowledge, experience, methods and abilities. It is also the whole process of students developing cognitive ability and shaping healthy personality. Teaching is the main contradiction in teaching; teaching design controls the teaching rhythm, teaching direction, teaching process, and determines the realization of teaching objectives. Teachers play a leading role in teaching. Learning is an important aspect of teaching. Especially in classroom teaching, students are the main body of learning, which is the main body of teaching objectives and the center of teaching activities. Teaching and learning are the two sides of contradiction and unity. This article focuses on this aspect of teacher teaching.

1.4.1 The development of teaching process theory

The teaching process refers to the development process of teaching activities. Teachers are based on certain social requirements and the characteristics of students' physical and mental development. With certain teaching conditions, they guide students to understand the objective world mainly by understanding the teaching content, and develop their own on this basis process. Through the teaching process, students learn to behave, learn to survive, learn to know, learn to develop, and have both educational and developmental functions. The teaching process is a program structure in which the initiation, development, change, and end of teaching activities are continuously developed in time.

1.4.1.1 The Sprouting Period of Ancient Teaching Process Theory

People's understanding of the teaching process has gone through a long historical development process. In ancient China, there was the germination of the theory of teaching process. Confucianism generally regards the teaching process as a unified process in which students learn knowledge and cultivate morality under the guidance of teachers. From the transcendentalism of idealism, Confucius affirmed the idea of "being born with knowledge", but the dominant idea was to advocate "learning with knowledge", and to combine "learning", "thinking", "learning" and "doing". Xun Kuang developed Confucius's idea of "learning to know". Starting from the epistemology of simple materialism, he regarded learning as a unified process of "hearing", "seeing", "knowing" and "doing". Cheng Hao, Cheng Yihe and Zhu Xi, the scholars of Song Dynasty, inherited and brought into play Mencius' idealistic epistemology and teaching ideas of "self-satisfaction" and "self-seeking" which had a great influence on the teaching practice at that time and later generations. In the ancient West, there were many great thinkers and educators. Socrates attached great importance to the teaching of knowledge and virtue. Socrates formed his own unique teaching method through long-term teaching practice, called "midwifery", which is to give birth to ideas and guide people to produce correct ideas. He takes the form of teacher-student question-and-answer. When he teaches students to acquire a certain concept, he does not directly tell the students about it, but first asks them questions to answer. If the students answer incorrectly, he does not directly correct it. Instead, he puts forward other questions to guide the students to think, so that they can get the correct step by step. The conclusion lays a foundation for heuristic teaching. In his Principles of Eloquence, Kun Tiliang summarized his experience in training speakers and put forward three progressive learning process theories: imitation, theory and practice. In this process, attention should be paid to the methods of intuitive knowledge acquisition, the improvement of theoretical level and skills training, and the research and improvement of teaching methods. In addition, his emphasis on early childhood education and morality, as well as the cultivation of individual differences, the requirements of kindergarten teachers, and the education method of combining work and leisure, contains many penetrating and profound opinions, which are worthy of our reference.

1.4.1.2 The Development Period of Modern Teaching Process Theory

The more rational and systematic teaching theory developed gradually after the Western Renaissance. Comenius rebuked the traditional scholastic style teaching methods, arguing that these methods, regardless of children's learning aspirations, forced children to memorize and put forward that "people can only become human beings through education", and that in the course of education, students should be estimated. The age characteristics should pay attention to the child's personality characteristics, and should be targeted to develop children's talents. Comenius emphasizes that education should conform to the natural nature of human beings, that is, the law of children's physical and mental development. One of the most important contributions of Comenius to modern education is the class teaching system and its teaching theory established by him. It proposes the principle of natural adaptability of teaching, the principle of intuitiveness, the principle of consciousness and enthusiasm, the principle of systemicity, and the principle of consolidation. The principle of quantity and the principle of teaching students in accordance with their aptitude. Another great thinker is Rousseau. The core of his educational thought is the theory of natural education. The purpose of nature education is to cultivate the "natural person" whose natural nature is fully developed. It emphasizes that education must conform to the natural course of children's natural development, that is, to follow the child's body and mind. The characteristics of development, but also respect the child's personality characteristics. He established a dynamic view of children or students, taking children as the main body of learning and teaching, and pioneering discovery learning. Natural education thought has far-reaching influence on later educators and modern education and teaching reform. The German philosopher and educator Herbart started from the idealism theory that all the psychological activities of the students in the teaching process are the movement of ideas, that is, the systematic connection between concepts and concepts, the main concepts and the subordinate concepts; as for the concept itself, it is not a reflection of the objective world, but a human's inherent transcendental rational generalization of the mind, which is endowed to the objective world through meditation. He attaches importance to comprehensive and systematic knowledge teaching, and divides the teaching process into four stages: clear, joint, systematic and method. It is clear that students are required to concentrate on learning the various elements of a new subject and achieve a correct understanding; unity is to establish a connection between a new concept and a known concept; the system highlights the main ideas and organizes the knowledge into a systematic system; the method guides students to think independently, use system knowledge to practice exercises. What he emphasizes is the systematic teaching of book knowledge, ignoring the role of perceptual knowledge and practice in the teaching process, and making the theory out of practice. His teaching stage is separated from the characteristics of specific teaching content, with a formalistic nature. However, Herbart used psychology to explain the teaching process. He first proposed and discussed the problem of teaching stage, and clearly regarded teaching as a process to study, which has certain progressive significance.

1.4.1.3 The Period of the Formation of Modern Teaching Process Theory

Since the end of the 19th century and the 20th century, the development of political economy has promoted the development and reform of education, and has formed the arguments of modern education and traditional education, which has promoted the continuous development of teaching theory and practice.

The pragmatic teaching theory represented by the American educator Dewey conforms to the development of the times. It is proposed that the child's personal life practice or direct experience must be the center of learning in the teaching process. It is required to learn knowledge around specific life affairs, that is, to learn by doing. Dewey divides the teaching process into five elements that form different stages: students must have a real experience situation, have a continuous activity that is interested in the activity itself; create a real problem within the situation, as a thinking stimulating; he has to possess knowledge, perform the necessary observations, and deal with the problem; he must be responsible for the step-by-step method of solving the problem he has come up with; he has the opportunity to test his ideas through the application, so that the idea is clear and let him discover if they are effective. He created a five-step teaching method of difficulties, problems, assumptions, verification, and conclusions. He values the active activities of students and their personal experience, and his educational theory is of epoch-making significance. However, Dewey despised the teaching of book knowledge of the system, so that the actual deviance from the theory of generalization and guidance.

Another famous educator is Kailuo of the Soviet Union. Kailov affirmed that the teaching process must follow the process of human cognition, from vivid intuitive to abstract thinking, from abstract thinking to practical process, but the teaching process also has self-characteristics, such as teaching students to receive known and acquired truths for human beings; through textbooks, students can acquire a large amount of knowledge in a short period of time. Textbooks are the main source of knowledge for students. Kailov clarified six teaching principles: the principle of intuitiveness, the principle of combining theory with practice, the principle of systemicity and coherence, the principle of popularity and acceptability of teaching, the principle of student's consciousness and enthusiasm, and the principle of consolidation.

Zankov is another great educator in the Soviet Union. He focuses on the relationship between education and development and has successfully applied the research methods of psychology organically to the study of teaching theory. He put forward his own unique views on teaching purposes, teaching principles, classroom life and teacher work. He opposes only paying attention to the mastery of knowledge, skills and skills, and advocates that teaching should promote the development of students. He tried to stimulate students' enthusiasm and initiative by improving the difficulty and speed of teaching, and promote the general development of students. He uses materialist dialectics as the guiding ideology of teaching theory, and keeps close contact with students from the reality of life and practice as an important guiding principle of teaching theory.

Bruner is an outstanding educator in the United States. In his view, the development of students ' minds, although somewhat influenced by the environment and affecting his environment, is mainly to follow his own unique cognitive procedures. Teaching is to help or form the growth of students' wisdom or cognition. The task of educators is to transform knowledge into a form that adapts to the developing students, and to characterize the order of system development. He divides children's intellectual development into three stages, the pre-operational stage (before 5—6 years old), the specific operation stage (before 10—14 years old) and the formal operation stage. The teaching process should promote children's intellectual development, develop students' theories of discovery and creativity, and therefore advocate discovery and learning. Emphasize that students' knowledge learning should be in charge of the subject's knowledge structure, while the knowledge structure is mainly composed of basic concepts and basic principles. Bruner's spiral curriculum structure in his teaching theory, arranging the best learning experience for students, organizing knowledge content for students' understanding, presenting the best order of knowledge for students, teaching procedures to stimulate students' thinking, and Emphasizing the motivation of students' internal learning motivation and correctly applying teaching ideas and measures such as rewards and punishments to help students understand knowledge and cultivate creative ability, all reflect the correct thinking of imparting knowledge and cultivating students' thinking and ability. It has important practical guiding significance for teachers' classroom teaching.

The epistemology of dialectical materialism comprehensively summarizes the development history of human cognition and reveals the universal law of cognition process: it believes that human social practice is the source and purpose of cognition, and human cognition is the reflection of subjective action on objective world, which is driven by perceptual knowledge. The process of gradual ascending and transforming into rational understanding; understanding and in turn actively guiding and promoting the development of practice, practice and understanding are processes of interaction and cyclical ascent. The elaboration of this law provides a scientific methodological basis for the teaching process. The student's learning process is a special form of human cognitive process. Learning is based on mastering the basic knowledge of culture science and technology known to mankind, and is taught and guided by teachers in order to enable the younger generation to reach the level of contemporary science and culture in a relatively short period of time. The teaching process is a special cognitive process with purpose and plan. It follows the law of unity of perceptual knowledge and rational understanding, and the unity of understanding and practice. This can avoid the one-sidedness of the theory alone and prevent the narrow pragmatic experience. According to the epistemology of dialectical materialism, the teaching process can be from concrete to abstract, from abstract to concrete; it can be realized by practice, but also by practice to understanding. It generally guides students to acquire perceptual knowledge, guide students to understand knowledge, guide and organize students to practice, check and consolidate knowledge.

Modern teaching theory believes that the teaching process is not only the process of imparting and learning cultural science knowledge. It is also a process to promote the overall development of students. There is an intrinsic and inevitable connection between teaching and development. Teachers are required to guide students to master the knowledge, while comprehensively developing students' intelligence and physical strength, cultivating independent learning ability, learning interest and good study habits, and the ability to engage in creative activities; in the process of learning knowledge, gradually form a proletarian world view and Communism moral quality. Teaching should not only adapt to the age characteristics of students, but also promote their physiological and psychological harmony and full development as much as possible. While promoting the general development of students, it promotes the special development of individual talents. In the relationship between teaching and learning, we must give full play to the leading role of teachers and guide students to become masters of learning and subjects of development.

1.4.2 Teaching Modes

The teaching mode can be defined as a relatively stable teaching activity structure framework and activity program established under the guidance of certain teaching ideas or teaching theories. As a structural framework, it highlights the teaching model from the macroscopic level of the overall relationship between teaching activities and the internal relationships and functions between the various elements; as an activity program, it highlights the orderly and operability of the teaching model. Any teaching mode points to and accomplishes certain teaching objectives. The teaching objectives are at the core of the structure of the teaching model, and it plays a restrictive role on other factors that constitute the teaching model. It determines the operating procedures of the teaching model and the teaching and learning of teachers and students. The combination relationship in the activity is also the standard and scale of teaching evaluation. It is precisely because of this strong internal unity of the teaching model and the teaching goal that the personality of different teaching modes is determined. Different teaching modes serve the completion of certain teaching objectives.

The teaching mode is the embodiment of teaching theory, and it is the generalized form and system of teaching practice. Different educational concepts often propose different teaching modes. According to the theoretical roots of the teaching model, it can be divided into four types of information processing teaching mode, personality development teaching mode, social interaction teaching mode, and behavior modification teaching mode. The more common ones are as follows:

1.4.2.1 Pass—receive

Influenced by the training psychology of Skinner's operational conditioning, emphasis is placed on controlling learners' behavior to achieve a predetermined goal. By linking - feedback - to strengthen the repetitive cycle process to shape effective behavioral goals, the teaching mode aims at imparting system knowledge and medium-based skills. The basic teaching procedure is to review old lessons—inspire learning motivation—to teach new lessons—consolidate exercises—inspect evaluations—interval review. The application of this model enables students to receive a large amount of information in a short period of time and cultivate students' abstract thinking ability. However, it is difficult for students to truly understand the information they receive. It is not conducive to the development of simplistic and modeled personality, which is not conducive to the development of innovative thinking and the ability to solve practical problems.

1.4.2.2 Self-study-coaching

The self-study tutoring mode is a mode of independent learning under the guidance of teachers. This kind of teaching mode can cultivate students' independent thinking ability, and many teachers use it in teaching practice. Starting from humanism, it pays attention to the subjectivity of students and aims at cultivating students' learning ability. This teaching model recognizes the value of students' trial and error in the learning process and develops students' ability to think and learn independently. Self-study—discussion—inspiration—summary—practices are used to consolidate teaching procedures. In the teaching, according to the student's recent development area, the teacher arranges some learning tasks related to the new teaching content to organize the students to self-learn. After the self-study, the students exchange ideas and discover the difficulties they encounter, and then the teachers conduct the students according to these situations. Dial and inspire, sum up the rules, and then organize the students to practice consolidation. The advantage is that it can cultivate students' ability to analyze and solve problems; it is conducive to teachers' teaching according to their aptitude; can exert students' autonomy and creativity; and help to cultivate students' spirit of mutual cooperation. However, if students are not interested in self-study content, they may have nothing in the classroom; this requires teachers to be very keen to observe the students' learning situation, to inspire and motivate students' learning enthusiasm when necessary, to explain and teach different students, so it is difficult Conducted in large class teaching.

1.4.2.3 Inquiry teaching

Inquiring teaching is centered on problem solving, focusing on students' independent activities and focusing on the cultivation of students' thinking ability. It is based on Piaget and Bruner's constructivist theories, focusing on students' pre-cognition, focusing on experiential teaching, and cultivating students' ability to explore and think. The basic procedure of teaching is problem-hypothesis-inference-verification-summary improvement. It is suitable to establish a democratic and tolerant teaching environment and give full play to students' thinking ability. Teachers should master the students' pre-cognitive characteristics and implement certain teaching strategies. It has the advantage of cultivating students' ability to innovate and think, the spirit of democracy and cooperation, and the ability to learn independently. However, this kind of teaching method can only be carried out in small classes, and a better teaching support system is needed. The teaching takes a long time. In the inquiry teaching mode, teachers must respect the subjectivity of students and create a teaching environment that is tolerant of democracy and equality. Teachers should give certain encouragement to students who break the rules, and do not easily say right or wrong to students. Teachers should be guided by the main, we must not easily inform students of the results of the inquiry.

1.4.2.4 Concept acquisition mode

The goal of this model is to enable learners to develop their thinking skills by experiencing the formation of the concepts they have learned. It reflects the cognitive psychology of Bruner et al., emphasizing that learning is the organization and reorganization of cognitive structures. Cognitive structuralists believe that classification is a means of treating different things as equal, simplifying and systemizing the surrounding world, and thus establishing certain concepts to understand the complicated world. The concept acquisition model consists of the following steps: the teacher chooses and defines a concept—the teacher determines the attributes of the concept—the teacher prepares to choose positive and negative examples—introducing the student into the conceptualization process—presenting the example—student summarizing and defining—providing more examples—further study and form the correct concept——the use and expansion of concepts. When using this teaching model, teachers help students to acquire concepts effectively is one of the basic tasks of school education. The concept acquisition model is a form of thinking that adopts "inductive-deductive". First, let the students discover some common attributes of the concept through some examples, and grasp the essential characteristics of this concept different from other concepts. Students need to understand the concept after obtaining the concept, that is, to guide students to understand concepts from the connotation, extension, genus, species, and differences of concepts. In order to strengthen students' understanding of concepts, concepts related to concepts, logical related concepts, corresponding concepts, etc. should also be distinguished. Using this model, students can develop their inductive and deductive abilities, form clear concepts, and develop students' rigorous logical reasoning skills. However, a large number of positive and negative examples are needed. Pre-school teachers need to be carefully prepared, especially for content with strong conceptual content. Teachers should carefully comb the connotation and extension of the concept before class.

1.4.2.5 Cooperative learning model

The study of cooperative learning began in the United States in the 1950s and emerged in the 1980s. It was marked by the "cooperative education" theory introduced by the Soviet Union, and formed a variety of cooperative learning models. Among the most famous are the Sleven student team learning model, the Johnson Brothers' common learning model, Sharon's group inquiry model, and Barnes's cooperative method model. The so-called cooperative learning refers to a form of teaching in which two or more individuals form a cooperative learning group to learn together in order to improve learning outcomes. Cooperative learning is based on social psychology. Good interpersonal relationships can promote students' cognitive, emotional and behavioral levels of learning. Group cooperative learning creates an opportunity for students to actively interact in the classroom. It is of great significance for students to form good interpersonal relationships and develop a good sense of cooperation and foster cooperation in communication. Johnson (1989) proposed that cooperative learning must have five major elements: individual positive interdependence; individuals have direct communication; individuals must master the materials of the group; individuals have collaborative skills; and adopt group strategies. Cooperative learning is conducive to the development of individual thinking and motor skills, enhances communication and inclusiveness among students, and fosters teamwork and students' academic performance. Collaborative learning in the classroom also has shortcomings, such as the difference between students who learn slowly and learn fast, the difference between students with strong ability and weak ability, the difference between positive and negative students, which often leads to cooperation neglect. Individual differences affect the learning progress of students who feel unnatural about cooperation. Moreover, the group's achievements depend too much on the individual's achievements. Once an individual has insufficient ability or is not interested, it will lead to cooperation failure.

1.4.2.6 Discovery mode

Bruner proposes cognitive discovery learning theory, opposes the use of stimulus-response (SR) connections and animal behavioral learning to explain human learning activities, but focuses on the internal cognition of students' access to knowledge. How processes and teachers organize classrooms to promote students' "discovery" of knowledge. Discovery learning is a teaching model that trains students to explore knowledge and discover knowledge as their main goal. As a teaching method, the discovery method is more concerned with the students' learning, with the students' independent learning and cooperative learning as the main features. In the learning process, the students are based on the original cognition. Its metacognition, motivation, and behavior can be actively and effectively involved. Discovery mode helps to improve students' knowledge retention, provides students with information to solve problems in teaching, and increases students' intellectual potential. Discovery learning can stimulate students' intrinsic motivation and stimulate their interest in knowledge, thus enabling students gain the skills to solve problems. However, this method is more suitable for teaching in the lower grades, and it is too time-consuming to use in the classroom.

1.4.2.7 Example teaching mode

The example teaching model is proposed by the German educational practicer M. Wagenschein. It follows the cognitive rules of human beings: from individual to general, from concrete to abstract, in the teaching, generally from some paradigm analysis, the principle of perception and Regularity, and gradually refine and summarize, and then carry out migration and integration. The basic process of example teaching is: clarify the "one" case—an exemplary clarification of the "class" case—the example of mastering the principle of law—the methodological significance of mastering the principle of law—the application of training in the principle of law, must select the essential factors, fundamental factors, typical case of factors, through the study of the examples, enables students to learn from individual to general, from concrete to abstract, from understanding practical understanding, to mastering patterns with universal rules and principles. In the process of teaching, this kind of individualization, into the class, and then from the class, refine the essential characteristics, and finally rise to the law and principle, help to cultivate students' analytical ability, students' ability to understand the law and principles. It is more suitable for teaching some principles and laws in the social sciences. The examples must be representative and best to stimulate students' interest.

1.4.2.8　Gagne Information Processing Mode

According to the information processing theory, Gagne believes that the conditions of learning are divided into internal conditions and external conditions, and internal conditions are further divided into basic prerequisites and supporting prerequisites. Supportive prerequisites play a supporting role in the learning process, but learning without these conditions can occur, and without basic prerequisites it is not acceptable. Different learning categories require different learning conditions and can produce five types of learning outcomes: verbal information, intellectual skills, cognitive strategies, motor skills, and attitudes. Speech information includes names, symbols, facts, and principles. Gagne's theory of learning hierarchy is mainly applied to the study of intellectual skills. He believes that learning any new wisdom skills requires some kind of prior learning, and learning is cumulative. According to the degree of complexity, from simple to complex, Gagne divides the wisdom skills into eight levels: signal learning, stimulus-response learning, chain learning, speech association, discrimination learning, concept learning, rule learning, and advanced rule learning. He proposed a nine-step teaching method in accordance with the steps of computer processing information (environment—receiver—registration—encoding—reactor execution monitoring—effector—environment): attracting attention—informing the target—stimulation of recollection prerequisites—presenting stimulating materials—providing learning Guidance—triggering performance—providing feedback on the correctness of performance—evaluation—enhancing retention and migration. Gagne believes that teachers are the designers and managers of teaching activities, and also the assessors of student learning effects. At each stage of learning, information processing activities are carried out inside the learner's mind, transforming information from one form to another, until the learner reacts in a homework manner. The teaching process must be based on the basic principles of learning. After the learning outcomes (ie, verbal information, cognitive strategies, intellectual skills, motor skills, attitudes) are determined, they must be arranged in the appropriate order of the teaching objectives. Effective teaching requires teachers to create or arrange appropriate external conditions based on their internal learning conditions to promote effective learning to achieve the desired teaching goals.

1.4.2.9 Ausubel Mode

Ausubel is a practical user of the theory of cognitive structure. He believes that cognitive structure is the form in which book knowledge is reproduced in the minds of students, and is the result and condition of meaningful learning. His meaningful learning theory emphasizes the status of cognitive structure, and it focuses on the cognitive learning structure of upper learning, lower learning, related generic learning, parallel learning and creative learning. On the basis of in—depth study of the type of learning, the "learning" is divided into two types: "meaningful learning" and "mechanical learning" according to its effects. The so-called meaningful learning is to obtain the understanding of the nature of the things reflected in the knowledge and the relationship between the things through learning. The key is to learn some new concepts, new knowledge and the original cognitive structure of the learners. Non-arbitrary substantive links are established between aspects (representations, concepts or propositions). As long as the connection can be established, it is meaningful learning, otherwise it will be a memorable mechanical learning. Ausubel believes that the establishment of this connection between old and new knowledge is the single most important factor affecting learning and one of the most basic and core principles of educational psychology. There are two different ways or means to achieve meaningful learning——accepting learning and discovering learning, all of which can achieve meaningful learning, and also how to implement meaningful learning strategies in these two teaching methods. Research has been carried out and outstanding results have been achieved——the "first organizer" teaching strategy. The basic model is to propose the advance organizer—gradually differentiated—integrated. In addition, he noticed another important factor affecting the learning process, namely the role of emotional factors. He believes that the influence of emotional factors on learning mainly works through motivation in the following three aspects:

- Motivation can affect the occurrence of meaningful learning. Motivation does not participate in the establishment of new and old concepts, the connection between old and new knowledge, so it does not directly affect the occurrence of meaningful learning, but the motivation can make the learner "focus attention". The "strengthening efforts" "learning persistence" and "frustration tolerance" play a greater role in strengthening the interaction between new and old knowledge (acting as a catalyst), thus effectively promoting meaningful learning.

- Motivation can influence the retention of learned meaning. Because motivation does not participate in the establishment of the relationship between old and new knowledge and the interaction between old and new knowledge, so it can not directly affect the retention of learned meaning, but always maintain through the review process. In the review process, motivation can still improve the clarity and consolidation of new meanings by enabling learners to exert greater potential in "concentration attention" "strengthening efforts", and "persistence", effectively promotes retention.

- Motivation can affect the extraction of knowledge (recall). The motivation is too strong, and it may have an inhibitory effect, so that the knowledge that can be extracted can not be extracted (cannot be recalled). Because of psychological stress and excessive motivation during the test, it affects the normal level. An example: on the contrary, sometimes the motivation is too weak to mobilize the full potential of the learner's nervous system, and it also weakens the extraction of existing knowledge. This is his "motivation theory".

Ausubel's theory of meaningful speech learning is suitable for explaining students' knowledge learning, and it is the learning process of declarative knowledge. It is not suitable for the learning process of interpreting procedural knowledge, such as speech skills, operational skills, behavioral methods, etc. The teaching methods and teaching models based on this theory are also applicable to classroom knowledge teaching, but there is insufficient teaching in terms of ability training and skill training.

1.4.2.10 Butler Learning Mode

In the 1970s, the American educational psychologist Butler proposed the seven elements of teaching and proposed the "seven-segment" teaching theory, which has a great influence on the international community. The basic teaching procedure is to set up the situation—the engine—organization teaching—application of new knowledge—test evaluation—consolidation exercises—expansion and migration. Starting from the information processing theory, Butler pays great attention to the adjustment of metacognition, uses learning strategies to process learning tasks, and finally generates learning results. When teachers use this model, they should always remind students to reflect on their learning behavior. This is a relatively universal teaching model. According to different teaching contents, it can be transformed into different teaching methods. As long as the teacher is flexible, he can achieve the teaching effect he wants. However, teachers should be required to be a research-oriented teacher. They must have knowledge of pedagogy and psychology. If they master metacognitive strategies, they can use this teaching model flexibly.

1.4.2.11 Anchored teaching

The theoretical basis is constructivism. It is believed that the learner wants to complete the meaning construction of the knowledge he has learned, that is, to achieve the deep understanding of the nature and laws of the things reflected in the knowledge and the connection between the thing and other things. The solution is to let the learner feel and experience in the real world of the real world (that is, learn by acquiring direct experience), rather than just listening to other people (such as teachers) about the introduction and explanation of this experience. Because anchored teaching is based on real-life examples or problems, it is sometimes referred to as "instance-based teaching" or "question-based teaching" or "situational teaching". Anchored teaching consists of several links:

- Create a situation: enable learning to occur in situations that are basically consistent or similar to reality.
- Identify the problem: In the above situation, select the authenticity event or problem that is closely related to the current learning topic as the central content of the learning.
- Self-learning: It is not the teacher who directly tells the students how to solve the problem, but the teacher provides the students with relevant clues to solve the problem, and pays special attention to the development of students' "self-learning" ability.
- Collaborative learning: discussion, communication, complemen- ting, correcting, and deepening each student's understanding of current issues through confrontation between different perspectives.
- Effect evaluation: Since the learning process of anchored teaching is the process of solving problems, the process can directly reflect the learning effect of students.

This method can cultivate students' ability of innovation, problem-solving, independent thinking, cooperation, etc. , but the application must pay attention to the situation setting and the problem. The problem is difficult and moderate, and it must have a certain degree of authenticity. In the teaching, the student's subjectivity should be fully exerted.

1.4.3 Teaching evaluation

Teaching evaluation is an activity that judges the value of the teaching process and results according to the teaching objectives and serves the teaching decision-making. Teaching evaluation is the process of studying the teaching of teachers and the value of students' learning. Teaching evaluation generally includes evaluations of teachers, students, teaching content, teaching methods, teaching environment, and teaching management factors in the teaching process, but it is mainly the evaluation of students' learning effects and the evaluation of teachers' teaching work process. Teaching evaluation methods include quizzes, reconciliations, observation questions, homework examinations, lectures, and class evaluations. There are two core links in teaching evaluation: the evaluation of teachers' teaching work (teaching design, organization, implementation, etc.) and the evaluation of students' learning effects. Teaching evaluation has:

- Diagnostic role, comprehensive and objective evaluation work can not only estimate the extent to which students' achievement has achieved the teaching objectives, but also explain the reasons for poor performance and identify the main reasons.
- Incentives, evaluations have a supervisory and intensive role for teachers and students. Within a certain limit, frequent test scores have a great incentive effect on students' learning motivation and can effectively promote classroom learning.
- Regulating the role, evaluating the information sent can enable teachers and students to know their teaching and learning. Teachers and students can modify the plan according to the feedback information, adjust the teaching behavior, and work effectively to achieve the specified goals. This is the evaluation.
- Teaching role, evaluation itself is also a teaching activity. In this activity, students' knowledge and skills will be advanced, and their intelligence and morality will progress.

According to the difference in the role of evaluation in teaching activities, teaching evaluation can be divided into three types: diagnostic evaluation, formative evaluation and summary evaluation. Diagnostic evaluation refers to the measurement evaluation of the evaluation preparation level before the start of the teaching activity, so as to take corresponding measures to make the teaching plan smoothly and effectively implement the measurement evaluation. The implementation time of a diagnostic evaluation is generally required at the beginning of the course, semester, school year, or teaching process. There are two main functions: one, to determine the student's readiness. Second, appropriate placement of students. Formative evaluation is the evaluation of the student's learning outcomes in the process of teaching, in order to adjust and improve the teaching activities and ensure the realization of the teaching objectives. At present, on the subject of evaluation, students' self-evaluation is emphasized more; in the evaluation function, more emphasis is placed on the educational function of evaluation; in the type of evaluation, more emphasis is placed on the implementation of formative evaluation; in the evaluation method, more absolute evaluation is adopted. The development trend.

1.5 Summary of curriculum theory

The course is a concept that is constantly evolving. In a narrow sense, the curriculum is a teaching design program that realizes the training objectives of all levels of schools. It is a set of knowledge, skills, values and behavioral norms that exist in the specific form of the teaching plan. The broad curriculum includes information clarified and arranged by the teaching plan, outline and textbooks, as well as potential or implicit content, that is, the content conveyed by the quality of life of the school, the attitude of the teacher, and the moral background of the teaching activities. The broader curriculum includes both on-campus and off-campus education, namely formal education and non-formal education.

1.5.1 The development and genre of the curriculum

Curriculum development is often subject to changes in social development, scientific development, and personal development needs, and curriculum research has evolved. It is mainly divided into three stages: from the late 1960s to the late 1960s, curriculum research has increasingly become an important area of educational research. Early research was deeply influenced by positivism and pragmatism, which saw teaching as the process of "transferring" pre-determined knowledge to learners. The research at this stage is mainly influenced by the natural science paradigm, emphasizing the "technical" of the curriculum, the controllability, predictability and practical efficiency of the teaching process. The traditional curriculum theory was challenged in the late 1960s. The process model of the British educator Steinhaus and the structural model of Bruner of the American educator emerged. Structuralism focuses on the study of the nature of education, and treats the curriculum as a more defined area, emphasizing the broader content of the curriculum. From the late 1960s to the early 1970s, anti-school movements and anti-rational cultural thoughts led to the emergence of ideological courses. From the standpoint of humanism, they reflected on the non-humanized school curriculum that suppressed the development of learners' subjective consciousness. criticism. The curriculum genre is the interpretation and practice of curriculum researchers based on their understanding of the connotation of the curriculum. It is generally divided into the following curriculum genres:

1.5.1.1 The School of Intellectualism (Intellectualism)

It is a curriculum concept based on the knowledge-based educational doctrine. The epistemologist represented by Herbart emphasizes moral education and knowledge-based. He believes that morally noble people have moral knowledge, moral thought and moral judgment. People who advocate the setting of school curricula should be commensurate with the multifaceted interests of people, including:

- Interest in experience: interest relating to natural, geographical, physical, chemical and other disciplines.
- Speculative interests: interest relating to grammar, mathematics, logic, etc.
- Aesthetic interest: interest relating to literature, poetry, music and other disciplines.
- Sympathetic interests: interest relating to classical foreign languages and modern foreign languages.
- Religious interest: interest relating to theological discipline.

Intellectualism has greatly influenced the practice of school moral education in countries around the world, and this trend is likely to continue. However, morality is a complex integration involving knowledge, emotion, and behavior. One-dimensional subjectivism cannot truly take into account the overall picture of individual moral development, and it is difficult to achieve individual development of individual morality. However, cognition is not the only element of morality, and intellectual education is not the whole of moral education. This is the limit of the auto-conformity of the moral education of the subject.

1.5.1.2 Experience naturalism curriculum genre

The genre of experience naturalism courses originated from the educational thoughts of Rousseau, Pestalozzi and Frobel, and was formed in Dewey's educational philosophy - "experience naturalism". In the curriculum philosophy, the combination of enlightenment spirit and romanticism is emphasized, emphasizing the nature center theory, child center theory, empiricism theory and development theory. In the specific proposition of the curriculum, emphasis is placed on the children's center curriculum, that is, the integration of children, nature, knowledge, and society. In the relationship between children and nature, children are nature, and nature is the curriculum. In the course content, emphasis is placed on the transformation and reorganization of experience, focusing on children's active work in the form of curriculum. In curriculum development, children, knowledge, society, and the relationship between the three must be respected.

1.5.1.3 Externalism curriculum genre

The epoch-making curriculum genre appeared in the United States in the 1920s. The main representatives were American educator Hutchins, French Alan, and British Livingstone. As an educational philosophy, externalism insists that the things of the past are excellent, and justifies the unchanging essence of the universe, humanity, knowledge, truth, goodness and beauty, and believes that everything that is worthy of yearning is eternal. The externalists emphasize that reason is the foundation of human nature. The stability of social order depends on a rational culture based on the principles of eternal truth, goodness and beauty. Disregarding these rational cultures, society will be unstable due to the collapse of the spiritual pillar. Therefore, in the principle of the curriculum, emphasis is placed on the "retro" claim; in the curriculum form, the subject curriculum is emphasized; in the course content, it is advocated to learn classical language, read ancient masterpieces, and attach importance to "humanities education".

1.5.1.4 Elementalism curriculum genre

The elementalism course theorists represented by Harvard University professor Bagley and Principal Conant think that "true education is the training of wisdom". Teaching should be based on the training of "smart" and academic excellence as the standard. The "common elements of culture" of human beings are the core of knowledge. In the course of curriculum development, high-level academic rational requirements are put forward, and the core curriculum development model of "knowledge center" is emphasized. The curriculum content should be organized systematically in the logical order of knowledge and the internal system of the discipline. This method has a certain historical progress, but with obvious instrumentalism.

1.5.1.5 Structuralism curriculum genre

Bruner's view of structuralism emphasizes the meaning of "discipline structure" and teaches the basic structure of subject knowledge. He advocates the spiral curriculum development technology, and believes that the curriculum evaluation is "a tool to guide curriculum construction and teaching" and advocates the discovery of learning teaching methods. Bruner believes that knowledge is always structured. Knowledge is a subjective model of people's construction of objective things. " It makes the regularity of experience have meaning and structure. Emphas on early education and promotes the development of children's cognitive ability. Bruner has proposed a famous hypothesis: "Any discipline can effectively teach children at any stage of development in an honest way. " As long as the knowledge structure is "translated" into a level that the cognitive structure of children of all ages can understand, early education can also receive the desired effect. To this end, he proposed the theory of spiral programming. Bruner The focus of the teaching task is on developing students' cognitive ability, that is, intelligence. He believes that intellectual development is the guarantee of mastering the structure of knowledge. The teaching method advocates the "discovery method" and believes that: "Discovery is not limited to the requirement that human beings are not yet aware of the behavior of things. To be correct, discovering includes all forms of acquiring knowledge in person with your own mind. "Discovery learning is to let students use the materials provided by the teachers to personally discover the conclusions or laws that should be drawn. The basic procedures are generally: Create a situation for finding problems—Establish a hypothesis to solve the problem—Verify the hypothesis—Make a match scientific conclusion—transformed into abilities. Using discovery methods can reduce students' dependence on teachers and teaching materials, thereby cultivating students' curiosity, developing students' reasoning ability and observation ability, and making them master the methods of inquiry. A representative of the structuralist education school, Bruner, with his unique claims, has had an important influence on the educational reforms in the United States and many countries in the world. For example, he has included cognitive psychology in the exploration of educational issues for education. Scientific research has opened up a new path. His research on selected textbooks, developmental intelligence, discovery method teaching, and spiral curriculum arrangement still have an impact on Western curriculum theory. However, there are also some shortcomings in his educational proposition. For example, his disciplinary structure is still too subjective and there is no objective standard. The "discovery method" is too far away from the teacher-student level, the teaching content is separated from the actual social life, and so on, which eventually leads to the "discipline structure movement".

1.5.1.6　Humanistic curriculum genre

The humanistic curriculum genre represented by American psychologist Rogers attaches importance to the individual consciousness of the curriculum, emphasizes the role of student emotion and individual experience in the curriculum implementation, and proposes the principle of appropriate curriculum selection and the integrated curriculum organization. The choice of curriculum should not only pay attention to the development of the individual, but also pay attention to the solution of social problems. It not only pays attention to the psychological characteristics of children, but also attaches importance to the logic of the curriculum system. The course "integration" mainly refers to three aspects: the first is the agreement between the learner's psychological development and the textbook structure logic; the second is the integration of the emotional field; the third is the integration of relevant disciplines under the guidance of experience. Integration means breaking the boundaries of fixed textbooks and traditional content systems, emphasizing the breadth of knowledge rather than depth, and caring about the application of knowledge rather than form. The organization of this curriculum compensates for the lack of one-sidedness of traditional courses and promotes the mutual penetration and interaction of knowledge and experience.

1.5.1.7　Constructivist curriculum genre

Constructivism believes that children are gradually constructing knowledge about the outside world in the process of constantly interacting with the external environment, thus constructing their own cognitive structure. Therefore, in the content of the course, to choose the task of authenticity, the content of the course cannot be handled too simplistically, so as not to be far from the real problem situation. In the organization of the curriculum, the boundaries of weak chemistry emphasize the intersection between disciplines.

1.5.1.8 Postmodern curriculum genre

The post-modern curriculum theory represented by Pina and Dole believes that the essence of the curriculum is complex, chaotic, limited, temporary and pluralistic. Therefore, the post-modern curriculum design emphasizes the design of the open system, and continuously absorbs the changed material and energy from the external environment as feedback to promote internal transformation and renewal. Curriculum implementation emphasizes transformational change, integration and interaction. In the specific curriculum proposition, 4R curriculum requirements——richness, recursion, relations and rigor——are proposed.

1.5.2 Course objectives

The course objectives refer to the indicator system for a task to be completed in a teaching subject or a teaching activity. It includes skills, knowledge, attitudes and values, and is a means of achieving the purpose of teaching. In a narrow sense, the objectives of the course do not include the "educational policy", which only includes "educational purposes" "training objectives" "course objectives" and "teaching objectives". The objectives of the course are mainly divided into behavioral orientation goals, generative curriculum objectives, and performance curriculum objectives. The behavioral orientation of the course is to anticipate the student's learning outcomes. It has a guiding function, a control function, an incentive function and an evaluation function. The behavioral goals are more specific, clear, easy to operate and evaluate, and are suitable for learning course content based on training knowledge and skills. The course goal theory of behavioral goal orientation mainly includes Taylor's curriculum goal theory and Bloom's educational goal taxonomy. The generative goal is not a goal that is pre-specified by the outside, but a goal that is naturally generated in the educational context as the educational process unfolds. It focuses on the process of learning activities, rather than focusing on results as the behavioral goals. Consider the differences in students' interests and abilities, and emphasize the adaptability and generations of the goals. The performance goal refers to the individualized creative performance of each student in the various situations of the educational situation. Pay attention to the creative spirit and critical thinking of students, and it is suitable for the curriculum arrangement based on student activities. The basic theory of the course objectives:

1.5.2.1 Taylor's curriculum principles and evaluation principles

Taylor introduced the evaluation into the curriculum development process, pointing out the inseparable relationship between goal formulation, curriculum content arrangement, teaching organization and outcome evaluation. Taylor's curriculum principles and evaluation principles are goal-centered. In his view, the goal is not only to state how the student should behave, but also to state the goal in the most precise way, in order to more clearly tell us whether the course and teaching are successful or not.

1.5.2.2 Bloom's educational goal classification system

The educational goal classification system represented by Bloom believes that the three basic areas of learning include cognitive, emotional, and motor skills. He believes that the goal of education is primarily to contribute to "the choice of content and behavior that constitutes the structure of the curriculum and provides the basis for evaluating the success of a particular educational program". Bloom is based on the cognitive process of human beings from simple to complex, from the specific to the abstraction as the theoretical basis for the classification of educational goals. Bloom believes that as long as two simple and similar behaviors are linked, both become incomparably complex. Under the guidance of this concept, Bloom has carried out a new classification from the simple to the complex development of educational behavior, which is to construct a complete theoretical system of the classification of educational goals in the cognitive field. He emphasized that the classification of objectives is not an end in itself, but a means of providing measurement for evaluating teaching results. It also helps to make various assumptions about the teaching process and changes in students, to stimulate thinking about educational issues, and to help teachers properly arrange Various types of teaching content provide guidance for curriculum development.

1.5.2.3 Gagne's "Conditions of Learning" theory

Gagne puts forward the classification system theory of learning results in "Conditions of Learning", classifies the learning results, and proposes five kinds of learning results: speech information, intellectual skills, cognitive strategies, motor skills and attitudes. He pointed out five aspects of cognition and response conditions (Table 1-1).

Table 1-1 Five aspects of cognition and response conditions

Classification of learning outcomes	Necessary conditions	Supportive conditions
Intelligence skills	Components of simpler intellectual skills (Rules, concepts, discrimination)	Attitude Cognitive strategy Speech information
Cognitive strategy	Some basic psychological ability and cognitive development level	Intelligence skills Speech information Attitude
Speech information	A well-organized and meaningful message	Speech skills Cognitive strategy Attitude
Attitude	Intelligence skills (sometimes) Speech information (sometimes)	Other attitude Speech information
Action skills	Some action skills (sometimes) Operating procedure rules (sometimes)	Speech information Attitude

1.5.3 Course content

The content of the course is the knowledge, skills, values and behavioral norms that enter the field of school education. It is the content of school education and is the experience that learners have acquired in the school environment. There are two main types of views on choosing course content:

Firstly, the concept of knowledge and the content of the curriculum mainly believe that the nature of knowledge restricts the choice of curriculum. One view is that knowledge is an objective principle that exists outside of learners. Education is to enable learners to gradually learn and master this knowledge. Therefore, educators should provide courses to learners; another view is that knowledge is the creation of the individual's mind and the knowledge that individuals form when forming and organizing experiences. Therefore, educators should arrange courses with students.

Secondly, the classification of course content is considered to be an important issue about the content of the course. Spencer divides human activities into five categories, including courses in physiology, logic, psychology, history, fine arts, and music. He believes that the education required for various activities has its own curriculum. Hearst believes that education is to teach students a variety of knowledge and develop their abilities, and knowledge and cognitive abilities have multiple logical forms, and the curriculum is the same. He divides knowledge into seven forms, namely mathematics and formal logic, natural science, moral understanding and moral judgment, aesthetics, philosophy, religious experience, and understanding of oneself and others' psychology. In addition, there are Bernstein's curriculum taxonomy and British curriculum center.

There are three main forms of organization and arrangement of course content: linear, circular and spiral. Straight line is to organize the elements of the course into a logically coherent straight line. The speed of knowledge presentation is relatively fast and does not repeat before and after. The circular arrangement emphasizes the arrangement of course elements, especially the knowledge and skill elements from the center to the edge, without repeating the previous content. The spiral curriculum development emphasizes that the basic concepts, principles and adoptions in a subject are repeated at various stages. The so-called spiral curriculum is to place the disciplinary structure at the center of the curriculum in a form consistent with the child's way of thinking. The promotion has continued to expand and deepen the basic structure of the discipline, making it spiral upward in the curriculum.

The method of its preparation adopts the basic concepts and principles in a discipline at various stages, and gradually expands the scope of knowledge, deepens the way of expression and the level of knowledge. Because this arrangement absorbs the advantages of the first two methods, and also conforms to people's cognitive development rules, has become the dominant way of textbook layout.

1.5.4　Course evaluation

Course evaluation refers to whether the objectives, compilation and implementation of the course have been achieved, and the degree of achievement has been achieved to determine the effectiveness of the course design, and to make decisions to improve the course. Course evaluation is a process of value judgment. The course evaluation includes various course elements such as "planning, implementation, results, etc". That is to say, the scope of the course evaluation is very wide. It includes both the curriculum plan itself, as well as the teachers, students and schools participating in the implementation of the curriculum. It also includes the results of the curriculum activities, that is, the development of students and teachers.

The theoretical perspectives of curriculum evaluation mainly have the following development periods:

(1) Early development: the period of educational measurement and evaluation.

In the mid-nineteenth century, psychology gradually became independent from philosophy, and the measurement method was initially used as a tool for psychological research. The representative of Sondike, known as the "father of education measurement", screens the memory status of individual knowledge by testing or measuring, thus measuring the teaching effect and developing the testing technology to a rather complicated degree.

(2) "Science" Development——Education Evaluation Description Period. The representative character is Taylor——"the father of educational evaluation", and the evaluation is essentially "description", which is to describe the consistency of educational results and goals. The criterion for determining the effectiveness of a course is to see to what extent the educational goal is achieved. The key to evaluation is to identify clear, actionable behavioral goals, not just "tests". In the evaluation method, two types of summative evaluation and formative evaluation are formed. Obviously, education evaluation is moving towards scientific development at this stage.

(3) The "judgment" period of evaluation——the Stoke period. The Stoke curriculum evaluation model expands the concept of evaluation, emphasizing the evaluation of things. The fundamental problem is to judge things. As a process of judging things, evaluation is not just a description of the results according to a predetermined goal. The intended goal itself also needs value judgment, and the procedurality of the evaluation is determined.

(4) Construction of evaluations——the era of new evaluators. The core of the curriculum is the "diversity and complexity of the learning environment". Evaluation is not a measurement and judgment of the expected educational outcome, but a comprehensive and in-depth study of the entire program, including premise assumptions, theoretical deductions, program design, implementation effects, and difficult issues. What this theory actually cares about is how to understand the phenomenon of the curriculum rather than clarifying its causal link, and therefore opposes the use of purely scientific and measurement techniques.

1.5.5 Course theory

The main theories about subject curriculum since the 1960s are: the structuralist theory of American educational psychologist Bruner, the paradigm of German educator Vagenschein, and the former Soviet educator Zankov's developmentist curriculum theory.

1.5.5.1 Bruner's structuralism curriculum theory

Bruner's structuralism curriculum theory advocates that the curriculum content is centered on the basic structure of each discipline. The basic structure of the discipline is composed of the basic concepts and basic principles of scientific knowledge. In the curriculum design, it is advocated to arrange the basic structure of the subject according to the characteristics of the child's intellectual development stage. He also advocates discovery law learning. Many of Bruner's ideas reflect a strong spirit of the times, and still have a strong practical significance for today's curriculum research and school education. At the same time, there are also deficiencies, such as one-sided emphasis on the academic nature of the content, which makes the teaching content too abstract; the positioning of students is too high, it seems that every student should be trained as an expert in this subject, and in dealing with knowledge, skills and intelligence The relationship is not very successful.

1.5.5.2 Wagenschein's paradigm

Wagenschein's paradigm approach emphasizes the basic, basic and paradigm of the curriculum. It advocates teaching students' basic knowledge, concepts and basic scientific rules. The teaching content should be suitable for students' intellectual development level and existing life. Experience, textbooks should be selected with typical and exemplary content. Its characteristics are as follows: First, it takes the example of knowledge structure theory to draw materials. Its content is both refined and specific, and it is easy to be inferior to the third. It is analogous to the analogy. Second, the example is that the theory is naturally combined with the actual. Third, to solve the practical problem, the content is comprehensive, not single. Fourth, paradigm teaching can cultivate students' ability to analyze and solve problems more typically, concretely and practically.

1.5.5.3 Zankov's development curriculum theory

Zankov's development curriculum theory regards "general development" as the starting point and destination of its curriculum theory, which is called "development curriculum theory". The so-called "general development" refers to the development of intelligence, emotion, will, quality, and personality, that is, the development of the whole personality. Main points: First, the course content should be as difficult as necessary. Second, we must pay attention to the role of theoretical knowledge in teaching materials, and teach regular knowledge to students. Third, the course materials must be carried out at the necessary speed. Fourth, the organization of teaching materials should enable students to understand the learning process, that is, let students master the interrelationship between knowledge and become conscious learners. Fifth, the curriculum materials should be oriented to all students, especially to promote the development of poor students.

1.6 Review of learning theory

1.6.1 Basic concept

1.6.1.1 Learning

Learning is a broad concept that refers to the longer-lasting changes in an individual's behavioral potential due to practice or repeated experience in a given situation. It refers not only to the study of knowledge and skills, but also to all learning behaviors in people's daily lives. Learning is caused by experience. This change is caused by the connection between the individual and the environment or repeated experience. Only when the individual has undergone behavioral changes under the influence of experience can the study be considered and cannot simply be considered as long as the behavior changes, it means learning.

1.6.1.2 Learning theory

Learning theory is a psychological theory that explores the nature of human learning and its formation of tact. It focuses on the nature, process, motivation, and methods and strategies of learning. It is a sub-discipline of pedagogy and educational psychology that describes or describes the types of human and animal learning, processes, and theories that influence the various factors of learning.

1.6.1.3 Concept learning

A concept is a symbol of a class of things or concepts that have common characteristics. Conceptual learning is the process of learning to bring together things with common attributes and to name them, and to exclude things that do not have such attributes. The main factors affecting conceptual learning are: the defining characteristics of the concept, the prototype, the way of teaching the concept, the connection between concepts, the learner's age, gender, intelligence, motivation, emotion, experience, ethnicity, language ability, values, and use learning. Individual differences in strategy, etc.

1.6.1.4 Principle learning

The principle refers to the expression of a relationship between two or more concepts, that is, the description of the relationship between concepts. Therefore, principle learning is based on conceptual learning. It is generally divided into two types: discovery learning and acceptance learning. Discovery learning means that under the inspiration of teachers, students independently discover the relationship between concepts; accepting learning means that the teacher presents the principle directly to the student in the form of a proposition, and establishes contact with the existing knowledge of the student, so that the new principle is integrated into the student's existing in the cognitive structure. Principle learning emphasizes the internal conditions of the learner such as the learner's learning and understanding of the concept, the learner's cognitive development level, verbal ability and learning motivation, and the external conditions of the learner's learning situation. Mainly the teacher's guiding principle plays the important role of learning.

1.6.1.5 Problem solving

The problem is that when an individual is doing something, he does not know the series of actions to be taken to do it, including the situation, the existing knowledge and skills, the obstacles and the methods. Problem solving is to form a new answer or solution to the problem, which is a process of thinking. Problem solving must face new problems and form principles or rules for solving problems, and become an integral part of the cognitive structure. It is an advanced form of learning.

1.6.1.6 Learning to migrate

In psychology, learning transfer refers to the effect of learning on another type of learning, that is, the knowledge experience, cognitive structure, motor skills, strategies, and methods that learners have acquired, and new knowledge and new skills. The impact of the occurrence. That is, it is the effect of the skills, knowledge, or attitudes acquired in one context on the acquisition of skills, knowledge, or attitudes in another context. Migration exists not only within a certain experience, but also between different experiences, and between knowledge and skills. For example, the mastery of vocabulary knowledge in language learning will promote the improvement of reading skills, and the improvement of reading skills can promote the acquisition of more vocabulary knowledge.

1.6.1.7 Mechanical learning and meaningful learning

The former means that the current study does not establish a meaningful connection with the existing knowledge; the latter refers to the establishment of a substantial and meaningful connection between the current learning and the existing knowledge. So how does learning happen, what are the rules, and how is learning done? These are all issues that educators have been studying. Researchers classify learning from different perspectives. From the perspective of learning objectives, Bloom divides learning into educational goals, emotions and motor skills cognition; Gagne divides learning into speech information learning, intelligent learning, cognitive strategy learning, attitude learning, and sports skill learning from the perspective of learning outcomes; Ossupor divides learning into learning and discovery learning from the perspective of learning style. Researchers have studied learning from different angles, explored the nature of human learning and its formation of tact, and formed some learning theories, which are mainly divided into two categories, one is the connectionist learning theory; the other is cognition.

1.6.2 Learning theory

1.6.2.1 Connectionist learning theory

The theory of connectionist learning believes that all learning is a process of establishing a direct connection between stimulus (S) and reaction (R) through conditional action. Strengthening plays an important role in the establishment of stimulus-response linkages. In the stimulus-response connection, individuals learn habits, and habits are the result of repeated practice and reinforcement. Once the habit is formed, as long as the original or similar stimuli appear, the learned habit response will automatically appear.

(a) Sandyk's trial and error. The American positivist psy- chologist Sandyke used scientific experiments to study the law of learning and put forward trial and error. Sondike's experiment of eating food through the pedals of hungry cats in the cage shows that the so-called learning is the process of continuously reducing the mistakes of animals (including humans) by constantly trying to form a stimulus-response connection. He believes that learning is the connection, and the heart is the connection system of people. The essence of learning is to form a connection between stimulation and response, namely S-R connection. The process of this association is gradual, trying to go wrong until the process of success. According to his own experiments, Sandek proposed three learning laws: preparation law, practice law and effect law. The preparation law is that the learner is prepared to give the activity and is satisfied. On the contrary, it is troublesome to prepare for inactivity or unprepared to impose the activity; the practice law is that the application of the connection will enhance the strength of the connection, that is, for the learner has formed some kind of connection, and repeating this reaction correctly in practice will effectively enhance this connection. On the contrary, it will lead to weakening or forgetting of the connection; the effect law means that any behavior that leads to satisfactory results will be strengthened, and vice versa. The various positive or negative feedbacks that learners receive during the learning process will strengthen or weaken some kind of connection that the learner has formed in the mind. Sondike has two major contributions to psychology. He is a pioneer of animal psychology. He studies animal behaviors, studies his behavior and proposes learning theories to transform traditional philosophy education psychology into science education psychology. Scientific research is important, but over-emphasis can be counterproductive. In addition, his theory is difficult to adapt to the actual needs of education.

(b) Pavlov's classic conditioning. The Russian physiologist Pavlov proposed classical conditioned reflexes through experiments. The combination of conditional stimuli and unconditional stimuli makes conditional stimuli also cause unconditional stimuli. This learning process is divided into two types, maintaining and regressing, and differentiation and generalization. Pavlov's response to the dog's reaction to ringing and food found that the vocal reflex behavior (saliva secretion) of the dog continued to persist after the animal established conditioned reflexes, and continued to present the ring to the unconditional stimulus (food). However, when there is multiple accompanying conditional stimuli (rings) and there is no corresponding food, the saliva secretion of the dog will decrease with the increase of the number of experiments, which is the regression of the reaction. Generalization refers to the phenomenon that an organism reacts to other stimuli similar to the conditional reflector after a certain conditional reflection is formed. The differentiation is that the organism's response to the conditional stimuli is further refined, the target stimuli are strengthened, and the unconditioned stimuli are resolved. Pavlov's doctrine explains the behavior of many learning situations, but it is less used.

(c) Skinner's reinforcement theory. American behaviorist psychologist Skinner used white mice as experimental objects to further develop the stimulus-response theory of Sandek and proposed operational conditioning. Sondike focuses on the S-R connection of research and learning, while Skinner further explores the reasons why the white mouse pushes the joystick (the joystick will be eaten by the joystick), and calls this behavior an operational condition. Reflection or instrumental conditioning. He refers to this process or process that further stimulates the organism to take certain actions, and any event or stimulus that enhances the behavior of the organism is called a reinforcement, and the stimulus that causes the probability of behavior to fall is called punishment. Skinner divides reinforcement into three types: positive reinforcement, negative reinforcement, and natural regression. Positive reinforcement, also known as positive reinforcement, means that when people take certain actions, they can get some kind of results that make them feel happy. This result in turn becomes the force to promote people's tendency to or repeat such behavior, to strengthen the desired personal behavior. Negative reinforcement, also known as negative reinforcement, refers to the negative consequences of an unpleasant behavior caused by an unqualified behavior. Punishment is a typical way of negative reinforcement. Natural regression, also known as attenuation, refers to the withdrawal of a certain behavior that was previously acceptable. Since it will not be strengthened for a certain period of time, this behavior will naturally decline and gradually fade away. The purpose of negative reinforcement and natural regression is to reduce and eliminate undesired behavior. These three types of reinforcements are interrelated and complementary, forming an intensive system and becoming a special environmental factor that restricts or influences human behavior. Skinner is the psychologist who has the greatest influence on learning psychology in the later stage of behaviorism. It inherits the traditions of behaviorism such as science, objectivity, control and prediction. It builds learning theory based on experiments and has certain theoretical guidance in practice.

(d) Gagne's information processing theory. Using the idea of computer simulation, Gagne absorbed the viewpoints of behavioral and cognitive learning processes, proposed the basic model of the learning process, and demonstrated the information flow in the learning process, as shown in the figure 1 −1:

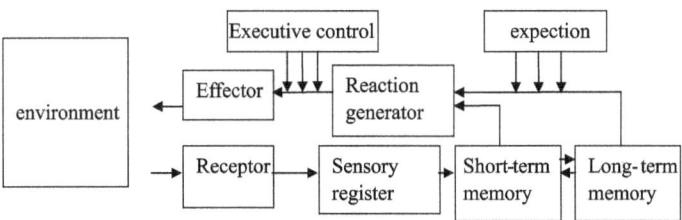

Figure 1 −1 Gagne's learning model

Gagne's learning model has noticed the characteristics of human learning, and is a relatively representative learning model at present, which also has a certain guiding role for teaching. In this information flow, Gagne believes that learning is a program for learners to ingest information. It is the first step in learning that learners receive stimuli from the environment and activate receptors. After careful attention, the external information is converted into a stimulus signal, which is selectively perceived by the human being, and maintained in the human sensor register (0. 25 to 2 seconds); the converted information is then entered into the short-term memory by sound or shape 2. 5 to 20 seconds). The information of these meaningful organizations is continuously saved by the continuous retelling of the learners and enters the human long-term memory system. Learner's spontaneous control and positive expectations are two important factors that can stimulate or change the processing of information flow. Gagne divides the teaching process into eight stages, that is, the motivation stage in which the teacher stimulates the student's learning, and the learner points the attention of the learning to the various stages of the stimulation related to his learning objectives, and helps the learner to use the better coding. The strategy is to learn the acquisition stage of knowledge, and use teaching methods to encourage students to store information in the retention phase of long-term memory, review the repeated recall phase, summary phase, operation phase and feedback phase.

1. 6. 2. 2 Bandura's theory of social learning

American psychologist Bandura accepted the relevant results of cognitive learning theory based on the simple learning model of stimulus-response emphasized by behaviorism. It is suggested that learning theory must study the reaction process occurring in the learner's mind. The viewpoint forms a cognitive-behavioral model of comprehensive behaviorism and cognitive psychology, and proposes a social learning theory of "people learn in society". He believes that the acquisition of children's social behavior is mainly done by observing and imitating the behavior of important people in real life. The process of observation and learning of any organism takes place under the interaction of individuals, environment and behavior. Behaviors and environments can be changed through specific organizations. The influence of the three on the shaping of children's behavior depends on the environment at that time and the nature of the act. He divided this behavior of observing social learning into four phases, namely the attention phase, the retention phase, the replication phase, and the motivation phase. And the enhancement of the behavior of organisms is divided into direct reinforcement, substitution reinforcement, and self-reinforcement. Bandura's social learning theory is different from behaviorism. He not only does not deny that cognitive function is a determinant of human behavior, but also pays attention to the internal causes of human behavior, and attaches importance to the role of symbolism, substitution, and self-regulation. His theory combines the views of behaviorism and cognition, often referred to as cognitive behaviorism.

1.6.2.3 Cognitive learning theory

Cognitive learning theory believes that learning does not passively form a stimulus-response (S-R) connection under the control of the external environment, but actively constructs a cognitive structure within the mind; learning is not a reaction habit formed by practice and reinforcement. It is acquired through epiphany and understanding; the current learning of the organism depends on his original cognitive structure and the current stimulating situation, and the learning is guided by the subject's expectations, and is not subject to the habit.

(a) Kohler's insight. Psychologist Kohler is one of the founders of the Gestalt school, and he came up with an epiphany based on experimental research on chimpanzees taking bananas. Cao Le pointed out that learning is the reorganization of perception. The process of change in perceptual experience is not a gradual attempt to try the wrong process, but a sudden realization, that is, epiphany, and the essence of epiphany learning is to construct a psychological end within the subject. shape. Epiphany said that the emphasis is on the organizational role between stimulus and response, and that this organization appears to be a sudden reorganization of the old organizational structure or an insight into the new structure in the perceptual experience. Learning is epiphany, not by trying to make mistakes. The core of epiphany learning is to grasp the essence of things, not the unrelated details. The content that is learned through mechanics is not truly unrecognizable, and the content learned through epiphany can be part of the student's knowledge and skills, and can be used for similar problems in any situation at any time. Through the content of the epiphany, once mastered, it will never be forgotten, that is, the content of the epiphany is to enter the long-term memory.

Epiphany said that once it was proposed, it became popular in the United States, and it has certain explanatory and applicability in guiding teaching. However, it overemphasizes the epiphany and completely rejects the trial and error is one-sided. Because in the process of solving a complex problem, the two activities of epiphany and trial error are often alternated. Attempts to error often manifest themselves, and more manifestations of behavioral characteristics and operational methods; and epiphany is often manifested, more manifested in psychological activities. The process of solving problems generally begins with an attempt to make a mistake and ends with an epiphany. Moreover, epiphany cannot reveal the learning process from the mechanism of psychological activity, and is not a perfect theoretical explanation. In addition, Epiphany said that there is still a lack of research on other learning-related issues, such as learning motivation, learning methods, and the type of learning.

(b) Bruner's cognitive structure learning theory. Also known as cognitive discovery, Bruner believes that the essence of learning is that students actively promote the formation of categories and their coding systems through perception, comprehension and reasoning. A category is a group of related objects and events. He emphasized that learning is to master the structure of knowledge and how to learn how things are interrelated. Bruner emphasizes that "whatever we choose to teach, we must make students understand the basic structure of the subject". The so-called "basic" means "having both broad and strong applicability". The basic structure of the discipline includes basic concepts, principles, and laws. That is, each subject should focus on teaching students the "three basics", emphasizing general importance of principle learning.

Promote the formation of effective learning methods. In Bruner's view, human beings have the ability to classify different things. People's learning is to incorporate the content of the new learning into the psychological framework (or the actual model) formed by the previous learning according to different categories of knowledge.

The process of forming a learner's knowledge system. Bruner believes that the process of human perception is the process of categorizing objective things. Therefore, he advocates that teachers should not only provide the necessary information in the process of helping learners to learn, but also teach students to master and comprehensively apply the methods of classifying objective things. He believes that the learner's inquiry is not actually the way to classify the various events in the world, but the way to create classifications. In the specific learning process, these related categories constitute the coding system. The coding system is a way of grouping and combining the knowledge that is learned. It is continuously changing and reorganizing in the continuous learning of human beings. In Bruner's view, knowledge transfer is actually the process by which learners apply the already existing coding system to other new information to effectively grasp new information. Therefore, it is very important for educators to objectively understand the coding system that learners have when teaching new knowledge.

Bruner's cognitive structure teaching theory is deeply influenced by Piaget's epistemology, which is believed to be formed through assimilation and adaptation and their mutual balance. However, he does not fully agree with Piaget's point of view. Piaget believes that cognitive structure is developed under the influence of other external influences, while Bruner repeatedly emphasizes the external tension of cognitive structure and believes that cognitive structure is an individual. A tool for knowing the world around you, it can be spontaneously perfected in constant use. Bruner's thoughts have a positive effect on teaching. The school's teaching work is mainly to help students master the knowledge of basic subjects, and to use this as an assimilation point to complete the update of knowledge structure, so that they can use the new cognitive structure to complete The perception of the surrounding world is the process by which the organism grows intelligently. Therefore, Bruner advocates teaching the basic structure of the discipline, mainly to allow students to master more general concepts or general principles to facilitate the assimilation and adaptation of subsequent new knowledge. Advocate the student's discovery and learning. The so-called discovery refers to all ways in which the learner personally acquires knowledge by following his own unique cognitive program. Bruner repeatedly emphasized that teaching is to promote the growth of students' wisdom or cognition. He advocates teachers to use the method of discovery learning in teaching. The use of discovery should follow six steps: presenting and clarifying issues of interest to the student; enabling the student to experience some degree of uncertainty about the problem; providing a variety of possible assumptions to solve the problem; assisting the student in collecting the available sentences Information; organize students to review relevant information, draw conclusions that should be; guide students to use analytical thinking to confirm conclusions. Of course, its theory also has certain limitations. Although it is found that learning has an incomparable advantage over learning, it cannot emphasize the role of discovery because it is related to the knowledge and experience of learners.

(c) Ausubel's theory of cognitive assimilation. Ausubel is a cognitive psychologist in the United States, and his outstanding contribution to educational psychology is concentrated in his expression of meaningful learning theory. On the basis of critical behaviorism simply equating animal psychology with human psychology, he creatively absorbed the cognitive assimilation theory of Piaget and Bruner equivalent psychologists, and proposed famous meaningful learning and advancement. Organizers and other theories, and organically combine learning theory with teaching theory. The core of Ausubel's learning theory is meaningful learning. He pointed out that the essence of the meaningful learning process is that the new knowledge represented by the symbol establishes a non-human and substantive connection with the appropriate concepts already existing in the learner's cognitive structure. Ausubel divides learning into learning and discovery learning, mechanical learning and meaningful learning, and clarifies the meaning of each type of learning and their relationship to each other. In order to effectively distinguish these four kinds of learning, Ausubel proposed two criteria for meaningful learning. One is that the concept of new symbols or symbols is substantially related to the relevant concepts in the learner's cognitive structure. The other is the non-human connection between old and new knowledge, that is, the connection between the new knowledge and the cognitive structure on a reasonable or logical basis. In addition, Ausubel further pointed out two major conditions for meaningful learning. First, the external conditions, that is, the material of meaningful learning, must conform to such non-human and substantive standards. The learning materials have logical meanings. The materials themselves and related concepts within the scope of human learning can establish non-human and substantive. Sexual connection. The other is the internal condition of meaningful learning, that is, the learner must have a meaningful learning direction, and associate the knowledge in the cognitive structure with the new knowledge, so that the new knowledge with potential meaning is related to its cognitive structure. Old knowledge interacts to achieve meaningful learning. Ausubel also divided meaningful learning into three categories, namely, representation learning, concept learning, and proposition learning. Ausubel's theory emphasizes the active spirit of learners' active learning, emphasizing the interaction between new ideas and existing cognitive structures. This is contrary to the theory that behaviorism only emphasizes external stimuli, but it is applied in teaching practice. No consistent research conclusions have been obtained.

  In general, the main contribution of the cognitive learning theory is: attach importance to the subject value of people in learning activities, and fully affirm the learner's conscious initiative. Emphasize the important position and role of awareness activities such as cognition, meaning understanding, and independent thinking in learning. In the practice teaching design process, it pays attention to the state of preparation of people in learning activities and advocates the creativity of people's learning. But there are also shortcomings, it does not reveal the psychological structure of the learning process. Learning psychology consists of two major components: intellectual factors and non-intellectual factors. The intellectual factor is the psychological basis of the learning process, and plays a direct role in learning; the non-intellectual factor is the psychological condition of the learning process, and has an indirect effect on learning. Only by combining intelligence with non-intellectual factors can learning achieve the intended purpose. Cognitive learning theory does not pay enough attention to the study of non-intellectual factors.

1.6.2.4 Humanistic learning theory

Humanism was an important educational trend in the United States in the late 1950s and early 1960s. The main representatives were A. Maslow, C. R. Rogers, and Kelly. They oppose the application of research results on white rats, pigeons, cats and monkeys to human learning, and advocate the use of case studies. They emphasize that the subjects of psychological research, growth and development are human instinct, people have the right to make choices actively and creatively, and people's emotional experience is very important.

The concept of humanity-based teaching believes that the nature of human nature is good, and that life has a good root. As long as the environment is appropriate, it will grow naturally; any behavior performed by human beings is not caused or determined by external stimuli, but rather Self-interest and comprehensive choices made by the inner and the parties' own emotions and willingness; human learning is the full development of personal potential and the development of personality. Therefore, the fundamental goal of education is to help develop individuality and help students realize that they are unique human beings and ultimately help students achieve their potential. The humanist emphasizes that school teachers should focus on helping students to clarify the goals of learning and the content of learning, create a good psychological atmosphere that promotes students' learning, and ensure that students are arranged through teachers in a situation full of satisfaction and security. Appropriate learning activities, discover the value and meaning of learning content, and make learners become fully developed people. Highlighting the subject's teaching process view: In the teaching process, it should be "student-centered", which is the inevitable outcome of its "self-realization" educational purpose. The teaching is centered on the learner, and the students become the real subject of learning. Humanism emphasizes that in the process of education and teaching, students should pay attention to the study of the inner world of students' cognition, emotion, interest, motivation, potential, respect each student's independent personality, protect students' self-esteem, and help each student fully tap their potential. Develop personalities and realize their own values.

Humanistic learners emphasize the emotional experience of people in the process of learning and have a certain enlightening effect on teaching. For example, teachers should pay more attention to the emotional experience of students in the teaching process, and understand the learning process and learning content from the perspective of students, help students understand the meaning of learning, establish the connection between learning content and individual learners, and guide students choose their own learning materials within a certain range, inspire students to develop learning tendency from self-propensity, cultivate students' spontaneous and conscious learning habits, and realize meaningful learning in the true sense. However, overemphasizing the subjective status of students in teaching, while ignoring the dominant position of teachers is equally counterproductive.

1.6.2.5 Constructivist learning theory

In the past two decades, with the rapid development of computer and Internet network education applications, a revolution is taking place in educational psychology, and the constructivist learning theory is gradually emerging, but so far, this theoretical system is still in existence. In the process of development, it is not yet mature. Constructivism emphasizes that the learner's original knowledge and experience should be regarded as the growth point of new knowledge, and the learner should be guided to develop new knowledge and experience from the original knowledge and experience. It focuses on how learners build knowledge based on their original experience, psychological structure, and beliefs, emphasizing the initiative, sociality, and context of learning. M. C. Wittrock believes that the learning process begins not with the sensory experience itself, but with the selective attention to the sensory experience. The learning and understanding of any subject always involves the learner's original cognitive structure. The learner always understands and constructs the new concept with his own experience, including the informal learning before formal learning and the daily concepts of scientific concepts, knowledge or information. Therefore, constructivists are more concerned with how to construct knowledge based on original experience, psychological structure and beliefs.

Constructivists elaborate their views from two aspects: the student view and the teacher view. The first is the concept of students. Constructivism emphasizes that learners build reality or explain reality based on their own experience. Second is the concept of teachers. The role of teachers should be the loyal supporters of students' construction knowledge, the senior partners or collaborators of students' learning. Although constructivism attaches great importance to the self-development of individuals, it does not deny the external influence of teachers. It believes that teachers should provide students with complex and real problems. Teachers must not only develop or discover these problems, but also must recognize the complex problems. An answer that motivates students to think about multiple issues. Teachers must provide students with metacognitive tools and psychometric tools, develop students' critical cognitive processing strategies, and construct psychological models of knowledge and understanding to help them master the knowledge, skills and strategies needed to cope with various challenges. The students should be independent and control the habit of learning, so that they could become independent thinkers and independent problem solvers. Teachers are not simple presenters of knowledge, but leaders who constantly encourage students to enrich and adjust their understanding. To this end, teachers must create a good learning environment in their teaching practice. Students in this environment can start their studies through experiments, independent inquiry, and cooperative learning. Teachers should become active helpers and guides for students to construct knowledge. In the process of constructing meaning, teachers should ask students to take the initiative to collect and analyze relevant information, put forward various assumptions on the problems they have learned and try to verify them, be good at making students connect the current learning content with their existing knowledge and experience, and think carefully about this connection.

Constructivist learners emphasize that learners grow new knowledge and experience from the original knowledge and experience, construct the meaning of new information and transform and reorganize the original experience. This is worthy of recognition, between teachers and students. The construction of the relationship puts forward new ideas and is conducive to the effective development of teaching. However, they believe that the meaning of things lies in the construction of individuals and overemphasizes the relativity of truth.

1.7 Summary of scientific research methods

1.7.1 General principle

What is the method? The term method is derived from Greek and means "road". It is not only a skill, but also an art. Its essence lies in the application of law, and it is a method to follow the law. It refers to the sum of the behaviors adopted in accordance with certain procedures in order to achieve a certain purpose, and is a general term for various specific ways and means of understanding the world and transforming the world. The choice of method must conform to the laws of the objective world development in order to achieve results. The principle of scientific methods and the category of thinking are not the tools of human beings, but the expressions of the laws of nature and human beings. Mastering scientific methods is a prerequisite for people to understand the world and transform the world.

What is research? Research refers to exploratory activities that create knowledge and organize and modify knowledge, as well as open up new uses for knowledge. It consists of two aspects: one is to create knowledge, to explore unknown problems, the purpose is to innovate and develop; the other is to organize knowledge, to analyze, sort and identify existing knowledge, to be standardized, systematic, and knowledgeable inherit.

What is educational science research? It refers to the use of certain scientific methods, following certain scientific research procedures, and exploring an educational activity through the interpretation, prediction and control of educational phenomena. Educational science research consists of three basic elements: phenomena and objective facts, scientific theories, methods and techniques. The purpose of educational scientific research is to explore the law of education, to solve important educational theories and practical problems; to have research hypotheses and specific statements on research issues. The research methods should be scientific and reasonable; the innovation of research should be.

Educational scientific research methods are ways of conducting educational research and constructing educational theories in a targeted, planned, and systematic manner. The application of educational scientific research methods is a set of systematic research processes aiming at educational phenomena, using scientific methods as a means, following certain research procedures, and obtaining knowledge of the regularity of educational science. It is also a process of understanding, the result of which is to explain or predict, discover or develop certain educational principles, principles and theories. It is both a system of knowledge and a rule of conduct.

1.7.2　Historical development

Educational scientific research methods mainly go through the following three periods:

The first period: before the 16th century, the period of intuition observation. In ancient China and Western countries, there were some summaries and records of educational experiences and methods. All the records were preliminary experience summaries, and did not form a systematic scientific research method, but also reflected certain rules and characteristics. The research method is mainly based on observation and induction, and is summarized from the observation of the material of the matter to draw conclusions. The expression of educational theory is mainly based on descriptive descriptions, which are more fragmented and fragmented, and do not form a rigorous theoretical system. The preliminary application of dialectics and the simple system view are the dominant ideas of this period. It is mainly reflected in the analysis and discussion of the dialectical relationship between literature and Taoism, words and deeds, learning and thinking, teacher and student, and the study of educational phenomena and problems. It focuses on the overall and neglected parts, pays attention to comprehensive and neglects analysis, and emphasizes the overall grasp of the phenomenon of understanding and the integration of subjective and objective. Socrates, Plato, Aristotle and so on are also the representatives of ancient dialectics. They mostly use idealism as the starting point and contain many reasonable dialectical cores. For example, they believe that truth is always specific and relativistic, under certain conditions, can be converted to the reverse side. The simple dialectical thoughts in ancient China, such as the Taoist thought represented by Lao Tzu, Lao Tzu once had "there is no life, it is difficult to form a phase, and the length and shape are the same, "the blessings of the blessings, the evils and the blessings of the blessings". In the book, the philosophy of softness, Yin and Yang is transformed, and everything is endless. Based on different philosophical, natural and social views, the educational concept and educational thought are also different. The ancient western educational thoughts must be traced back to the ancient Greek period. The ancient Greek philosophers Socrates, Plato, and Aristotle were outstanding representatives of ancient Western educators.

The second period: at the beginning of the 17th and 20th centuries, the scientific research method of modern education was in an analysis-oriented development period, which mainly showed the following characteristics:

(a) From the description of experience to the generalization of theory, the study of education as a development process not only describes the characteristics of phenomena, but also focuses on the connection and development of phenomena. Educational research methods are largely combined with epistemology, and initially formed two different research methods and research styles guided by different philosophical theories. This is the inductive method and the deductive method. Similarly, the opposition between deduction and induction in methodologies also drives the development of methodologies, especially logical methodologies, and becomes an important aspect of this development.

(b) Psychology thought has become the theoretical basis of educational science research methodology. Although the psychological thoughts of this period are limited to the main forms of empiricism, association theory and sensory theory, the method of explaining the psychological phenomena in terms of mechanic concepts and principles one-sidedly, but after all, the educational research methodology is scientific. The direction is a step forward.

(c) The experimental method enters the vision of educational scientific research methodology and provides an objective basis for examining educational issues. The experimental methods have different intuitive observation methods, although the educational experimental methods at the time were still verifiable, and there were no strict scientific procedures and analytical methods. However, the transplantation of "experimental methods" from the natural sciences to explore educational issues has marked the development of educational research methods.

The third period: in modern times, since the 20th century, it has been an independent discipline.

The educational scientific research method is developing towards the comprehensive direction of the system. The main characteristics of the educational research method in this period are:

(a) Educational research methods are differentiated from philosophical methods and become an independent specialized research field. The educational research method itself is the research object, which means the deepening of people's understanding.

(b) Two basic factions in the theory of educational research methods——progressive and traditional, empirical and speculative, practical and theoretical, and their respective development studies have opened up new areas for the development of methodology.

(c) Investigating the philosophical basis of the research methods in this period, due to the influence of Western irrationalism, scientism and pragmatic philosophical thoughts, in the discussion of research methods, the pragmatic tendency is clearly manifested.

(d) The emergence of Marxist dialectical materialism and the development of psychological research methods have provided an important foundation for the scientific development of educational research methods.

1.7.3 Research methodology

1.7.3.1 Basic steps of research

Educational science research is an orderly process involving a series of steps. This is the selection of research topics, the retrieval of literature materials, the formation of theoretical ideas, the development of research plans to implementation plans, and the collection, collation, and analysis of data obtained. Finally, draw conclusions and write a research report or paper. Specifically, you should always pay attention to:

(a) When selecting research questions, the choice of topics should be scientific. It must have both a scientific theoretical basis and a scientific practical basis. Generally, three criteria must be met, that is, it must be valuable, innovative, and feasible. The selected questions should be problems that have not been solved or have not been completely solved by the predecessors. The research should be innovative, new and contemporary; the choice of the project is feasible, that is, the problem can be studied, there is a realistic possibility; the expression of the problem be specific.

(b) The review of the literature, i. e. the retrieval of the literature, usually consists of three stages: first, the analysis and preparation stage, analysis of the research topic, clarification of the subject requirements and scope of the subject to be searched, and determination of the subject search mark to determine the required documents. The author, the type of the document, the words that express the content of the subject, and the categories to which they belong, and then select the search tool and determine the search path. Then there is the search phase. Search for documents related to research questions, and then select important and truly available materials to read in the appropriate order, and record the collected materials by means of excerpts, data cards, and reading notes. Finally, in the processing stage, that is, in order to ingest useful information from a large amount of documents collected, it is necessary to do some work on the literature, such as roughing, falsifying, and processing.

(c) The formation stage of the theoretical concept requires the researcher to first propose the research hypothesis, that is, an answer given in advance to the research question based on empirical facts and scientific theories, the prediction of the research results, and the relationship between the main variables involved in the problem. Make an assumption and then decide whether the research hypothesis needs to be formally determined based on the nature of the study. The theoretical concept is guided by certain scientific theories, based on the existing objective reality materials and theoretical research results, using a scientific way of thinking to explain the phenomenon, process, essence or cause of the problem to be studied. The theoretical concept makes education and scientific research have a clear direction, the theme and research objectives; it regulates the process of educational research, helps researchers to improve the scientific level of scientific research, and restricts the definition of research results, the form of results, and the evaluation of results. Explanation. In general, the content of theoretical ideas should accurately describe and clarify the objectives and specific problems of the research, define the core concepts of the research topic, such as defining the core concepts of the research questions through the definition of the method, and clarifying the definition, extension and essence of the concepts, features, etc., and form and present their own theoretical perspectives that constitute research ideas. The essence of theoretical conception is to form a theoretical hypothesis that needs to be proved. It is a deductive structural system composed of a series of concepts and principles according to a certain logical relationship. Generally, it adopts the following steps: through theoretical discussion, preliminary determination of the basic concept, content scope and research ideas of the research topic; establishment of an indicator system to make the theoretical concept concrete preliminary verification; through investigation and preparatory experimental research, to form The theoretical concept provides the factual basis; draw on the existing research results at home and abroad, and absorb the reasonable factors. However, in the theoretical conception, the historical and realistic materials on which it is based are comprehensive, sufficient and objective; research has the practicality and feasibility of guiding educational practice; the correctness of theoretical analysis; research must have new research ideas, perspectives and methods. And the accuracy of the basic concepts and the rationality of the theoretical architecture. In addition, the theoretical system structure formed in the theoretical concept should conform to the logical requirements, and must have a system that requires both the inherent connection of things and the rich diversity of things.

(d) After the research hypothesis is formed, the next step is to develop a research plan that is a comprehensive plan and arrangement for the entire educational research process, including:

Finalization of the subject and hypothesis;

Identify specific research methods;

Develop methods for extracting and distributing research objects;

Specify research steps and processes;

Determine statistical methods;

Identify the researcher and work schedule.

(e) In the process of implementing the research plan, firstly collect information extensively around the topic, provide scientific evidence basis and research methods for educational research, and innovate on the basis of inheriting the research results of the predecessors. Secondly, after comprehensively collecting the information, through reading, you can understand the main research results of the predecessors or others in the subject, the level of research achieved, the research focus, the research methods, experience and problems, and further clarify the research topics. Scientific value, find the breakthrough point of your own research, innovate, and form your own new theory.

(f) The summary and evaluation stages are mainly carried out in two aspects:

- Write a research report or academic paper. When conducting an educational research, the researcher must carefully analyze and summarize the entire research process and research results, and select appropriate forms to express the research results clearly and convincingly. Educational research results can be explained by facts through educational observation reports, educational strategy reports, educational research reports, educational experience summary reports, and educational experimental research reports. Deep philosophies and rigorous logical arguments can also be used to illustrate problems, such as academic papers, academic monographs, and academic papers.

- Identification and evaluation of research results are usually identified according to their academic and social values.

1.7.3.2 Educational scientific research methods

(a) Historical research method. The historical study method of educational science refers to a method of systematically analyzing and researching by collecting the historical facts of the development and evolution of an educational phenomenon, so as to achieve a rationalization, interpretation or evaluation and prediction task. In fact, it is a kind of research that uses historical research methods to study educational science, and collects historical facts of certain educational phenomena, functions and evolutions, and objectively analyzes them to reveal their development laws. The research questions mainly concern the history of educational activities, the historical law of the actualization and development of educational theory and educational theory, the cultural and educational policies, the implementation of education, the evolution of educational systems, and the changes in social education. The actual activities of educators, etc.; educational thoughts, theories, educational trends, and theoretical views of educational schools. The use of historical research methods is first to collect historical data, and to collect historical materials related to research issues as much as possible, including written historical materials and non-literal historical materials. Then it is to identify the historical data, that is, to identify the authenticity of the collected historical materials. Finally, using historical materials, we must use the perspective of historical materialism to analyze, concretely analyze specific things, critically inherit them, take their essence, and go to their dross. Through the study of educational history, we can reveal the laws and characteristics of education development, help us understand the essence of modern education, help us learn from historical experience, predict the direction of future education development, and help us explore new areas of educational research and research, and continue to improve the ability of researchers to judge and analyze. However, we must also recognize its limitations. For example, the historical literature records the reliability of lag and non-systematic impact studies. The subjectivity of the literature content causes historical data distortion, and historical research cannot be quantified.

(b) Research method. Under the guidance of scientific methodology and educational theory, education research is based on certain educational issues, planning and purposeful investigations, collecting relevant factual materials, making scientific analysis and making work recommendations for educational research activities. The researcher systematically and fully understands (including oral or written, direct or indirect) through the personal contact, and fully grasps the history, current situation and development trend of the actual education, and based on a large amount of first-hand materials. Conduct analysis and synthesis to find scientific conclusions to guide future educational practice activities. According to the choice of education respondents, they can be divided into general surveys, sample surveys, and case surveys. According to the purpose of the survey, it can be divided into current status survey, related survey, development survey and forecast survey. According to the survey means, it can be divided into questionnaire survey, interview survey, survey and questionnaire method. The survey method is generally carried out in a natural process, and materials such as research phenomena are collected through interviews, questionnaires, surveys, and tests. In the course of the in- vestigation, observations are often used as a means of investigating and reconciling materials. The investigation method can be used in conjunction with historical research methods and experimental methods when necessary. The survey method is widely used, and it has the characteristics of the wide range of survey objects, the diversity of survey methods, the operability and practicability of survey methods, and the delay of survey results. Investigation and research can help expose problems in the development of education, expose contradictions, and promote the development of education by continuously solving various contradictions inside and outside education, and help educators and researchers to discover and summarize advanced education ideas and advanced experiences. Better improve work, improve the quality of education, and provide education management and education prediction services for different levels and different requirements.

The survey method generally includes the following steps:
- Identify the topics of investigation and research.
- Identify the respondents. According to the overall category and the meaning of the sample, the researcher should select the respondents according to the topic and conduct scientific sampling to ensure the representativeness of the textbook.
- Design survey methods. That is, according to the specific content and implementation conditions of the survey topic, select the main survey method, and do the appropriate preparation work.
- Investigate research plans. That is to say, the initial idea of education

research and research is systematic and operational, and the purpose, significance, object, content, implementation time, location, data acquisition and organization methods of the investigation and research are specifically explained.

• Design a questionnaire or prepare an interview outline. The researcher does the preparatory work according to the survey method selected in the plan, designing the questionnaire or compiling the interview outline.

• Conduct a preparatory investigation. Conduct a pilot survey of the prepared questionnaire or outline to identify and correct problems in the design and ensure the perfection of the design.

• Conduct a formal investigation. The researchers used the revised survey outline to conduct a normal survey to obtain the information needed.

• Processing survey data. The researcher analyzes the data obtained from the survey, finds some biased questions, and provides the basis for the data to draw conclusions.

• Write an educational research report.

We use questionnaires, interviews surveys, measurement surveys, experimental researches, comparative researches, theoretical researches, and ethnographic researches etc. in practice.

Questionnaire

The questionnaire survey refers to a research method in which the researcher submits the questionnaire to the respondent to fill in the answer and then collects the analysis to understand the subject's perception of an educational problem or educational phenomenon.

A complete questionnaire consists of three main parts:

• Guidance language. The instruction is generally arranged at the beginning of the questionnaire. It acts as a communication, allowing the respondent to answer as required to obtain true, accurate and reliable information. Including a brief introduction to the identity of the investigator and the purpose of the research to facilitate the cooperation of the respondents; to write out the requirements and methods of answering, to avoid the error of the respondents in answering the questions in different ways; to write clear the purpose of the research to eliminate the suspect's doubts.

• Question. The question is the main component of the questionnaire. Whether the problem design is scientific and reasonable determines the quality of a questionnaire.

• Concluding remarks. The concluding remarks are written at the end of the questionnaire. The general content is to make some short comments on the questionnaire.

According to different investigation needs, the problem can be actually in the following forms:

● Open. At the time of design, only questions are raised, and the answer is not specified. Some respondents arbitrarily answer according to the requirements of the respondents.

Because the information obtained by the open questionnaire is non-standardized, statistical analysis is more difficult. At the same time, because the answering questions are more time-consuming, the recovery rate of the questionnaire is likely to decrease.

● Closed. The question designer determines in advance the answer that provides the choice, and the respondent selects a form of question to answer from the question answer.

The procedure for the preparation of the questionnaire:

● Decompose research topics into a series of research questions based on research purposes.

● Determine the type of information to be collected and the form of the problem to be compiled.

● Further decompose the problem and draft the questionnaire questions and answers.

● Arrange the drafted questions according to certain criteria and draft guidelines.

● Seek advice from relevant experts and make preliminary revisions.

● Test.

● Revise again. According to the test results, the instructions, the content of the questions, the way of asking questions, the answers and the arrangement of the questions are completely revised and supplemented.

The issues that should be noted in the preparation of the questionnaire.

● Fully analyze the content of the problem to prevent crossover, overlap or omission.

● The number of questions should be moderate.

● The arrangement of the questions generally follows the same type of combination. It is easy to make it easy afterwards. It is generally special, first big and then small, first closed and then open.

Questionnaires can be issued in the form of face-to-face, mailing, and organized distribution. The recovery rate is the ratio of the valid questionnaires recovered by the researcher to the questionnaires issued. Under normal circumstances, if the recovery rate is only 30%, the obtained data can only be used as a reference; when the recovery rate is 50%, the obtained data can be used as the basis for making recommendations; when the recovery rate is above 70%, the obtained data can be used as the research conclusion. Therefore, the recovery rate of the questionnaire is generally not less than 70%. If the recovery rate is low, you can make up the test, or you can investigate the area with very low recovery rate, understand the reason, and make the appropriate test. The questionnaire survey saves time and money, the sample size is not limited, and it is not limited by time and space and environment. It does not need to occupy too much time and energy of the other party, nor is it signed, and it is convenient for the respondent's answer. But it lacks flexibility, and the recovery rate cannot be guaranteed.

Interview survey

The interview survey is a research method that investigates the attitudes and opinions of the respondents on the educational issues or phenomena through the way of oral conversations, asking questions to the respondents and asking them to give verbal responses. According to the rigor of the interview process, it can be divided into structural interviews and non-structural interview surveys. According to the number of interviews with the same subject, it was divided into one-time interviews and repeated interviews. According to the number of interviewees, it can be divided into individual interview surveys and group interview surveys. In addition to the above types, there are also telephone interviews, child interviews and other methods. This research method is widely used because of its flexibility and the ability to use relatively complex interview outlines to obtain direct and reliable information and materials, without being limited by written language and easy to conduct in-depth investigations. However, the investigation efficiency is low, the scope and conditions of application are often limited; the analysis and processing of data is difficult; the investigation process is also prone to bias.

In the process of interview investigation, the interviewee is selected first. The choice of individual interviewees should pay attention to the typicality of the object, and the subject has more understanding of the research topic, in order to obtain more information. The choice of the group interview object should consider the representativeness of the object, and the familiarity with the situation is generally 6—12 people. Secondly, prepare the interview outline and interview plan, often expressed in the form of questions. Be cautious and properly arrange the order of the questions so that the interview can naturally move from one question to another. Finally, formal interviews were conducted. In the interviews, the investigators and investigators should show initiative, friendship, and talkative efforts, and strive to create a harmonious and harmonious atmosphere, so that the other party feels free and unconstrained, and naturally conduct interviews according to the scheduled plan. In general, the interviewer should take the initiative to approach the interviewee, introduce himself, explain the intention, and explain to the other party the purpose of the investigation, the scientific value and social significance of the survey. Listen carefully, actively make a reasonable response, and make interviews.

Measurement survey

Measurement survey is a survey and research activity that uses a set of test questions to determine an educational phenomenon or actual situation, so as to collect data for analysis. The measurement survey has a wide range of materials, a strict tooling process, a strict testing process, and generally uses the norm to explain the results and so on. Measurement surveys have diagnostic functions, establish and test scientific hypotheses, evaluation roles and predictions, and selection functions. In educational practice, students' academic achievement, intelligence, aptitude and personality are often tested. The types of test questions usually have selected questions, such as multiple choice questions, yes/no/false questions, matching questions, arrangement questions and correction questions; free-response questions, including short answer questions, fill-in-the-blank questions, paper questions, application questions, operations questions and association questions.

The implementation of the measurement survey generally includes:

- Determine the target of the measurement. The researcher should first determine whether the purpose of the measurement is for diagnosis or for establishing and testing hypotheses, or for evaluation, and secondly for the purpose of the measurement, and finally the specific measurement content.
- Develop a measurement plan.
- Prepare measurement topics (scales).
- Check the measurement questions to determine the quality of the questions.
- Conduct a formal test.
- Collect feedback information from the object.

When preparing test questions, it is necessary to have higher accuracy, reliability, and appropriate difficulty, as well as a common model for comparative analysis. Test reliability is the reliability of the test, which refers to whether the test results are stable and reliable. In other words, does the test score reflect the actual language level of the subject. For example, if the same set of tests in a number of tests on the same test subject, the subject's score is high or low, it indicates that the test lacks reliability. Whether the test itself is reliable depends mainly on the scope of the test, the number of questions, the degree of discrimination of the test questions, etc. The reliability of the test is usually expressed by a correlation coefficient (that is, the proportional relationship between two numbers), the larger the correlation coefficient, the letter the higher the degree. Reliability is only affected by random errors. The larger the random error, the lower the reliability. When the coefficient is 1.00, the reliability of the test is reached to the highest degree; and when the coefficient is 0.00, the reliability of the test is minimized. In general, the coefficient will not be as high as 1.00, nor will it fall to 0.00, but between the two. The requirements for the reliability index vary depending on the type of test. People usually require a reliability coefficient of 0.90 or higher for standardized tests. For example, the reliability of TOEFL is about 0.95, and the reliability coefficient of classroom test is 0. 70——the acceptability factor is between 0.80. One concept related to reliability is validity, which is a prerequisite for validity. Validity is the degree of validity of the measurement, the extent to which the measurement tool can measure the traits it is measuring. Simply put, it refers to the accuracy and usefulness of a test. The reliability of the test is closely related to the validity of the test. Generally speaking, only tests with higher reliability can have higher validity, but higher validity cannot guarantee higher reliability.

Experimental research

The experimental method refers to the research of educational experiment research, which is based on the purpose of the experiment, reasonably controlling or creating certain conditions, artificially transforming the research object, and thus verifying the hypothesis and exploring the causal relationship of the educational phenomenon. It can make observation and record more precise, and it is easy to understand the impact of each condition and ensure the accurate research work. The experimental method can be divided into laboratory experiment method and natural experiment method. The experimental method is generally divided into three types: a single group method, an experiment is conducted on one group or class, and the effect is different in applying an experimental factor with or without applying an experimental factor or applying another experimental factor at different times. The law applies different experimental factors to the two classes or groups with equal aspects in all aspects, and then compares the effects. The cycle method applies several different experimental factors to each of the different experimental factors in a predetermined order. Class or group, then add several effects of each factor together for comparison.

The basic procedures for educational experimental research are as follows:

• Identify research topics, experimental research topics should have high value, be feasible, and have clear experimental assumptions.

• Select the experimental design. The experimental design refers to the selection and grouping of the subjects in the experimental research, as well as the arrangement of the independent variables and dependent variables. For example, the sampling method selected by the participants is simple random sampling or other sampling methods. It is a single-group design or an equal-group design. It is a design that only has pre test or post-test. Different design methods produce different research validity. Therefore, when designing educational experimental research, it is necessary to consider various factors and determine the appropriate design.

• Formulate experimental protocols, including questions, briefly clarify the source of research topics, provide a general description of the research status of the research topics, clarify the basic assumptions of the research, etc. ; theoretical basis and guiding ideology of experiments; objects and methods of experiments The manipulation of independent and dependent variables; the specific steps of the experiment; the organization and leadership of the experiment.

• Specific measures of the experiment, this process is carried out according to the experimental plan, through training teachers, implementing the various measures of the experiment, making various experimental records, collecting the clock data, and completing the experimental tasks.

• Data collation and analysis, collating and analyzing the data collected during the experiment, finding valuable conclusions, and verifying the hypotheses proposed.

• Write an experimental report, comprehensively study the results of the experimental study, and write an experimental research report.

The educational experiment design is based on the nature of the experimental research topic and the subjective and objective conditions of the experimental research, the specific operations determined by the selection and grouping of the subjects, the operation of the independent variables, the measurement of the dependent variables, and the control of the unrelated variables program. It mainly considers the determination and arrangement of factors such as the test, the experimental treatment and the measurement of the dependent variable. The different arrangements of these three factors constitute different experimental designs, which are divided into the following types:

A single-group design is a method of performing an experimental variable on a group of subjects and measuring the resulting experimental results in three forms:

- The single-group post-test design is to perform experimental treatment on a group of subjects, then measure the dependent variable, and use the measured results to describe the effect of the experiment.

- Single-group pre-test design is to perform a pre-test on a group of subjects, then perform experimental treatment, and finally post-test, and determine the effect of the experiment by comparing the results of the two tests before and after.

- Time series design is to conduct a series of tests on a group of subjects at a certain time interval, and arrange the experimental processing between two of the series of tests. The effect of the experiment is to compare the results of each test before and after the experimental treatment. The difference is derived.

The equal group design is a method of performing different experimental treatments on two or more subjects, and using the difference between the test results of the test groups to illustrate the experimental results. The group design can be divided into the following three forms:

- Pre-test and other group design, this is the most basic and most commonly used design method. Randomly select experimental samples and randomly divide the samples into two groups; perform pre-test on both groups; perform experimental treatment in the experimental group. The normal method was used in the control group; the two groups were followed by the test. This design specifically requires that the conditions of the experimental and control groups be as close as possible, and the time and content of the pretest and posttest should be the same for both groups.

- There is only a post-test design, which is similar to the pre-test design, except that the pre-test is missing. Design steps: randomly select experimental subjects, and divide them into experimental group and control group; perform experimental treatment on experimental group, use common method in control group (control group); perform post-test on two groups.

• Multi-processing design, multi-processing design is an extension of the equal-group design, and is an experimental design for three or more test groups. Subjects were randomly selected and divided into experimental groups with the same number of subjects; pre-tests were performed on all subjects (or pre-tests were not performed); an experimental treatment was performed in each group of subjects. The group was tested after the test.

Multi-factor design is an experimental design to determine the effect of two or more experimental variables. The simplest multi-factor design is a 2 ×2 design, where each of the two factors has two different situations. If factor one changes to A1 and A2, and factor two changes to B1 and B2, a combination of two factors can produce four different groups. That is: A1B1, A1B2, A2B1, A2B2. If one of the two factors has two cases (A1, A2) and the other has three cases (B1, B2, B3), it constitutes a 2 ×3 factor design, forming six processing groups: A1B1, A1B2 A1B3, A2B1, A2B2, A2B3...and so on.

In short, a good educational experiment should have the following basic characteristics:

• There are clear and specific theoretical hypotheses. A good educational experiment, its hypothesis must be clear and specific, forming a relatively complete structure.

• Have reasonable control. On one hand, it is necessary to implement certain control, and also to ensure normal educational activities, to ensure the normal development of the mind and body of the educated; on the other hand, it is necessary to control the irrelevant variables reasonably.

• The design and procedures of the experiment are relatively standardized.

• It is helpful to improve the quality of education and teaching, and it is best to form (generate) certain patterns. That is to say, educational experiment skills guide education and teaching practice activities, and can promote the reform and development of education and teaching models, and constantly innovate and form characteristics.

Comparative research

The comparative method is a comparative study of the different manifestations of certain educational phenomena in different periods, different social systems, different places and different situations to reveal the universal law of education and its special performance. Comparative research is a comparative analysis of things that are related to each other according to certain criteria to determine their common points and differences, common laws and special essences, so as to draw conclusions that are consistent with objective reality. For example, research on learning interests, learning ability and academic achievement, research on family education methods and student personality characteristics, and so on. It has the contrast of things, the cooperation of research methods, and the profound characteristics of the results and descriptions. There are many comparison methods, such as horizontal and vertical comparative research methods, similar and heterogeneous comparative research methods, quantitative and qualitative comparative research methods, problems and regional comparative research methods. The various methods are skillfully combined and applied, and they are more comprehensive and profound, making the comparative research form lively, detailed and theoretical, and more convincing.

The comparative study method of education is understood from the operational level to include the following aspects: to identify the problems of comparative research; to collect the data of comparative research, data can be collected through field visits, literature review, survey interviews, discussion discussions, educational experiments, etc. ; comparative analysis. Based on the in-depth and meticulous analysis of the materials, the author makes a comprehensive evaluation of the comparative objects and further reveals the nature of the educational phenomenon.

Theoretical research

The theoretical research method is based on the existing objective reality materials and ideological and theoretical materials, using various logical and non-logical methods to process and sort out, and the general term of the objective law method of education is reflected in the knowledge form of theoretical thinking level. As early as the 18th—19th century, the issue of genetics was widely used to study education. This method is actually a longitudinal study that requires the separation of cognitive phenomena from some initial state, and then explores the various basic stages and trends in its development. In theoretical research, this method is mainly used to examine the origin, formation, change and development process of the educational phenomenon and its essence. It mainly uses the dialectical unity of analysis and synthesis and induction and deduction to study educational phenomena, including methods of induction, deduction, analogy, classification, comparison, analysis, synthesis, generalization, etc. , which can be divided into three categories. The first is from abstraction to specific methods. It is a way for people to completely reconcile the diversity of things by theoretically linking the various abstract stipulations in a certain logical order by grasping the inherent laws of all aspects of things. The second is the historical-logical method, which abandons all kinds of details and accidental factors in the historical process of the occurrence and development of things, and explains the laws of historical development in a purely theoretical form through a series of conceptual categories, thus establishing a scientific theoretical system. With this method, it is necessary to deeply study the form and structure of the educational object, analyze the intrinsic essential relationship between things, and reveal the historical regularity of the research process and the development process of the research object, and combine the historical research with the logical research. The third is the combination of systematic science methods and educational research. The systematic method is to use the object as a system to quantify, model and optimize the research methods. Conduct theoretical research from the perspective of system theory, and adhere to the basic principles of integrity, comprehensiveness, structural hierarchy, relevance, and dynamic balance, theoretical research methods are commonly used in educational research.

Ethnographic research

Ethnography is actually part of anthropology, which refers to an in-depth and analytical description of a particular cultural context. Educational ethnographic research refers to the scientific description process of educational systems, processes and phenomena in specific situations. It relies mainly on observation, description, qualitative judgment or interpretation of the phenomenon being studied. It is based on phenomenology, emphasizing the phenomenon from the perspective of experience, and carefully describing the phenomenon and understanding its essential aspects. Influenced by naturalism, ethnography studies the natural context of education without controlling variables, simulating or imposing a structure on it from outside, requiring that all data be interpreted in the context and context in which the data is collected. It is widely used in educational research.

Chapter 2
Theory and Practice of Foreign Language Teaching

2.1 Summary of the main schools of foreign language teaching methods

2.1.1 Grammar translation

The grammar translation method is a traditional foreign language teaching method that uses foreign language translation to teach foreign language written language, that is, a method of teaching foreign languages by means of grammar explanation plus translation practice. The grammar translation method is also called the traditional teaching method, the classical method, the old method (Old Method), the reading method, the Prussian Method, and the like. Its representatives are H. Ollendorff and Jacotot. The prototype of the translation method is that the foreign language teaching method originated from the Latin teaching method, and was popular in Europe in the 15th—17th century. At that time, it was called the "grammar imitation method". In the 18th and 19th centuries, some countries in Western Europe established the teaching status of the translation law. Before the 18th century, Latin was the international language of countries such as Western Europe. Latin teaching is characterized by memorizing grammar and essay. European culturalists in the Renaissance began to reform the malpractice of Latin teaching. The seventeenth-century educator Wolfgang Ratichius proposed that foreign language teaching should rely on native language, first explain in native language, and then carry out vocabulary, grammar analysis and mother tongue comparison. Johann Amos Comenius proposed to use inductive grammar, to pay attention to system knowledge and translation contrast, foreign language textbooks should list native language texts. After the eighteenth century, with the development of capitalism, Latin was gradually replaced by some modern languages. The comparative linguistic study of this period confirmed the kinship of the Indo-European languages and formed the mechanical atomic view of language, that is, all languages originated from one language, all languages were basically the same, and language and thinking were unified. This concept is reflected in the practice of foreign language teaching. The native language is translated into foreign languages word by word, or the foreign language is translated into the language word by word. The focus is on the reading and understanding of foreign language written language, ignoring oral teaching. Richards and Rodgers (2000: 5) argue that grammar translation has no theoretical basis. Zuo Huanqi (2002: 38) believes that the basis of his linguistics is historical comparative linguistics. It is also argued that functional psychology is the psychological basis of grammar translation, and some even believe that translation is based on psychological mechanism.

Grammar translation generally contains the following teaching processes:

- Review: dictate words; recite text passages.
- Teaching new words: List the words, phonetic symbols and mother tongue explanations of the new words in the lesson on the blackboard and explain them word by word. Students follow the teacher to read the words. The teacher speaks the meaning of the mother tongue and the student speaks English words.
- Teaching grammar: Explain the meaning of grammar and related rules, list related vocabulary in the text on the blackboard, and convert students according to grammar rules.
- Explain the text: The teacher reads the text step by step, and the students analyze the grammar and translate it into the mother tongue. The teacher corrects the error at any time.
- Consolidate the new lesson: Students follow the teacher to read the text step by step. The teacher asks questions according to the text, and the students answer according to the text.
- Assigning assignments: spelling words; filling in the grammar; memorizing the text.

The basic characteristics of this teaching method are:

- The purpose of teaching is to develop students' ability to read foreign language essays (especially classical literary works) and imitate essays for writing purposes.

- Use traditional grammar as the basis for teaching foreign languages. Grammar is regarded as the core of language, and is the main content of foreign language learning. The grammar explanation uses the deductive method, first explains the grammar rules, and then uses and consolidates the rules in the exercises. The main teaching methods are to explain and analyze sentence components and speech, vocabulary changes and grammar rules. Vocabulary teaching mostly uses synonym and antonym contrast and example sentence example method; explaining and analyzing grammar basically adopts deductive method, that is, the teacher gives rules or conclusions, requires students to remember and use the rules to explain the text.
- The arrangement of grammar materials is the grammar and the text. The text is composed of difficult pieces of literary works, accompanied by vocabulary with detailed notes in the native language and grammatical rules for detailed explanation. The grammar rules and texts in the textbook are arranged in two parts: present grammatical rules, words, example sentences, and then arrange the text.
- Translation is the basic means of teaching. The translation of a foreign language into a native language and the translation of a native language into a foreign language are the basic means of teaching. The translation, foreign language knowledge, practice, consolidation and reading skills are all translated.
- Classroom management adopts the teacher authority mode, and teaching is a one-way behavior in which teachers instill knowledge into students. The teacher system teaches, and students receive a full range of foreign language knowledge. Emphasis on the memory of lexical and grammatical rules, and believe that memorizing grammar rules is a shortcut to learning foreign languages, under such teaching method, students rarely ask questions and there is less communication between students.
- The literary language is better than the spoken language. Spoken language teaching is limited to enabling students to master the pronunciation of vocabulary, and do not pay attention to the practical use of language, only emphasize the reading ability of written language. Frequently take the form of a written answer to the question, the answer can be directly quoted from the original.
- Most of the classroom language is native language. Check the quality of teaching through translation. Practice methods include blanking a single sentence, making sentences, memorizing texts, and writing essays. Organize teaching in

Chapter 2 | Theory and Practice of Foreign Language Teaching

your native language. The use of the mother tongue as an important means of interpretation, explanation, practice and examination is rarely used actively.

The grammar translation method has its own advantages: through the translation and comparison of the mother tongue, the students can deeply understand the abstract meaning and complex sentence structure of the foreign language; the teacher systematically teaches the grammar knowledge, pays attention to the use of the students' understanding, and is beneficial to the inspiration. Thinking and training wisdom can help improve the teaching effect; the students have clear grammar concepts, the meaning of the words is more accurate, and the translation ability is cultivated; the students learn to master the grammar rules, which is conducive to cultivating students' ability to understand foreign languages and use foreign languages; reading, memorizing the original work to develop reading ability, and can cooperate with other reading and writing teaching methods to help students improve their reading and writing skills; this method is convenient for teachers, does not require any teaching aids and equipment, as long as they have mastered the basic knowledge of foreign languages. We can take textbook teaching, test students easily, and the class is easy to manage.

However, grammar translation method also has some shortcomings:

- It does not grasp the essence of language, only pays attention to written language, but ignores spoken language teaching, neglects the teaching of pronunciation and intonation, which leads to the lack of training of students' oral English ability, and students are prone to foreign language deafness.

- Teaching overemphasizes the role of translation, making it easy for students to develop the habit of relying on translation when using foreign languages, which is not conducive to comprehensively cultivating students' ability to use foreign languages for communication.

- Excessive use of translation also takes up a lot of teaching time, resulting in fewer practical opportunities.

- Too much emphasis on the role of grammar in teaching, from grammar explanation to example sentences, from the actual needs and language level of students, and grammar and text are out of touch, out of touch with real life.

- Excessive emphasis on reading ability, learning language materials are some fragments of literary works, vocabulary is very deep, away from the actual life of students.

- Emphasizing rote memorization, single teaching mode, dull classroom atmosphere, not easy to stimulate students' interest in learning and learning, it is difficult to cultivate students' ability to use language for communication.

- Teachers being in an absolute authority position hinders the initiative of students.
- Students who are passive in learning and difficult to learn often lack the confidence to learn a good foreign language.

Grammar translation is one of the longest and most widely used methods in foreign language teaching (Zuo Huanqi, 2002). This teaching method has dominated European foreign language teaching for hundreds of years, and reached in the 19th century. In its heyday, "ruling the whole of Europe" between the 1940s and the 1940s (Richards & Rodgers, 2000), the grammar translation method " created the theory of using the mother tongue in foreign language teaching, and became a foreign language teaching history. The earliest pedagogy system laid the foundation for the es- tablishment of foreign language teaching method as an independent scientific system (Lu Zongqian, 2001). Grammar translation is still a standard language teaching method (Brown, H. D., 1994). Although translation has been criticized for many years, until today, in some schools, especially in schools where teachers' English is not high and professional training is lacking, the use of translation in foreign language classes is still quite common.

2.1.2 Directed Method

The direct method appeared in Western Europe as the opposite of grammar-translation in the second half of the 19th century. The main representatives were MD Berlitz, B. Eggert and HE Palmer. The direct method is also called Natural Method, Psychological Method, Oral Method, Reformed Method, Compromise Method, Comprehensive Direct Method, Eclectic Direct Method, Step-by-Step Direct Method, etc. The translation method cultivates students' lack of listening and speaking ability. Although there are differences, they belong to the same category. The so-called direct method is to teach foreign languages directly in foreign languages, without the mother tongue of the students, without translation, or with formal grammar. Its teaching goal is not a standardized written language, but a foreign language spoken language. The main teaching principles and characteristics of the direct method are as follows:

(1) The principle of direct contact. The most basic thing in direct law is to establish language and connect with external experience. That is to say, in foreign

language teaching, each word is directly related to the things or meanings it represents, without translating the mother tongue. In doing so, students can lose the "heart translation" as soon as possible, and use foreign language thinking directly.

(2) Spoken language-based principles, oral teaching is the main means and purpose of the entry phase.

(3) The principle of sentence standard: teach foreign language to start with a sentence, take the sentence as the unit, the whole sentence into the whole sentence. In this way, both the words and the grammar were learned. Starting with a sentence does not mean neglecting the teaching of words and phonetics. The direct method places great emphasis on words and phonetics in sentences.

(4) The principle of imitation: repeat the learned sentences through various imitative means, develop habits, and achieve automation.

In addition to the above four main principles, the Direct Law has other teaching principles, such as the principle of selecting linguistic materials, the principle of gradual progress, and the interest. Its main features are: it is not allowed to use the mother tongue, and the meaning and sentence are explained by visual means such as movements and pictures. The direct method is very popular and has its own advantages. For example, the use of various visual aids in teaching and the extensive use of teaching methods close to the actual life of students help to cultivate learners' ability to use foreign language thinking; emphasize direct learning and direct application of language. Focus on language practice, students have high enthusiasm for learning and strong interest in learning. It attaches importance to oral and phonetic teaching and can effectively develop students' language skills. However, in the teaching, the use of the mother tongue is completely excluded, which makes the students difficult to understand some abstract and complicated concepts; the teacher does not have a clear grammatical explanation in the teaching, which leads to more grammatical errors.

2.1.3 Audio-lingual Method

It is said that the United States was born in the 1940s. After the outbreak of the Second World War, the U. S. military adopted a series of measures and means to train the soldiers in the short-term ability to master a large number of foreign language proficiency, and to strengthen the training of the soldiers' listening and speaking ability. After the war, the teaching method was promoted and applied to foreign language teaching in schools, and it was popular in the United States and Western countries in the 1950s and 1960s. Listening to the sayings, also known as "mouth grammar" "sentence pattern" "structural law" "military teaching method", etc. , is a teaching method that emphasizes the ability to cultivate oral listening and speaking skills through repeated sentence structure training. Its linguistic theoretical basis is American structural linguistics, which emphasizes that second language teaching begins with spoken language, begins with speaking, and learns the target language by mastering the language structure. Representatives are L. Bloomfield, C. Fries. Structural linguists believe that the task of linguistics is to strictly observe and describe human language in accordance with scientific principles, and to clarify the structural characteristics of these languages. They think that language is the first thing to say (speech), all people are before learning to read, you first learn to speak, and words are the expression of words. Its psychological basis is the stimulation of behaviorist psychology-reaction theory, which believes that speech acts are formed through the stimulation-reaction connection and reinforcement, emphasizing that second language teaching should develop new through a lot of imitation and repeated drills. Language habits. The main teaching process of listening to the saying is divided into five stages: cognition, imitation, repetition, transformation, and selection. The basic characteristics of teaching are mainly reflected in the following seven aspects:

(1) I heard that I am leading. Focus on speaking, "I heard" that I am leading, I heard that it is the basis of all speech activities. Spoken language is the first, literacy is derived on the basis of listening and speaking; the primary stage is to practice oral English, mainly to cultivate oral ability, supplemented by reading and writing.

(2) Repeated practice, using the methods of imitation, repetition, and memory to practice repeatedly to form an automated habit.

(3) Focus on sentence patterns. Sentence pattern is the foundation of language teaching and the center of foreign language teaching. Through sentence pattern practice, each sentence pattern can be used automatically to master the target language.

(4) Reject or restrict the use of mother tongue and translation, and try to understand and express it directly with the target language by means of visual means or by means of context and context.

(5) Compare language structure, determine teaching difficulties, and focus

Chapter 2 | Theory and Practice of Foreign Language Teaching

on the main strength of foreign language teaching. The comparison of language structure includes a comparative analysis of the structure of the mother tongue and the target language and an internal comparative analysis of the structure of the target language.

(6) Correctly correct the mistakes of learners in a timely manner and cultivate correct language habits.

(7) Extensive use of modern teaching techniques, such as slides, recordings, movies, television, etc., through a variety of ways to strengthen the stimulus.

I heard that the advantage of teaching method is that it is centered on spoken language, mainly to cultivate listening and speaking ability, and has a progressive side compared with translation method. Emphasizing the training of sentence patterns, it has created a set of listening, speaking, reading and writing through sentence pattern drill. The basic training method; it not only restricts the use of the mother tongue but does not exclude the mother tongue, which to some extent compensates for the shortcomings of the translation method and the direct method; it establishes the teaching focus and difficulty through the comparison between the mother tongue and the foreign language; and uses modern audio-visual means Teaching has its historical progress. However, this teaching method emphasizes listening and speaking skills and neglects literacy skills; and it is said that practice is a boring mechanical operation, and sentence pattern practice is often out of context, which is not conducive to cultivating students' creative ability to use language. However, in the history of the development of second language teaching methods, listening and speaking is a pedagogical school with a very strong theoretical foundation. It applies structural theory and behaviorism theory to foreign language teaching, and makes foreign language teaching based on contemporary scientific research results. On the basis of it, it has an epoch-making significance. The emergence of listening to the sayings has become a milestone in the history of the development of second language teaching methods, and promoted the development of second language teaching methods in both theory and practice.

2.1.4 Audio Visual Approach

The Audio Visual Approach was first created in France in the 1950s. It was a method of short-term accelerated teaching of foreign adults in France at that time. It developed with the application of teaching machines and calculators in teaching. The audio-visual teaching method utilizes the perceptual knowledge of human vision and hearing to deepen understanding and improve the teaching effect of teaching and learning methods. It emphasizes the senses of the ear, the eyes, the brain and the like as a whole to perceive the language materials. It uses a variety of electronic teaching equipment such as slides, movies, radios, televisions, video recorders, etc. to organize listening and speaking exercises, combining the auditory image with the visual image and the language. The three elements, shapes, sounds, meanings, words, sentences, and words of materials are also perceived as a whole to improve the efficiency of teaching. Therefore, it is also called the overall structure method. And because it emphasizes teaching in combination with the scenes in life, it is also called the situational method. The audio-visual method is based on structural linguistics. It emphasizes that language is first of all a spoken language system. Language is a system composed of structurally related ideographic components. Language learning is to analyze and master the structure of the language ingredient. Therefore, the audio-visual method emphasizes that listening and speaking is prior to reading and writing, and the principle of speaking is the first. Spoken language is the first, and written is the second. Foreign language learning can only rely on the actual words spoken by the native speakers. The audiovisual teaching method uses situational teaching to make the students feel the language as a whole, and practice repeatedly in the classroom to form a "stimulus" for the students to make "reactions" when they encounter similar scenes. It can also be seen that the production of audiovisual methods is also closely related to behavioral psychology. Influenced by the "stimulus-response" theory of behaviorism, it is believed that learned language is actually a language habit. The audio-visual method promotes the advantages of direct law and listening and speaking. It adopts the form of situational dialogue, starting from spoken discourse and emphasizing a structural and holistic approach to foreign language teaching. In essence, it is the development of listening and speaking. Its main teaching characteristics are the following five aspects:

- Language and context are closely combined. In addition to paying attention to listening and speaking, it also emphasizes "seeing", that is, watching pictures or scenes. Students look at the pictures while practicing listening and speaking, immersively learning foreign languages, and naturally connecting the scenes they see and the sounds they hear. deep impression.
- Pay attention to oral teaching and think that oral English is the basis of teaching.

Chapter 2 | Theory and Practice of Foreign Language Teaching

- Emphasis on sentence-type teaching, emphasizing the use of situational training of sentence patterns, so that students can master the set of living words commonly used in certain occasions.
- Daily life situation dialogue is the center of teaching. Starting from the needs of daily life situations, choosing to arrange language materials is more in line with the needs of students' verbal communication than listening and speaking.
- Exclude native language and words as an intermediary, and directly interpret and practice in a foreign language.

Audiovisual teaching makes the class more interesting. Because the audio-visual media has quite "tolerance" and "degree of freedom" in the expression of teaching content, it can be made into different image levels according to the abstraction degree of teaching materials. It has a broader and more vivid time and space than the teacher's dictation. It will enable students to maintain a concentrated and vigorous energy for a long time. It can display a variety of stimuli that stimulate students' motivation for seeking knowledge, attract attention, develop skills, improve thinking ability and guide thinking, and make it run through the whole learning process. This teaching method integrates the wisdom of subject experts, education experts and media experts, and the painstaking efforts to plan a reasonable audio-visual media, so that the human interference factors are overcome more, the teaching information presented has a high degree of "sharpness", and the transmission of information has a large capacity, thereby shortening the teaching time and improving the teaching effectiveness. But at the same time choose the appropriate teaching media, you can consider the choice of a variety of media to use, give full play to the advantages of various media. The use of multimedia, change the teaching methods, reduce the labor intensity of teachers. Due to the existence of audiovisual teaching media, teaching activities are no longer limited to classrooms or classrooms, and can be carried out in any time and space, breaking the limits of time and space. But there are also its shortcomings, such as overemphasizing the overall structure, ignoring language analysis, explanation and training, hindering the understanding and application of language; emphasizing audiovisual while neglecting the role of written language, artificially cutting the connection between spoken and written language.

The audio-visual method inherits and promotes the advantages of direct law and listening and speaking. The biggest contribution is that it widely uses modern equipment such as sound, light and electricity to make the language and image closely combined, and to perceive the sound and structure of the language as a whole. In the process of teaching methods, it is a leap. It not only makes a leap in teaching methods and concepts, but also has further requirements for foreign language teachers. The audio-visual teaching method requires teachers to help students find a more suitable method for learning the language in the process of English teaching. The traditional English learning method is to recite grammar and remember words, but the new social background is abandoning this English learning method. Teachers should guide students to find a more appropriate English learning method. The audio-visual teaching method also requires deeper requirements for English teachers to master the classroom. Teachers should do their best to organize audio-visual materials before class. Everything in the classroom should be used to encourage students to use language to imitate and communicate. Every effort is made to mobilize the enthusiasm of students to learn English, making the classroom life interesting and vivid, and it must be challenging. All in all, teachers not only play the role of knowledge transferor in English teaching, they are also organizers, managers and supervisors.

2.1.5 Cognitive approach

Cognitive law, also known as the "cognitive-symbol method", was born in the United States in the mid-1960s. This teaching method was produced as the opposite of listening and speaking. In the 1960s, the rapid development of science and technology, the fierce competition in the international political, economic, military and scientific fields required a large number of high-level talents who could directly conduct international scientific and technological exchanges. Inappropriately adapting to the needs of this situation, the foreign language teaching community requires higher and higher voices to replace the listening and speaking method. At this time, the basic theoretical disciplines such as psychology, education and linguistics in the United States have also developed greatly. This provides a solid foundation for the creation of a new foreign language teaching system. In this context, cognitive law came into being. The theoretical basis of his linguistics is Chomsky's theory of transformational generation. He uses the "language acquisition mechanism" hypothesis to explain the language learning process and distinguishes between language ability and language behavior. Its psychological basis is Piaget's epistemology and Bruner's disciplinary structure theory and discovery learning theory. Cognitive law advocates the role of learner intelligence in second language teaching. By consciously learning pronunciation, vocabulary and grammatical knowledge, it is possible to understand and grasp the rules of language, and to comprehensively and creatively listen, speak, read, and write. Cognitive method divides the process of foreign language teaching into three stages: language understanding, language ability training and language use. It also affirms the grammatical translation method that emphasizes grammar learning and development of intelligence, also known as modern grammar translation. Its representative is the American psychologist Karur.

Cognitive methods have the following characteristics:

- Student-centered, the role of the teacher is to stimulate students' motivation and interest in learning, to guide students to discover rules from verbal practice, and to provide students with opportunities and scenarios for creative use of rules, so that students can master the rules.

- Focus on developing students' language skills so that students can creatively understand and generate unlimited sentences using limited language rules.

- Focus on understanding, practice on the basis of understanding language knowledge and rules, and oppose mechanical memorization.

- Opposing the lead in listening and speaking, I believe that the voice and words of the language complement each other in the language learning activities. I advocate the comprehensive training of listening, speaking, reading and writing from the beginning, and the comprehensive development of listening, speaking, reading and writing.

- Tolerate students' language errors. It is advocated to analyze and confuse mistakes, only to change the main mistakes, and to oppose mistakes.

- Determine the focus and difficulty of learning through a comparative analysis of the mother tongue and the target language.

- Use the mother tongue if necessary to allow proper interpretation and translation in one's native language.

- The extensive use of visual aids and e-learning tools will help to create a language environment, and make local language teaching contextualized and communicative.

From the theory, cognitive law emphasizes student-centered, emphasizes meaningful learning and meaningful training, and pays attention to understanding has its progressive nature. However, some theories of its theoretical basis are still in the stage of formation and development. For example, how to apply the transformational grammar system to teaching practice needs further exploration, in practice, there is no supporting textbook that is compatible with the theoretical principle. The law is used in the United States to teach foreigners to learn foreign languages, but it is basically not necessary to teach other people to learn English at home and abroad. However, cognition is a major genre of second language teaching methods that is contrary to the law of listening and speaking. Cognitive law comes from translation, but it is not a mechanical repetition of translation, but a development and improvement. It applies the latest "cognitive theory" of contemporary psychology to the study of language teaching, and has initiated the study of learners, making the foreign language teaching method based on a more scientific basis, and making contribution to second language teaching.

2.1.6 Self-motive Method

After the 1930s, the former Soviet Union's orthodox foreign language teaching method has always been a conscious contrast method close to grammar translation. It emphasizes language knowledge, excessive use of contrast and translation, and neglects the practical ability of foreign languages, especially the cultivation of oral ability. In the late 1950s, the former Soviet Union had more and more frequent exchanges with other countries in politics, economy, culture, science and technology, and urgently needed a large number of foreign language talents. However, the result of consciously comparing teaching methods is that foreign language teaching is seriously out of touch with actual social needs. In the late 1950s and early 1960s, the foreign language teaching circles of the former Soviet Union carried out two major discussions on teaching reform, which finally formed a "conscious practice method" that preserved the traditional rational connotation, and fully reflected the spirit of reform. The conscious practice method, sometimes called the "consciously positive method", is a second language teaching method in which students develop their target language through a large number of verbal practice activities on the basis of consciously mastering certain language theory knowledge. It is a reasonable and comprehensive pedagogy system, inherits the rational core of grammar translation method and direct method, overcomes the one-sided and extreme aspects of the two, and actively absorbs the strengths of other pedagogical genres, making itself constantly Develop and mature.

The conscious practice method is a pedagogical system with a strong theoretical foundation. The linguistic foundation is the doctrine of the famous

Soviet linguist Shelba on the distinction between language, speech and speech activities. At the beginning of the psychological foundation, Belyyev's foreign language teaching psychology on foreign language and thinking relations was later mainly the speech activity theory of psychology in the former Soviet Union. The conscious practice method has the following basic principles.

2.1.6.1 The principle of consciousness

It is the most important pedagogical principle in the conscious comparison of the former Soviet Union. The conscious practice method inherits the idea of " practice under the guidance of linguistic theory" of the conscious contrast method, but it has developed and expanded the scope of consciousness. It recognizes that language theory knowledge has a positive role in promoting foreign language learning, but it is not theoretical knowledge that plays a decisive role in foreign language teaching, but a large amount of speech training. It is believed that not only must understand grammar rules, but also grammatical analysis, but also understand semantics and practical usage, from conscious to intuitive.

2.1.6.2 Practical principles

Emphasizing speech practice is the main way of foreign language teaching, requiring 80% of the time for speech practice, 20% of time for the explanation of language theory knowledge, and emphasizing that the purpose of teaching is to cultivate practical ability to communicate in a foreign language. The principle of practicality is the first principle of conscious practice.

2.1.6.3 The principle of communication

This principle is the development of practical principles and has become the dominant principle since the 1970s. Speech activities are fundamentally a kind of communicative activity. Therefore, teaching activities should mainly be the practice of verbal communi-cation. The purpose is to cultivate students' communicative competence. Communication should not only be the main purpose of foreign language teaching, but also should be the main teaching method and check the scale.

2.1.6.4 Situational principles

Advocating the transfer of knowledge and practice of verbal communication should be set in specific situations and occasions to maximize the proximity to real communication situations.

2.1.6.5 The principle of integrated teaching

The conscious practice method believes that foreign language teaching should be comprehensive first, but it does not hinder the artificial division of different aspects, such as speech, vocabulary, grammar, rhetoric, and folklore. Different aspects are divided, mainly for the convenience of teachers in the teaching according to the different language materials can be focused, and the actual teaching process is comprehensive, should not be carried out in isolation. It also emphasizes comprehensive teaching with sentences as the basic communication unit, including comprehensive teaching of four skills of listening, speaking, reading and writing.

2.1.6.6　Consider the principle of mother tongue

It advocates a large number of foreign language practices, and considers the positive transfer of the mother tongue, restricting the use of the mother tongue but not the mother tongue.

2.1.6.7　Consider the style principle

Foreign language teaching should pay attention to the language problem from the beginning. When teaching students to master foreign languages, they should also let them master the various styles and skills needed to use the target language for real verbal communication. This principle is actually an extension of the principle of communication.

2.1.6.8　The conscious practice method also proposes the principle of intuitiveness and the principle of "speaking ahead" for foreign language teaching at the primary and intermediate levels

The conscious practice method is a new reform method proposed to correct the shortcomings of modern grammar translation method-conscious comparison method. It is a reasonable and comprehensive teaching method system, inheriting the rational kernel of grammar translation method and direct method. Overcome the one-sided and extreme aspects of the two, and actively absorb the strengths of other pedagogical genres, so that they continue to develop and mature. Since the 1960s, the former Soviet Union has widely adopted the conscious practice method. After applying the conscious practice method, the quality of foreign language teaching in the former Soviet Union has been significantly and universally improved.

2.1.7　Communicative Approach

The Communicative Law, also known as the "Ideas Method", the "Functional Law" or the "Ideas-Functional Law". Produced in the early 1970s European Economic Community countries, the center is in the UK. The theoretical basis of linguistics is the sociolinguistics that formed the climax of the 1970s in the 1960s. In particular, the social linguist Heims' communicative competence theory and functionalist linguist Halliday's functional linguistic theory and discourse analysis theory, as well as Widdow's linguistic communication view. The language view of communicative approach holds that language is a system of expressing meaning. Its basic function is social communication. Linguistics should not only study the form of language, but also pay attention to the social function of language to be completed and the constraints of language in people's social interaction. Factors, therefore, the purpose of second language teaching is not only to enable learners to master language rules, to use language correctly, but also to master the rules of language use and to use language appropriately. The theoretical basis of psychology is the representative of the psychological school (Christalki). He believes that human language behavior is much more complicated than animal behavior, and language behavior can only be explained by human innate ability. From a psychological point of view, in order for students' learning to produce results, it is necessary to link the learning content and learning activities with the students' communication needs and their experiences. The students' motivation and learning enthusiasm are the most important for mastering knowledge and skills.

Communicative Method is a pedagogical system that uses language function items as a guide to cultivate communicative competence in language in a specific social context. The founder of this system is the British linguist Wilkins. Representatives include the British language educator Alexander, Widdow, and Van Eyck of the Netherlands. Communicative teaching has the following characteristics:

• With the aim of cultivating communicative functions, it is clear that the second language teaching goal is to cultivate the communicative ability of creative use of language, not only the correctness of language application, but also the appropriateness.

• Focus on functional ideas. According to the actual needs of the learners, the real and natural language materials are selected instead of the processed " textbook language".

• Communicating the teaching process, communication is not only the purpose of learning but also the means of learning. In the teaching, it creates a situation close to real communication and uses the form of group activities. Through a large number of verbal communication activities, it develops the ability to use language communication and communicates in class. Activities are combined with communication in extracurricular life.

- Use discourse as the basic unit of teaching. It is believed that language does not exist in isolated words or sentences, but in coherent texts.
- The combination of single skill training and comprehensive skill training is based on comprehensive training, and finally achieves the purpose of comprehensive use of language in communication.
- Have a certain tolerance for the language errors that learners have in the process of learning, do not affect the errors of communication, can not correct, do not correct, try to encourage learners to play the initiative and enthusiasm of speech communication activities.
- The Communicative Law emphasizes that students are the center, emphasizing that teaching should serve the students' communication needs, with language function as the key. According to the principle of applying the principle of learning, the teaching of "special language" is arranged for learners of different majors.
- Advocating the use of a variety of teaching methods, should not be just a textbook, but should be a "teaching package", that is, teachers' books, tutoring books, tapes, wall charts, videos, movies, television, etc.
- Let the students be in the situation, feel the atmosphere in an immersive way, and communicate in English, which is the essence of communicative teaching.

The communicative approach includes a variety of teaching methods, including the Total Physical Response (TPR). It is American James. James Asher was proposed in the 1960s. This approach advocates linking language and behavior, and teaching foreign languages through body movements. The systemic response method is mainly based on the different functions of the two hemispheres of the brain. The right brain is mainly image thinking, and the left brain is mainly logical thinking, emphasizing the development of abstract thinking on the basis of image thinking. Therefore, it emphasizes the need to teach in real situations. According to the laws of the language itself, from the perspective of children's language learning, the first is to learn the ability to listen, and then on this basis, gradually develop into the ability to speak, and then develop into the ability to read and write. Total physical response emphasizes the ability to train students first. After listening to a large amount of time, they will hear a certain foundation. When the children are willing to say it, they will start to talk about it. In this way, the students are not nervous, and it is natural to say that they must be produced on the basis of familiarity.

The suggestive teaching method is also called "heuristic foreign language teaching method", which is called a teaching method of "developing human intelligence and accelerating the learning process". It creates a high degree of motivation for students and establishes a psychological tendency to stimulate individual potential. From the perspective of a student as a complete individual, in the process of learning and communication, it strives to combine various unconsciousness. The principle of suggestive teaching is the principle of integrity. He believes that not only the brain, but also the body participate in the learning process; not only the left hemisphere of the brain, but also the right hemisphere of the brain; not only conscious activities, but also unconscious activities; not only intellectual activities, but also emotional activities. People usually divide themselves into several parts: body, brain hemisphere, conscious and unconscious, emotion and reason. They are always unable to coordinate or even conflict, thus greatly weakening people's learning ability. The suggestive teaching method is to integrate these parts organically and exert the overall function, and the overall function is greater than the partial combination. Implied teaching is to carefully design the teaching environment, establish unconscious psychological inclinations in various comprehensive ways such as suggestion, association, practice and music, create a high degree of learning motivation, stimulate students' learning needs and interests, and give full play to students' potential to make students get better results in a relaxed and enjoyable learning. This pedagogy was created by the Bulgarian psychologist Lozhanov to learn a language. This method has been adopted by people since 1966, and has been promoted to more than ten countries. In recent years, it has been introduced to China, and its effect in non-linguistic subjects is also very good.

The Silent Way is a foreign language teaching method designed by the educator Caleb Gattegno. The pedagogy believes that foreign language teachers should be as silent as possible in the classroom, and allow students to open as much as possible. The main point of the silence method is the use of color charts and cuisenaire rods. The main learning theory hypothesis are as follows:

- Better through discovery or creation, rather than through memory and repetitive learning;
- Learning through the corresponding objects helps the learning effect;
- Be Helpful to learn by solving problems related to learning materials.

In the Silence Act, the roles of students are diverse. Sometimes he acts as an independent learner and sometimes as a member of a group activity. Learners sometimes play roles as teachers, sparring, problem solvers, and self-evaluators. Students must decide for themselves what role they should play. In the silent law, the teacher's silence is its main feature. Therefore, teachers must learn to control themselves and change the traditional role of teachers as a model to provide help and responsiveness to students at any time. Gattegno pointed out that in the silence method, the student's learning is more important than the teacher's teaching. Stevick suggested that in the silence method, teachers have three functions: teaching, testing, and not obstructing students. In general, in the Silence Act, the role of the teacher creates an environment in which students encourage adventure and improve learning efficiency. The teacher himself is a neutral observer, an unbiased referee.

In short, the communicative approach draws on the strengths of the people, from the latest achievements in contemporary linguistics and psychology research, such as sociolinguistics, human linguistics, functional linguistics, pragmatics, discourse linguistics, intercultural communication, speech behavior theory, linguistic variant research until the influence of interlanguage theory. Communicative law is by far the most influential and most powerful foreign language teaching method genre, which has a great influence on foreign language teaching and teaching Chinese as a foreign language. The shortcomings are first of all the functional project questions: how to determine the functional project, determine what the standard of the language functional project is, how many language functional categories are required for different second language teaching, how to scientifically arrange the teaching sequence of functional projects, etc. These problems are not very good. The ground is solved; the second is the teaching problem that fails to deal with the grammar knowledge: the functional category can not completely replace the traditional grammar knowledge, emphasizing that grammar teaching only uses (use), not usage (usage), which is actually Nowhere; and cultivating grammatical awareness will affect the cultivation of abilities. In the development of foreign language teaching methods, there are two trends of diversification and eclectic (comprehensive) development trends. Due to the existence and development of these two trends, various schools or systems have emerged in the science field of foreign language teaching methods. On the other hand, various genres have made up for each other's strengths and mutual penetration. You have a strong presence in me and me. The tendency of compromise. But one thing is certain is that the teaching method will continue to improve.

2.2 A review of first language acquisition research

First-language acquisition is studied by observing the process of children's mother tongue. The first language acquisition we often talk about is the acquisition of children's mother tongue. It refers to the process and method of children's unconsciously natural mastery of the mother tongue. They master the language in communication through a large number of contact languages. No one teaches him specifically, and no one teaches him. Deliberately correct his mistakes, pay attention to the language form and pay attention to meaning. The mastery of the language law is unconscious, from unconscious to consciously learning the language process. This language acquisition is different from the concept of language learning that we often say. Language learning mainly refers to the process and method of consciously mastering the second language in the school environment. It focuses on the language form, and the process is from self-consciousness to unconsciousness, which is what we often call second language learning. However, the difference between learning and acquisition is relative and cannot be separated. When the second language learner starts, the learning component is more. As the language level continues to increase, the acquired components gradually increase.

2.2.1 Phased

Through observation and research on children's language learning, the researchers divided the process of children's language acquisition into five stages:
- The whispering stage: also called the pre-linguistic stage, 6 months to 1 year old, learn the language, imitate the words of the adults, can understand some words and sentences, can use a specific voice to express a certain meaning.
- Word sentence stage: 1 year to 1 year and a half, really learn words, a word, word discourse.
- Double-sentence stage: 1 year and a half, two words together (one for the axis and one for the open word).
- Telegraph sentence stage: about 2 and a half years old, real word stage, only real words, no virtual words. Gradually use pronouns, prepositions,

conjunctions, verb endings, auxiliary verbs, etc.

- Adult sentence stage: 3 years and a half to 5 years old, the initial stage is basically completed. Be aware that there is a system of rules that can be reused. Start to understand and master the social functions of language.

2.2.2 Sequential

Linguists have found that children's language acquisition process has a certain order. The study of the order of the first language morpheme acquisition is mainly based on the study of the acquisition order of English as a mother tongue.

In the horizontal direction, including speech, syntax/lexical, semantic/pragmatic research. For babies, Jakobson proposed a discontinuity hypothesis. He believed that the baby's squeaky voice was non-verbal. For the acquisition of the phoneme system, an irreversible binding law is proposed. He believes that the phonetic opposition in children's speech appears in a fixed order. For the acquisition of tones, Li & Thompson pointed out that children can learn tones earlier, even earlier than vowels and consonants. For the acquisition of syntactic relations, Braine believes that the syntactic category is derived from the concept of semantics. Pinker thinks that the syntactic category is in the children's grammar from the beginning. For the acquisition of clauses, some scholars believe that (Sheldon, 1974; Bever, 1970; Chomsky, 1969) children cannot analyze these complex structures because their grammar does not yet have such a complex structure. Other scholars believe that (Goodluck & Tavakolian, 1982) children do not understand and use the attributive clauses in the pragmatic factors and complexity of these sentences. As long as these interference factors are eliminated, children can better decompose the attributive clauses. Longitudinal researchers have Brown (1973). A study of 14 English morphemes in three English-speaking children found that three English-speaking children learned English morphemes in a fixed order of acquisition.

The horizontal researchers are Villiers J. & P. De Villiers (1973). They have learned English morphemes of 21 English children and found that English learners with different backgrounds and ages have very similar English morpheme acquisition. The sequence, in turn, validates Brown's findings. According to Brown (1973), the order of acquisition is basically the current (-ing), preposition in, on, plural (-s), irregular verb past tense, belonging (-'s), non-abbreviated Connected verbs (is, am. are), articles (a, the), regular verbs past (-ed), verb third-person rule changes (-s), verb third-person irregular changes, etc. from simple to complex process. Other scholars have also studied the order of language acquisition from different perspectives such as frequency and complexity.

The study of first language acquisition has the following conclusions:

- Children's language learning experience is the same, although the acquisition speed is not necessarily the same.
- Children establish systems and rules in the language to govern language knowledge and language applications.
- The language rules established by children do not necessarily correspond to adult language rules.
- There is a tendency to over-generalize grammatical morphemes.
- There are some language processing constraints that govern language acquisition and application.
- Correction does not always work.
- Language acquisition is not determined by intelligence.

2.2.3 Theoretical explanation

The researchers also found that children born in different verbal communities are equally able to choose the language of their community. If a child of a non-native English parent is born in an English-speaking community, he will naturally acquire English and be his native language. And children's language acquisition has some common characteristics:

- Learning a native language is very fast but very laborious. Children are usually proficient in mastering their mother tongue when they are five years old. Children's learning of their mother tongue has never been as conscious and hard-working as studying subjects such as mathematics and chemistry. More importantly, children's initial language acquisition is often carried out without formal and clear instruction.
- Although children's learning environment is very different, their process of acquiring language has gone through the same stage: vague speech periods, unorganized speech periods, word sentence periods, and double-word sentences are forming. The grammatical stage, the grammatical level that is close to the adult, thus gaining full language proficiency. Regardless of the differences in the environment in which children learn the language, they are able to achieve roughly the same level of language.
- Children have a complete knowledge of language grammar from a limited

discourse (usually non-standard) for a limited time. They can not only understand and create sentences they have heard, but they can also create sentences that they have never heard before. What they have mastered is not a single sentence. It is rather a set of grammatical rules.

In order to explain all these phenomena, linguists have conducted in-depth research and discussion, and proposed different theoretical explanations. There are three main types of representative hypotheses:

Firstly, stimulation-response theory. This doctrine is influenced by the theory of behaviorism. The founder is American psychologist Watson, and the representative is American psychologist Skinner. Behaviorists believe that psychology must study the behavior of individuals in a scientific way. They interpret human behavior by studying the results of animal behavior. It is believed that the constituent elements of all human behaviors are only a combination of reactions or multiple reactions. Most of the reactions are formed by a stimulus-reaction junction in the environment. The philosophical foundation of stimulus-response theory is Locke's whiteboard theory, which emphasizes the importance of acquired experience and believes that language is also an act. Learning a language is to develop a habit in the acquired environment. Children's language ability comes from a series of Stimulation (adult language), they respond by imitation, if the response is correct, they will be strengthened, and certain stimuli and corresponding reactions will become habits and learn language.

Stimulus-Responsiveness can explain the acquisition of vocabulary and word formation, but there is also criticism of this theory: children do not rely on imitation in the process of language acquisition, because sentences are infinite and cannot be obtained by imitation and reinforcement. The expression of abstract concepts and feelings cannot be imitated, the complexity of speech acts is neglected, the linguistic potential of human beings and the particularity of speech acts are negated, the motivation of brain processing external information is negated, and animals are simply placed in the laboratory. The stimulus-enhancement-reaction is simply copied to children's language acquisition, and it cannot explain the critical period of children's language. Why does the stimulus-enhancement effect diminish after the critical period? The reinforcement is limited, how is the grammatical rules learned by children obtained through reinforcement? These questions are difficult to find through this theory.

Secondly, Innate theory. Children are generally born with the ability to learn a language that is not just for one language but for all languages. Chomsky pointed out that human beings are born with a "language acquisition mechanism" (LAD) suitable for language learning. The innate ability of human beings to acquire a language is manifested in a child's mind with a genetically determined LAD that is unique to humans. Normal children should last from birth to about 12 years old. This special mechanism is divorced from other human functions. Independent existence, even with intelligence, the environment only plays a role in triggering language acquisition mechanisms. It consists of two parts: the language principle that is common in human language in the form of parameters to be determined, also known as "universal grammar"; the ability to evaluate linguistic information, that is, the actual language that is exposed (Liu Wei, the core part of 2000 : 161—162) is the setting of the language parameters. Chomsky believes that children can value the language parameters they are exposed to. When children hear specific words, they first make assumptions about the structure of a language based on the general characteristics of the language, and then use the evaluation ability to verify the hypothesis. And evaluation to determine the specific structure of the mother tongue, that is, to give specific values to the general categories and rules of the language, the baby has the ability to acquire a native language. That is to say, the grammar rules are not derived from the input materials, but are derived from the universal grammar in the language acquisition mechanism. Language acquisition is the process of determining the values of the parameters to be determined in the universal grammar. The parameters activate the principles in the universal grammar, thus making the acquisition process possible. The grammar rules of a specific language can be seen as a set of specific parameter values, while the universal grammar is the overall system of all possible rules, principles and parameters. It also emphasizes the innateness of language ability in terms of the sequence, stage and critical period hypothesis of children's acquisition of language.

This theory can explain the acquisition of complex grammar. Congenitalism focuses on children's acquired innate factors of language and children's initiative and creativity. It changes the viewpoint of passive imitation of behavioral children. It can explain why any child with normal development does not need any systematic education can master the main aspects of the complicated first-language rule system in 3—5 years. It can understand the words he has never heard, say sentences he has never heard, and explain why children are born. The mistake of "over-generalization". But the congenital hypothesis has also been questioned: Firstly, this theory is a product of speculation. It is impossible to prove whether there is a language acquisition mechanism in children's minds. This is just a hypothesis of genius, neither can prove nor deny it. Secondly, is there a common grammar? This is also a matter of debate. If children have a universal grammatical category and rules in their lives, it is difficult to explain that children spend so much time learning grammar. Children's ability to acquire language in nature is easily accepted, and the general grammar is for further study. Thirdly, innate theory separates the language acquisition mechanism from other human functions. It believes that language ability has no direct relationship with intelligence. The development of language ability is not restricted by intelligence and cognitive ability. It can be prior to the development of intelligence. Not convincing. Also, innate theory is too underestimating the role of the acquired environment. Language is a customary, children leave society, even if there is a mechanism, but can not identify or use grammar rules.

Thirdly, Cognitive theory. Jean Piaget's theory of cognitive development has got rid of the controversy and entanglement between genetics and environment, and proposed the development view of the interaction between internal and external factors, that is, psychological development is the result of the interaction between subject and object. He believes that the essence of intelligence is adaptation, wisdom is "adaptation" and "the most advanced form of adaptation". He elaborated his theory of adaptation and construction theory with four basic concepts of schema, assimilation, adaptation and balance. The schema is the cognitive structure, which has the function of sorting, classifying, transforming and creating the object information, so that the subject can adapt to the environment effectively. The construction of cognitive structure is carried out through assimilation and adaptation. Assimilation is the process by which a subject incorporates and integrates information from the environment into an existing cognitive structure. When the schema of the subject cannot adapt to the requirements of the object, the process of changing the original schema or creating a new schema to adapt to the needs of the environment is to adapt, which makes the schema change qualitatively. Assimilation shows that the main body transforms the object, and the process of transformation shows that the subject is transformed. Through the assimilation and adaptation to construct new knowledge, we will continue to form and develop new cognitive structures. Piaget also emphasizes the initiative of the subject in the process of cognitive development, that is, the process of cognitive development is the active construction process of subject self-selection and self-regulation, and balance is the driving force of active construction. Therefore, he pointed out that language originates from intelligence, cognitive structure is the basis of language development, language structure develops with the development of cognitive structure, and the development of language is subject to the development of cognition. Children's language ability is not innate, nor is it learned from the day after tomorrow. Humans have an innate cognitive mechanism, but this innate cognitive mechanism is not Chomsky's language ability consisting of universal grammar. Children do not have special language learning ability. The so-called children's language ability is only a part of the general human cognitive ability.

In addition, there is a function theory represented by Halliday that language is a social behavior and a semantic system. Therefore, the process and essence of language acquisition should be analyzed and interpreted from the perspective of sociology and social function of language. Language acquisition is the result of the interaction between the individual's inner learning ability and the environment.

2.2.4 New trends in research

The study of first language acquisition emerged as an independent discipline in the 1950s, and has grown considerably in recent years. The more prominent research results are Pinker's Language Instinct (1994) and Helen Goodluck's Linguistics Language Acquisition (2000), David Crystal The Cambridge Encyclopedia of Languages, Jackendoff's "Language, Logic and Concepts", and some new research theories and trends.

The Optimality Theory, the Theory of Optimum (OT), is a new theory proposed by Prince and Smolensky in 1993. It began with a study of phonology, but its assumption that the constraints interacted to determine the output form was gradually applied in other fields. The study of language knowledge and language learning is also an important area for the optimization theory to validate its hypothesis. It is believed that there is a set of constraints in children's language and adult language; children's language and adult language are different because of the different levels of the same constraints; children's language can develop into adult language. In addition, there is research on language acquisition for bilingual children. Volterra & Taeschner proposed the Unitary System Hypothesis, in which only one system exists in the minds of bilingual children. Ye Caiyan and others confirmed that there are two distinct language systems in the minds of bilingual learners, and examples show that the two systems have sufficient opportunities to influence each other. This effect is manifested in the fact that bilingual children can clearly distinguish between different voices, word order and syntax. However, no one can still answer the definition of the second language in the bilingual environment: Are the two languages acquired by bilingual children all native speakers, or the first language acquired is the mother tongue and the language acquired later is the second language? There is also a further study of Chomsky's innate theory. Lewis (1993; 1994) conducted a detailed follow-up and experimental investigation of early children's grammatical structures. They believe that early childhood grammar reflects a specific verb rather than a general syntactic rule. The structure of the center. Their corpus shows that children's syntactic development is not a very rapid parameter setting process, but in the early stages, quite a few children's phrases are coagulation units. Based on these phrases, children gradually derive the rules of grammar through induction.

Psychological and linguistic circles in China have studied Chinese children's language acquisition from different perspectives. Relatively speaking, research from the perspective of psychology develops rapidly and has great power, while research from the perspective of linguistics is slightly weak and has few theories, and most of them are explaining foreign theories.

2.3 Summary of the second language acquisition research

2.3.1 Basic concept

2.3.1.1 First language (L1) and second language (L2)

The native language is usually the first language that a child first contacts and learns after birth, and is often referred to as the "first language". Since the mother tongue is the language used by the family or the ethnic group or society, it is also called the "native language". Linguists often use the language system of the native language as the research object and pay attention to the laws of the language system itself, which is called the first language acquisition research. Of course, there are also special circumstances. For a Chinese Han child born abroad, the "first language" he contacts is not Chinese, but the language spoken by the birthplace community, for example, English. In this case, his native language or native language is Chinese. However, his "first language" is English or Chinese. Some experts think that it is English, while some experts think that it is Chinese, and so on.

The second language acquisition research takes the second language "student's language system" as the research object, pays attention to the learner's language system, and reveals the second language learner's acquisition process and acquisition mechanism. Second language acquisition research is closely related to linguistics. There is controversy in the division of disciplines. Some linguists attribute it to applied linguistics. Some linguists believe that it is not a linguistics. It is an interdisciplinary subject. Because it is also closely related to psychology and psycholinguistics, it is neither psychology nor psycholinguistics. However, although it does not belong to the above-mentioned disciplines, some of the research areas of these disciplines are related to each other due to some commonalities of the research objects, which fully demonstrates the interdisciplinary characteristics of second language acquisition research.

2.3.1.2 Learning and acquisition

In the L2 acquisition study, "Acquisition" and "Learning" are a pair of corresponding concepts. Scholars use this pair of concepts to distinguish between two different language acquisition processes or ways in which language is acquired. Krashen (1981, 1982) argues that adults acquire a second language in two different, independent ways. One way is through "acquisition", which is similar to how children learn their mother tongue, and the other is through "learning". "Acquisition" refers to the conscious and informal learning of language in a natural state. "Learning" refers to consciously and formally learning a language. Learning in this state is a kind of "Metalanguage Knowledge", which is the rules that learners consciously learn language, such as grammar rules. This kind of learning takes time and effort compared to acquisition. Krashen sees the process of obtaining language through these two ways as independent learning processes. Learning is mainly to obtain explicit knowledge, and acquisition is to acquire implicit knowledge. Ellis has always used these two concepts interactively, and he believes that these two processes are difficult to distinguish in practice. In his view, second language acquisition includes both subconscious and conscious processes, both natural acquisition and classroom language learning. Klein divides acquisition from psycholinguistics into: spontaneous acquisition (naturally, without obvious learning behavior). The learner concentrates on communication rather than language form in the process of natural acquisition, and thus is an inadvertent learning, Learner's Guided Acquisition in the context of instructional guidance, focusing on certain aspects of the language system, such as speech, vocabulary, grammar, etc.

2.3.1.3 Target language and interlanguage

The target language is a non-native language that a person is learning. Interlanguage, also known as "interlanguage" or "interlanguage", refers to the formation of a target language based on a certain learning strategy in the process of second language acquisition. A dynamic language system that differs from its first language to the target language and gradually transitions to the target language as the learning progresses.

2.3.1.4 Second language acquisition and foreign language acquisition

Ellis (1994) clearly distinguishes second language acquisition from the concept of foreign language acquisition. He believes that second language acquisition refers to learners learning the target language in the target language country. The target language learned by learners is a recognized communication tool in the target language countries, and certainly a tool used by learners to communicate. For example, learners study English in the United Kingdom or the United States, English should be called a second language in this environment. An other example is that Chinese students studying English in China are foreign language learning.

2.3.1.5 Language ability and language expression

Chomsky (1965) considers these two to be completely different concepts. "Language Competence" is composed of the psychological representation of the internal grammatical rules of both sides of the communication. Simply put, language ability is a psychological grammar that reflects the language knowledge of both parties. "Language Performance" refers to the representation of the internal grammar of both parties in the process of language understanding and generation. Language ability is knowledge about language. An ideal native speaker generates an infinitely recursive sentence based on a "recursive rule". The man saw the dog which bit the girl who was stroking the cat which had caught the mouse which had eaten the cheese which ... The language expression is about the use of language. In the specific language expression, the native speaker cannot generate the above sentence due to various non-linguistic factors such as fatigue, lack of concentration and memory limitations. The language generated by native speakers in actual language use is only part of the entire discourse, and some of these actually generated discourses may be grammatical. In other words, these practical words do not necessarily reflect the ideal language ability.

2.3.2 Second language acquisition hypothesis

Second language acquisition research generally goes through the following stages of development: before the 1970s, the early stage of theoretical creation of second language acquisition research; after the early 1980s, the theoretical development stage of second language acquisition research; after, although there are still many new theories emerging, most scholars conduct research on the basis of existing theories and test, supplement and develop existing theories. The following hypotheses have emerged and contributed greatly to the theory of second language acquisition.

2.3.2.1 Contrasive Analysis Hypothesis (CAH)

Beginning in the 1940s, linguists have noticed the " Phase of Mother Language" in foreign language teaching, resulting in several comparative analysis articles. Benjamin Lee Whorf (1941) first used the term contrast linguistics in his article. However, the first book on the comparative analysis hypothesis of second language acquisition and the establishment of a comparative analysis theory system is Lado's Intercultural Linguistics published in 1957. It is pointed out in the book: when students are in contact with foreign languages, they are as simple as the learner's native language, and it is difficult to learn in a different place than their native language. Therefore, if the teacher compares the target language with the student's mother tongue and finds the difference between them, it will clearly understand what is difficult in the student's learning, and therefore there is a way to teach. That is to say, the comparative analysis compares the learner's mother tongue and the target language system to predict the difficulties in learning caused by the difference between the two languages, so as to take preventive measures in teaching and establish an effective first Second language teaching method. The publication of this work marks the establishment of comparative analysis theory.

There are three theoretical foundations for comparative analysis.

The first is the theoretical framework of structuralism and behaviorism, and it is based on the structuralist linguistics of behaviorist psychology and American descriptive school. Structuralism sees language as a static, self-contained system that emphasizes the objective description of the structure of language. Language can be broken down and broken into small fragments or units. These decomposed small units can be described, contrasted, and recombined into a whole in a scientific way. It is precisely because of this detailed description of the language structure that the contrast between different languages has a basis. For behaviorist scholars, language learning is also a habit. Learning a new language means forming a new set of habits. In the process of forming new habits, the original habits will undergo a transfer function, so the theory of mother tongue migration has emerged (the 1950s and 1960s). In psychology, "migration" refers to the psychological process in which people already have the knowledge to play a role in the new learning environment. Positive transfer is often produced when certain features of the native language are similar or identical to the target language. However, when some characteristics of the mother tongue and the target language are different, the learner will use the rules of the mother tongue to generate a negative transfer phenomenon. The purpose of comparative analysis is to try to promote positive migration and prevent negative migration through comparison.

The second is the theoretical framework for transformation generation (60s and 70s). The theory holds that the abstract deep structures of all languages in the world are all the same, but the surface structure is different, so it is possible to reasonably describe and interpret the median-valued discourses with different structures between languages.

The third is a pragmatic theoretical framework that focuses on the comparison between functions and ideas at the transcendence or form (in the 1980s). The comparative analysis based on the first theory in the above three theories has a long history and many research results, and it is also widely used in language teaching.

As a method of language research, the comparative analysis hypothesis was very popular in some countries in the United States and Europe in the early and mid 1960s. Many universities have established language comparison research centers to expand the scope and scale of language comparison. A number of representative figures have appeared, such as Charles Fries, Robert Lado, Stockwell, Bower, etc. Among them are the influence theory and the difficulty hierarchy proposed by Martin (Hierarchy of but Difficulty) and Clifford Prator (1967) grammar grading system, which is divided into 0—5 grades from simple to complex; Ronald Wardhaugh's strong and weak sense, using contrast analysis ways to analyze difficulty levels and prediction difficulties; Oller and Ziahosseiny proposed subtle differences (Subtle Differences) comparison analysis hypothesis. The results of comparative analysis reveal many special linguistic phenomena, enriching the theory of general linguistics. At the same time, it has accumulated a wealth of language materials and reference materials for the research of translation field and the compilation of bilingual dictionaries. In the aspect of foreign language teaching, through the comparison of the target language with the learner's mother tongue, it provides important information for the second language teaching: discovering the difficulties in the students' learning, revealing the teaching focus, strengthening the pertinence of teaching, and strengthening the teaching of the speech system. More effective development of the outline, the preparation of teaching materials, the establishment of test projects, etc. have played a significant role. However, comparative analysis theory also has some weaknesses and shortcomings, mainly as follows:

- Comparative analysis theory believes that as long as the difference between the target language and the mother tongue is found, people can predict the mistakes that the learner may have during the target language learning process. However, the results of a large number of experiments and field observations indicate that many of the learning errors predicted by the comparative analysis did not occur, and some of the learning errors that were not predicted occurred. In other words, the ability of comparative analysis theory to predict learner errors is very limited.

- One of the main principles of comparative analysis is that the greater the difference between the mother tongue and the target language, the greater the difficulty of the learner, and the greater the possibility of making mistakes, that is, the similarity of L1 and L2 is equal to the acquisition, and the difference is equal to the difficulty. This practice of equating "difference" with "difficulty" has been criticized by many people. Critics point out that "difference" is in the form of language, and "difficulty" is a concept in psychology that can be equated without any psychological basis (W. Littlewood, 1984). Since the late 1960s, due to the emergence of cognitive psychology and transformational generative linguistics, the psychological and linguistic foundations of comparative analysis have been challenged. People began to shift from the comparative study of language to the study of foreign language learning process.

- It is influenced by behaviorism and believes that language learning is a habit. However, Chomsky believes that the process of language acquisition is not just a habit but a process of innovation.

- Long and Sato believe that it is not enough to rely solely on the analysis of language products to explain the process of psycholinguistics.

2.3.2.2 Interlanguage

In the 1960s, due to the influence of Chomsky's language acquisition mechanism, people conducted a lot of experimental research on first language acquisition. The results show that children's early speech is unique, different from the language used by adults, and in the process of continuous development. In the late 1960s, applied linguists and psycholinguists used the research results obtained in the first language to re-examine the learner's second language behavior and attempted to study interlanguage from different perspectives. Selinker (1969) first used the concept of interlanguage, and in 1972 proposed the interlanguage hypothesis. The interlanguage hypothesis attempts to explore the language system and the acquisition law of the second language learners in the acquisition process. The so-called interlanguage refers to the transitional language between the mother tongue and the target language constructed by the second language learners. Put forward the "transition ability" hypothesis, the so-called "transition" means that the learner's language system continues to develop in the direction of the target language. According to this hypothesis, the starting point of learners of second language acquisition is similar to the initial stages of child language acquisition "simple code" (Simple Code). This simple code is complicated by the development of the acquisition process. This process is a "restructure" process in which complex structures are constantly replaced with simple structures and continuously integrated to gradually approach the rules of the target language. It is in the process of continuous development and change, and gradually approaches the target language. He believes that is responsible for interlanguage construction there are five cognitive processes: migration language (Language Transfer), training of migration (Transfer of Training), second language learning strategies, second language communication strategies and target language materials overgeneralization. The knowledge system of interlanguage formed by learners is actually a series of mental grammars that learners use to interpret and produce speech. These psychological grammars are dynamic and easy to change. As learning progresses, the knowledge system of interlanguage contains more and more complex mental grammar. This theory focuses on three issues in second language learning:

- What cognitive processes are responsible for the construction of interlanguage?
- What is the nature of the interlanguage knowledge system?
- Why do most second language learners not fully acquire the language skills of the target language?

He studies interlanguage from the perspective of cognitive process and considers interlanguage to be the product of the five main cognitive processes of learners in second language learning. These five cognitive processes include:

- Language transfer, that is, some items, rules and subsystems in the interlanguage are directly transferred from the first language;
- The transfer of training will transfer some features of the language training process to the interlanguage;
- Learning strategies, that is, some components in the interlanguage are derived from certain learning methods;
- Communicative strategy, that is, some components in the interlanguage are generated from certain specific ways of communication;
- Over-generalization, which is a general use of rules in the target language material.

Selinker believes that the development of interlanguage is different from the development of the first language. After the interlanguage develops to a certain stage, it is easy to become rigid, which is why most second language winners have difficulty in perfecting the target language ability. Language transfer is the main reason for the rigidity. However, children do not become rigid in the process of obtaining the first language, and they end up with the same language skills as adults. Selinker believes that there is a phenomenon of fossilization in the process of second language learning. It means that some non-target language grammar, speech, etc. exist in interlanguage for a long time, and it is not easy to change. Due to the phenomenon of language rigidity, most learners cannot fully acquire the language ability of the target language.

Some scholars also study interlanguage from other perspectives. Damian Adriano leaves the interlanguage system as an act of rule-governed language studies carried out. In his view, the interlanguage grammar is also subject to the language common grammar. He paid special attention to the study of the plasticity of interlanguage. Tarone et al. used interlanguage as a set of styles to study that interlanguage can be a set of different styles governed by context, and its speech behavior changes with context. In the second language communication, the learner uses the language according to different contexts, which leads to different styles of the interlanguage. Both Taron and Ademeyan agreed that the development of interlanguage is limited by the commonality of language, so it is also possible to analyze interlanguage using conventional language methods. Selinker's interlanguage theory focuses on the discussion of three characteristics of interlanguage:

- Intermediary is permeable, that is, the rules that make up the interlanguage are not fixed. It can be infiltrated by rules or forms from the learner's mother tongue and target language. This kind of initiative makes the interlanguage system always in the process of constant modification and expansion. The learner constantly accepts the new rules in the process of obtaining the second language, makes new hypotheses, and gradually modifies the hypotheses, so that the interlanguage gradually transitions to the target language.
- Interlanguage is variability, that is, the interlanguage is constantly changing. This change does not suddenly jump from one stage to the next, but continuously uses the "hypothesis-test" means to slowly modify the existing rules to adapt the process of the new rules of the target language. Virtually all natural languages are flexible, and they constantly evolve and evolve over time. The difference between an interlanguage and a natural language is the degree of flexibility.
- Interlanguage is systematic, that is, interlanguage is a relatively independent language system, which has a unique set of rules of speech, grammar and lexical rules.

Interlanguage theory is a theoretical model for explaining second language learning with cognitive perspectives earlier. Its significance is mainly because it regards second language learning as a psychological process and provides a theoretical framework to explain this psychological process. And this theory provides a theoretical basis for the later study of the second language using experimental methods. Secondly, from the perspective of cognitive psychology, interlanguage is actually a representation of linguistic knowledge. Therefore, the concept of this concept is to further explore the nature of this representation in cognitive theory, and the role of this representation in the second language learning lays a theoretical foundation. The lack of interlanguage theory mainly includes the following aspects:

- Research is limited to morphemes and syntactic aspects, and research on semantic and pragmatic knowledge acquisition is insufficient. Moreover, it is not scientific to determine the order of language acquisition based on morpheme research, because the standard of using a certain morpheme as a standard of acquisition is not supported by psychological evidence.
- Ignore the self-standards of learners learning foreign languages. The study of interlanguage uses the target language as the frame of reference, and the research on the standards that the learners themselves refer to is not enough.

- Ignore the different standards of interlanguage and other language variants.
- Research methods, such as longitudinal research and cross-over research, have some technical problems that have not been resolved, and the conclusions obtained are not completely reliable. In addition, it does not clearly explain how the interlanguage system develops and changes, nor does it explain how the interlanguage system affects language output, and further research is needed.

In addition, some scholars have further developed on the basis of intermediary theory. Error Analysis theory is one of them, produced in the 1960s, and flourished in the 1970s. It is based on cognitive theory and Chomsky's universal grammar theory. Error analysis is the first theory to focus on the learner's language system. It proposes a research method to investigate the learner's language system, which opens a window for observing the learner's language acquisition process. Mistake refers to the deviation of the second language learner from the target language when using the language. It is the error or imperfection of the target language. This kind of error is systematic and regular, reflecting the speaker's language ability and belonging to the language ability category. The analysis of the errors analyzes the errors made by the students in the process of learning the second language, and discovers the rules of the second language learners' biases, including the types of errors and the causes of the errors. According to the development process of interlanguage, Corder divides the errors into three categories:

- Pre-system bias: refers to the bias before the formation of the language system of the target language. The learner is in a rule and system that has not yet grasped the target language, is at the extreme of exploration, and has more errors;
- System bias: refers to the rules and systems that learners are gradually discovering and forming the target language in the process of second language acquisition, but they cannot use these rules correctly, and thus the regularity errors appear.
- Post-system bias: refers to the bias after the formation of the target language system.

At this point, the learner has basically mastered the relevant language rules, and generally can use it correctly, but sometimes there will be errors and errors. Reasons for bias include:

- Negative mother tongue migration. When learners are not familiar with the rules of target language, they can only rely on native language knowledge, so learners of the same mother tongue background often have similar nature.

- Negative migration of target language knowledge. The learner improperly applies the limited and insufficient knowledge of the target language he has learned to the linguistic phenomenon of the target language by using analogy, which causes bias, also known as over-generalization or over-generalization.
- Cultural factors are negative. Some of the errors are not entirely the problem of the language itself, but the language form bias caused by cultural differences, or the bias in language use.
- The impact of learning strategies and communication strategies. It means that learners encounter difficulties in learning the target language in a positive way to deal with the solution. At the same time, the learning strategies that cause bias are mainly migration, over-generalization and simplification (ie, the above), causing bias the communication strategy is avoidance and language conversion.
- The impact of the learning environment. Refers to biases caused by external factors, such as teachers' inadequate interpretation and guidance, improper organization of textbooks and other external factors.
- Transfer of language training.

Some of the "intermediary" components are the result of repeated training in the training of the teacher and the teaching.

Corder (1974) also proposed five steps in the analysis of bias:
- Collection of learner language samples;
- Identification of biases;
- Description of bias;
- Explanation of bias;
- Evaluation of bias.

The theory of bias has a certain guiding effect on practice:
- Re-evaluate the value of comparative analysis and recognize that there are certain limitations in comparative analysis of foreign language teaching practice.
- People have changed their understanding of the nature of error, and have raised the status of mistakes from the need to avoid, and need to be corrected to the position as a guide to understanding the internal processes of language learning.
- Formed a set of effective error analysis methods and procedures to establish a correct understanding of the bias through the understanding of the nature of the bias, the bias is a normal phenomenon in the second language

acquisition, accompanied by the acquisition process. At all times, learners learn language by constantly overcoming biases; using comparative analysis and bias analysis, teachers can understand in advance the possible errors and sources of biases of learners, and take the initiative in the teaching process. At the beginning, provide the correct demonstration, let the learners learn to take less detours; teachers can adopt scientific attitudes and appropriate methods to correct the learners' biases, and inspire students to discover and correct the mistakes themselves.

- Error analysis also has its limitations;
- The definition of the error and the criteria for differentiation are difficult to determine;
- The wrong classification lacks a unified standard;
- It is difficult to explain the situation of avoidance.

The other is Dickerson (1975) and others who study the language variation of learners and propose how to explain the variability of learner language system while expounding the systematic nature of interlanguage. (Mainly concentrated in two areas, namely system variation research and non-system variation research.) Systemic variation includes variations caused by the context of Linguistic Context, Situational Context, and Psycholinguistic Context. The so-called non-systematic variation refers to the expression variation of the learner's language and the phenomenon of "free variation". Although non-systematic variation is not as easy to observe as systemic variation, its phenomenon is still common in second language acquisition. One possible variant is the environment in which second language acquisition takes place. Marton (1980) argues that since interference is not a major aspect of natural acquisition of a second language, it often appears in classroom teaching and foreign language learning, and second language habits under natural conditions. In this way, learners have the opportunity to have extensive and in-depth exposure to the target language, but the second language acquisition learners in the classroom always use their first language, which will enhance the proactive inhibition; another variant may be the learner's. At the level of development, Taylor (1975) argues that the biases of students at the primary and secondary levels are very different. The former is mostly caused by migration, and the latter is mostly caused by the generalization of the target language rules. (For example, use the past suffix -ed generalization after an irregular verb, such as "goed"). Ellis (1994) argues that not all variants are systematically altered by context. The generation of free variability is conditional.

Ellis (1985c) argues that the conditions for free mutation include five aspects, that is, two or more forms appear randomly in: (1) the same context, (2) the same context, (3) the same In the discourse environment, (4) in the context task with the same restrictions, (5) exercise the same language function. When learners acquire new rules in the initial stage, it seems very accidental to use more than two language forms to express the same meaning. In fact, this phenomenon is also regular. That is to say, the learner interacts with the existing form in the initial stage of acquisition, that is, as a non-system variant. Later, due to the economic principles of language, the learner is encouraged to abandon the form that does not conform to the rules of the target language, using a form that conforms to the rules of the target language. The study of free mutation in the language system of second language learners helps to understand the dynamic development process of interlanguage.

Acquisition order research and creative construction hypothesis

The learner acquires a certain regularity in the first language. Then, is there a certain rule in the second language acquisition problem and then learn some other rules? Or does the learner learn that the second language rule follows a Order of Acquisition? Does the learner learn whether a particular linguistic rule also follows a Sequence of Acquisition? Is the "accuracy order" equal to the "acquisition order"? Is L1 equal to L2? These issues are also issues that researchers have been discussing.

The behaviorist school attributed the acquisition of language to the process of obtaining speech behavior habits through simple stimulation-response. Therefore, the second language acquisition process is to continuously eliminate the interference of the mother tongue, through the process of imitating and strengthening the formation of new speech behavior habits. In the 1970s, the cognitive psychology school challenged the behaviorist school and believed that language ability was not obtained through simple imitation of external stimuli. The intrinsic factor of learners is the determinant of language acquisition, and human language ability is obtained through a universal language acquisition mechanism. Therefore, the acquisition order study is also influenced by N. Chomsky's theory of transformation-generating grammar, which is that language is generated and created. Children have a language acquisition device (Language Acquisition Device) and a universal grammar (Universal Grammar), which is an inherent grammatical rule inherent in human beings. Chomsky scores language learning as two levels, Competence and Performance. Competence refers to the

Chapter 2 | Theory and Practice of Foreign Language Teaching

linguistic knowledge of the target language, including the natural and acquired linguistic knowledge of the native language; performance refers to the practical use of linguistic knowledge, including the principles of creating and understanding sentences, and the reasons for analyzing grammatical errors and misuse . On the one hand, speech generation theory attacks the simple mechanical model of behavioralism, and on the other hand emphasizes the cooperation between linguistics and psychology, and explores the inner psychological mechanism of language behavior. Applied linguists led by Dulay and Burt attempt to explore whether there is a universal language acquisition mechanism through a series of studies on English morpheme acquisition. This intrinsic acquisition mechanism guides learners to the different stages of the acquisition process and ultimately the ability to acquire a second language. Dulay and Burt (1973), Dulay and Burt (1974), Bailey, Madden and Krashen (1974), Larson-Freeman (1976), Krashen (1978), etc. studied the following series of hypotheses, and finally reached the following conclusions:

- Learners who use English as a second language acquire English morphemes, both children and adults, in a fixed order of acquisition;
- The second language acquisition order is the same regardless of whether the learner's native language background is the same;
- Different learning tasks have a certain impact on the acquisition order, but different modes of operation have no effect on the acquisition order;
- All studies have shown that the second language acquisition order is different from the mother tongue acquisition order.

The creative construction hypothesis holds that the psychological process of driving second language acquisition is basically the same as the psychological process of driving children to acquire their mother tongue. Second language acquisition is highly programmed as native language acquisition, and such procedures are pre-existing. The input of linguistic information is only a trigger for activating this pre-existing, highly programmed acquisition mechanism. Dulay and Burt (1974), Bailey, Madden and Krashen (1974), Larson-Freeman (1976) and others have shown that the second language acquisition mechanism is basically the same as the mother tongue acquisition mechanism; regardless of the native language background of the learner, the acquisition order of the second language structure is basically the same; the mother tongue has little influence on the second language acquisition. Studies have shown that the second language acquisition order is roughly similar to the native language acquisition order, ie L1

=L2. The acquisition order obtained by Dulay and Burt (1974b) was compared with Porter (1977) in the order of acquisition of English-speaking children, and the order of acquisition was related. Cazden's (1972) study of the order of acquisition of native-language questions also shows that the order of acquisition of English-speaking learners is very similar to the order in which learners of English as a second language are acquired. However, it is also concluded that the opposite example does not support the theoretical assumption of L1 = L2. For example, Sharwood Smith (1994: 55) proposed the so-called " same development order, different paths". The views of Dulay and Burt are actually the challenges of the theory of the mind school as a weapon to the traditional theory of migration. This kind of challenge is of great significance to the development of second language acquisition theory. At the same time, Dulay and Burt's views went to the other extreme, and the cognitive psychology acquisition theory itself was also severely challenged. This hypothesis holds that the learner's correct acquisition of the English morpheme (Accuracy Order) reflects the learner's English morpheme acquisition order (Acquisition Order). Hypothetical logic: When the learner uses the target language, the higher the correct rate of the target language rules, the easier it is to grasp these rules, so the learned is earlier; vice versa. Hakuta (1974) Rosansky (1976) questioned that the assumption that the " correct order" is equivalent to the "acquisition order" lacks sufficient theoretical basis. The research method used in the study of morpheme acquisition order is doubtful. It is the acquisition order obtained through the "Bilingual Syntax Measurement", which is a false sequence. The acquisition order obtained by the Krashen et al. (1977) study refuted this view through an instant discourse rather than a "double sentence scale". Sharwood Smith (1994) argues that ignoring the potential impact of mother tongue on second language acquisition is a major issue of creative construction assumptions. Because the conclusions of these studies are contradictory, even Dulay and Burt's own research conclusions are not consistent with the ideas of creative construction hypothesis, which has caused scholars to theoretical controversy about their basic viewpoints, and further exploration of truth-seeking is needed.

2.3.3　Some important theoretical models

Second language acquisition is relative to first language acquisition. He studies how learners learn another language after their mother tongue is acquired. The study of language learning begins with the acquisition of the first language and the methodology of second language acquisition. And many of the main topics discussed follow the first language acquisition study, so a key question is to clarify whether the second language acquisition is the same or different from the first language acquisition process. Second language acquisition is very influenced by the learner's first language. This is a very popular view. The most supportive view is that learners have a "foreign" accent when speaking a second language. When a French people speak English, his English sounds like French. The learner's first language also affects the learning of other language components such as vocabulary and grammar. This may lack direct evidence, but most language learners and teachers will verify it.

2.3.3.1 Language monitoring mode

American linguist S. D. Krashen proposed the famous and controversial second language acquisition model in the early 1980s—"monitoring model", which includes five hypotheses, namely acquisition and learning hypothesis, natural order hypothesis, monitoring hypothesis, input hypothesis, and emotional filtering hypothesis. Krashen summed up his five hypotheses and made detailed descriptions and arguments, especially the importance of the input hypothesis. He believes that the input hypothesis "may be the single most important concept in the current second language acquisition theory", because it answers a key question in language learning, namely how to acquire language, especially foreign languages. He believes that simply advocating corpus input is not enough. Learners need Comprehensible Input, and "understandable input" is a necessary condition for language acquisition. The so-called "understandable input" is an understandable language material that the learner hears or reads. The difficulty of these materials should be slightly higher than the language knowledge that the learner has now mastered. This concept is similar to the Zone of Proximal Development proposed by Soviet psychologist Lev Vygotsky. Krashen defines the current state of language knowledge as i and the next stage of language development as "i +1". The 1 here is the distance between the current language knowledge and the next stage of language knowledge. Only when learners are exposed to language materials belonging to the i −1 level can they have a positive effect on the learner's language development. If the language material contains only the knowledge or language material that the learner already has, it is too difficult for language acquisition. The role of language input is to activate the acquisition mechanism in the brain, and the condition of activation is the appropriate understandable language input. Krashen also emphasizes that language use skills, such as spoken language, are not taught, but are naturally acquired over time, in contact with a large number of understandable corpora, and also obtain the necessary grammar. It can be seen that language input is the key to acquiring language. The teacher's greatest responsibility is to allow students to accept as many understandable corpora as possible.

2.3.3.2 Information processing mode

Influenced by Gagne's information processing theory, it is considered that second language acquisition is an information processing process, through the cognitive processing of information perception, understanding, storage and output. The mode is shown in the figure 2 −1.

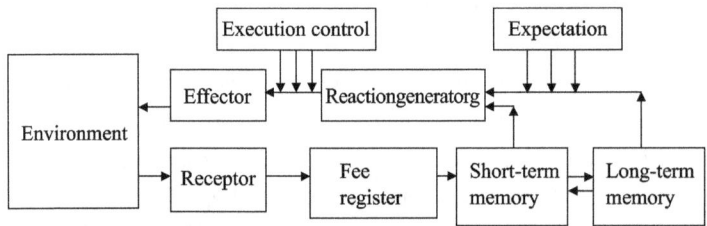

Figure 2 −1   Information processing mode

Gass (1988) depicts a flow chart of the language acquired by the human brain cognitive mechanism from the perspective of cognitive psychology. Gass distinguishes language input from the noted language input (Noticed Input) and the understood language input (Comprehended Input). She believes that the language input that is noticed is the first stage of language acquisition. It is composed of the characteristics of the language input that can attract the attention of the learner and the current second language knowledge of the learner. Not all the language input that has been noticed can be learned. Understand. Similarly, not all of the language input that has been understood is absorbed by the learner's brain. Gass believes that there is a process of ingesting the language in the process of target language input and internalization of learner rules. Once the language input absorbed by the learner is integrated, these language inputs become part of the learner's tacit knowledge. In addition, Gass also believes that some language input, if processed, can not be integrated into the interlanguage system, it will be stored in the explicit representation of the second language project and rules, become explicit knowledge, it can promote language output through monitoring, and can promote the formation of language absorption (See Figure 2 −2).

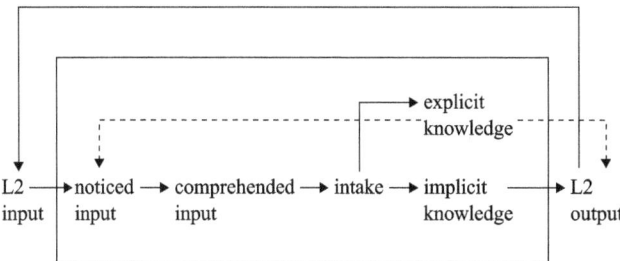

Figure 2 – 2   A flow chart of the Language Acquisition

2. 3. 3. 3   Competition mode

The competition model proposed by MacWhinney (1984) explains what kind of knowledge is used by learners in information processing in actual language use. Mac Whinney believes that language communication is the result of the mutual projection of two levels of language (formal and functional), and the projection of both levels is achieved by clues (such as temperament, morphological markers, word order, lexical semantics, etc.), and various clues may activate and interact with each other. The ability of human language learning and other abilities are equally dependent on the same cognitive system. The learner's mastery of the target language grammar is the result of the interaction between language input and cognitive mechanism. He believes that in order to achieve communicative function, learners create, control, restrict, and acquire the form of natural language. Any language form can be used to implement multiple functions. Conversely, any language function may also be implemented in multiple languages. The learner's task is to find the match between form and function in the target language. Language input provides the learner with four clues, namely word order, vocabulary, form and tone, and the usefulness of each clue is determined by reliability, availability and competitive validity. Reliability refers to the extent to which a clue causes the same form to always match the same function; availability refers to how often the clue appears in the language input; the validity of the competition refers to a certain environment in a competitive environment. The clue is to win or lose.

Ellis (1994) The Variable Competence Model argues that language use is divided into planned communication and unplanned communication. Planned communication refers to communication that is prepared before expressing information. Unplanned Communication refers to pre-prepared communication, often referred to as the usual form of everyday communication and spontaneous dialogue. Ellis further believes that knowledge activation and use requires some process, and can be divided into major processes and secondary processes. The main process is used when the learner conducts unplanned communication. The knowledge involved is relatively undecomposed and automated; the latter is used when the learner conducts a planned communication, involving unexploded to decomposed knowledge in the knowledge continuum that deviates from the end. Therefore, first activate language projects and planning in planned communication, and then gradually use L2 projects and rules in unplanned communication. At any stage of the learner's language development, the preposition is composed of competing rules. In some cases, these competing rules are systematic, while in other cases, these rules are used arbitrarily. Produce a free variant.

2.3.3.4 The multi-development model

The multi-development model is proposed by five phases and two dimensions:
- First stage: "Canonical Order" stage

Subject + verb + object: The children play with the ball.
- The second stage: the Adverb Preposing stage

Adverb + subject + verb: There children play.
- Third stage: Verb Separation

Subject + auxiliary verb + object + verb: All the children must the pause make.
- Fourth stage: "Inversion" stage

Adverb + auxiliary verb + subject + object + verb: Then has she again the bone bringed.
- The fifth stage: the "verb ending" (Verb – End) stage, in which the qualified verbs are displaced at the end of the sentence.

Such as: er sagte dass er nach hause kommt.

(he said that he to home comes)

The two dimensions are shown in the Figure 2 −3:

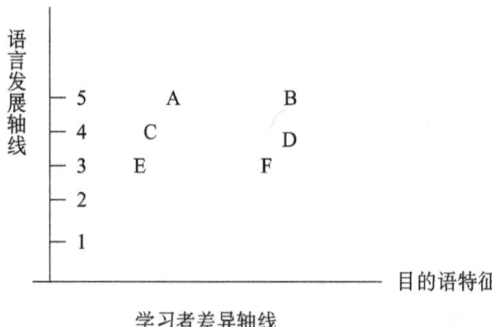

Figure 2 −3 Two Dementions Under the Multi-development Model

Three language processing strategies include:
- "Typical order strategy" refers to a strategy in which the learner maintains the second language "basic word order" (SVO) at an early stage.
- The "first position/tail position strategy" does not involve the displacement and change of the internal components of the sentence structure, but the component before the sentence or the component after the sentence.
- "Subordinate sentence strategy" refers to moving a sentence component in the main sentence, but does not move the sentence component inside the subordinate sentence.

The concept of "processing constraints" combines language development order research with speech processing strategies and provides an objective interpretation of the language development sequence.

The above three strategies reflect the depth of the learner's processing of the target language in different stages of language development, and also form the restrictions and constraints on the learner's entry into the next stage of development.

2.3.3.5 Cultural adaptation model

Cultural adaptation model refers to the process in which learners gradually adapt to new cultures (Brown, 1980) the social and psychological integration of learners and target language associations (Schumann, 1978). When social and psychological distances are large, learners are easy to after the initial stage of acquisition, it is stagnant, and the language form is "pidginized".

2.3.3.6 Universality Hypothesis

Language universality mainly studies whether the target language is universal and affects the difficulty of acquisition. Chomsky defines the universality of language by studying a language, that is, universal grammar. Greenberg examines the commonality of language in different languages to define the universality of language, that is, type universality.

Appendix: List of second language acquisition research theories

SLA Theories

Contrastive Analysis by Lado, R.	Bialystok's Model of Second Language Acquisition
Error Analysis by Corder, S. P.	Homogeneous Competence Paradigm by Adjemian
Classifications of Errors by Richards, J.	Tarone's Capability Continuum
Language Transfer	Ellis's Variable Competence Model
Interlanguage Theory	Preston's Sociolinguistic Model

Acquisition Sequence Theory	Functionalist theories of SLA by Tomlin
Universal Grammar Theory	Functional-Typological Theory by Givon
Learnability Theory	The Competition Model by MacWhinney
U-shaped Pattern of Development Theory by Kellerman	Form-Function Mapping Theory
Silent-Period Theory	Operating Principles Theory by Andersen
Critical Period Theory	Nativization and denativization theory by Andersen
Behaviourist Theory	The one-to-one principle by Andersen
Mentalist Theory	The multi-functionality principle
Cognitive Processing Model Theory	Formal determinism principle
Structural and Semantic Simplification Theory	Distributional bias principle
Natural Order Theory by Krashen	Relevance principle
Pronominal Copy Theory	Transfer to somewhere principle
Inter-learner Variability Theory	Relexification principle
Interlanguage Continuum Theory	The Multidimensional Model by ZISA
The Labovian Paradigm	Skill Learning Theory

2.4 Data analysis method and use of SPSS

2.4.1 Method of data analysis

Data analysis of educational research usually adopts methods of qualitative analysis and quantitative analysis.

2.4.1.1 Qualitative analysis

Qualitative analysis refers to the process in which the researcher makes logical and meaningful analysis on the basis of systematic review, summary and classification of the collected information, such as words, sounds and pictures, so as to reveal the intrinsic characteristics of things. Qualitative analysis is a process of classification, description, induction and abstraction of data. The object of analysis is descriptive data. Qualitative analysis pays attention to the analysis of overall development, aiming at grasping the qualitative stipulation of things. Therefore, it must be based on the overall analysis of the object of study to obtain a complete image of the object of study. Since the object of qualitative analysis is qualitative descriptive data, it is necessary to generalize and logically analyze the data. There are also some limitations when using quantitative analysis. Firstly, the research procedure of qualitative analysis is not strict and flexible, because education is a dynamic process with diversity, which leads to frequent changes in qualitative analysis process with great flexibility. Secondly, qualitative analysis is based on descriptive materials which reflect the nature of things. These materials are usually written, pictures and other forms of expression. They are obtained by qualitative research methods in natural situations, often with greater ambiguity and uncertainty. Thirdly, qualitative analysis is a kind of value research, which is easy to be influenced by the researcher's personal factors, thus integrating the researcher's subjective factors. Therefore, qualitative analysis is more suitable for the following situations: focusing on the process rather than the results of the study, case studies, descriptions of differences in comparative studies, qualitative evaluation and analysis, the analysis of materials related to the concept of consciousness.

  The process of qualitative analysis includes three stages: information review, classification and induction analysis. Data review mainly starts with the authenticity, accuracy and validity of the data to ensure the objectivity of the researchers, the appropriateness of the research methods, and the scenarios of the research objects. The validity of data refers to the consistency of the collected data with the research topic, that is, whether it is "relevant". Data classification refers to the process of distinguishing different data according to the nature, content and characteristics of research data and merging the same and similar data into one group. Classification should be carried out in accordance with the same standard. If the classification criteria are not uniform, the same data will cross and repeat in different categories, which makes inductive analysis difficult. It should be classified according to a certain level, and there are different categories in each level, so as to prevent the same category from being mixed up at different levels. Inductive analysis is a way of thinking that generalizes general or universal conclusions from known facts or individual premises. The inductive method can use complete induction, simple enumeration and scientific induction (causal relation induction). There are many methods of induction and analysis, such as seeking the same method, seeking the different method, seeking the same and seeking the different method, covariant method, residual method and so on.

Covariance method is to study the cause of the phenomenon if a certain condition changes to a certain extent under other conditions unchanged. Residual method refers to the study of a composite phenomenon is caused by a composite cause, in addition to the known part of the causal relationship, there may be causal relationship between the remaining parts.

2.4.1.2 Quantitative analysis

Quantitative analysis refers to the process by which researchers use the means of teaching to statistically analyze the collected data to reveal the quantitative characteristics of things. The main means of quantitative analysis is statistical analysis, that is, using a variety of statistical techniques to describe and interpret the collected data, and to infer the corresponding overall characteristics from the sample characteristics under certain conditions. Quantitative analysis is often used in education research for data description, judgment and comprehensive analysis. It is to organize the data, describe the distribution of the data with meaningful charts, and use certain statistical means to describe the concentration trend of the data, discrete trends or correlations. Distribution characteristics, then using the theory and method of probability and its distribution, inferring the overall characteristics from the sample characteristics and estimating the error range, and finally using the quantitative relationship between the series of data to comprehensively analyze the data features, and predict and interpret the variables between relationships or the extraction of common factors from a number of variables provide quantitative support for the induction of data, leading to scientific conclusions. Quantitative analysis of quantitative analysis has certain accuracy. However, it also has certain limitations. For example, this method of statistical analysis relies on the user's understanding, mastery and appropriate selection of various statistical techniques, requirements, conditions, and specific formulas associated with them. Otherwise, It is invalid. The probability of the data on which the statistical inference is based will have a certain error, not absolute accuracy. The significance of statistical analysis results sometimes does not represent the significance of true educational significance, and the complexity of educational phenomena leads to the ambiguity of quantitative analysis.

Quantitative analysis is a process of processing data with scientific methods. It is a rigorous and systematic process. It requires accurate and reliable analysis of data. Therefore, the premise of quantitative analysis is to examine the objectivity, completeness and validity of data. Research topics suitable for statistical analysis include deductive and descriptive topics. In descriptive subjects, researchers only need to understand the basic data characteristics of the object of study, and do not need to make further statistical analysis. Generally speaking, the data analysis of educational investigation is performed. In inferential subjects, researchers need to infer the characteristics of the population or compare whether there are differences between the two populations according to the characteristics of the sample, which requires the use of parameter estimation, hypothesis testing and other methods. Most educational experimental subjects belong to deductive subjects. Statistical analysis methods have strict restrictions on the use of conditions, not all applicable, the choice of methods must be clear about the specific application of various methods, to prevent misuse or inappropriate use.

In quantitative analysis, statistical tables, statistical charts, centralized quantities, difference quantities, position quantities and correlation coefficients are often used to describe the distribution patterns, data characteristics and transformation relations of original data. The inference of data is to extract a part of the sample according to certain rules, and infer the overall characteristics by studying the characteristics of the sample. Data standards include two parts: overall parameter estimation and hypothesis testing. Population parameter estimation refers to the use of the data obtained from the sample to infer the overall data characteristics. The total parameter estimation is divided into total estimation and interval estimation. Hypothesis testing refers to the process of testing a hypothesis with the idea of contradictory evidence, and accepting or rejecting another hypothesis by testing the rejection or acceptance of the hypothesis. Hypothesis test is divided into parameter test and non-parameter test, parameter test includes Z test, T test and F test, non-parameter test includes X-2 test. The comprehensive analysis of data is to make use of the quantitative relationship between series of data, analyze the data characteristics comprehensively, and predict and explain the relationship between variables or extract the same factors from multiple variables to provide quantitative support for data classification. There are many methods for comprehensive analysis of data, including: variance analysis, factor analysis, principal component analysis, clustering analysis, discriminant analysis, multiple regression analysis and so on.

2.4.1.3 Reliability and validity of quantitative and qualitative analysis

Reliability, or reliability, refers to the consistency or stability of research methods and results. Reliability is divided into internal and external reliability. Internal reliability refers to the consistency of data collection, analysis and interpretation under the same conditions; external reliability refers to whether a study can be repeated in the same or similar scenarios and get roughly the same results. Reliability analysis of qualitative analysis is difficult to pursue absolute accuracy and objectivity, with a certain degree of fuzziness and flexibility, which is the particularity of reliability analysis.

Validity refers to the validity of research results, that is, the degree to which a study can achieve its goals. Validity was divided into validity and external validity. The intrinsic validity refers to whether the research results can be reasonably and accurately studied; the extrinsic validity refers to the extent to which the research results can be extended to other situations, that is, the extension degree. The object of study in qualitative research is constantly changing. The research data and results are formed by the continuous communication between researchers and research objects. There is no absolute truth. Therefore, the validity analysis in qualitative analysis has its own particularity.

2.4.2 The application of SPSS in foreign language empirical research

Statistical Program for Social Sciences (SPSS) is one of the three famous statistical software packages of Social Sciences in the world.

2.4.2.1 Basic concepts

(a) Statistics: theories, methods and methodologies for data analysis.

(b) Meta-analysis: a method of comprehensive evaluation and analysis of a large number of individual research results on a problem by means of statistical analysis program. By means of meta-analysis, the inconsistency caused by subjective factors in the analysis can be avoided so as to obtain universal and general conclusions.

(c) Distribution and Normal Distribution: A set or batch of data consisting of all the numbers or observations of a variable is called a distribution. If a random variable obeys a probability distribution with a position parameter and a scale parameter, and its probability density function is

$$f(x) = \frac{1}{\sqrt{2\pi}\sigma} \exp\left(-\frac{(x-\mu)^2}{2\sigma^2}\right)$$

(d) Then the random variable is called a normal random variable, and the distribution of the normal random variable is called a normal distribution. The probability density function curve of a normal distribution is bell-shaped, so people often call it a bell curve.

Chapter 2 | Theory and Practice of Foreign Language Teaching

(e) Descriptive Statistics describes the full picture of the data, including data grouping, using statistical charts to describe the grouping and distribution of data, and calculating data parameters.

(f) Inferential Statistics infers the overall characteristics locally based on random sample data.

(g) The concentration quantity is the positional value of the distribution and is a point in the distribution that indicates the position on the measurement metric in the distribution. The average, median, and mode are the most commonly used concentration quantities.

(h) Variables are a key factor in research activities. Relative to a constant (a feature or condition that remains constant throughout the study).

(i) Independent Variable and Dependent Variable: The independent variable refers to the variable that the researcher actively manipulates to induce the change of the research object, the cause of the change or the change, and the hypothetical cause variable manipulated by the researcher. A dependent variable, also known as a reactive variable, refers to a behavior, factor, or characteristic that changes as a result of an independent variable. For example, in teaching experiments, teaching methods are often regarded as independent variables, and student achievement is regarded as dependent variable.

(j) Eextraneous Variable: Also known as a control variable, a variable that affects the change of the dependent variable at the same time as the independent variable, but has nothing to do with the purpose of the study and needs to be controlled.

(k) Interdependent Variable: Also known as a mediator variable, it is a variable between the cause and the result, which is hidden and not visible, and acts as a medium. Moderator Variable, also known as a slowing variable. It is a special kind of variable that has the function of an independent variable, also called a "secondary independent variable".

(l) Overall and sample: The whole of the research object is the whole, and the basic unit that constitutes the whole is the individual, and some individuals extracted from the whole according to certain rules are samples. There is no strict quantitative limit on the Sample Size. A sample with a sample size of less than 30 is generally referred to as a small sample, and a sample of greater than or equal to 30 is a large sample. Regional studies generally have an average sample size between 500 and 1 000; national studies generally have an average sample size between 1 500 and 2 500.

(m) Standard score: Convert the raw score to an isometric scale, and the score obtained is called the standard score. It measures the dispersion between each score and the average score in units of standard deviation. The distribution pattern of the standard score is basically the same as the distribution of the original score. Regardless of its original score, the mean value of the Z score is equal to 0, the variance is 1, and the standard deviation is its positive square root, which is also 1.

(n) Correlation coefficient: The relationship or degree of association between two variables, called correlation. The correlation coefficient is a measure of the relationship between two variables. It is a widely used descriptive statistic that describes the relationship between two variables. It is also used for prediction. Another variable is estimated based on the case of one variable.

2.4.2.2 Application

(a) Understanding of the SPSS interface. SPSS's main window is named SPSS for Windows, including the main menu (including 11 items), shortcut editing menu, data management window (including data input and variable definition), status bar, and status bar at the bottom of the window (SPSS Processor is ready), output window (output). If you are not used to see the output of English, you can change it from Edit → Options → Language to Simplified Chinese and change it to Chinese output. Figure 2−4 and Figure 2−5 2 show a comparison of the SPSS data input and the Excel data input window.

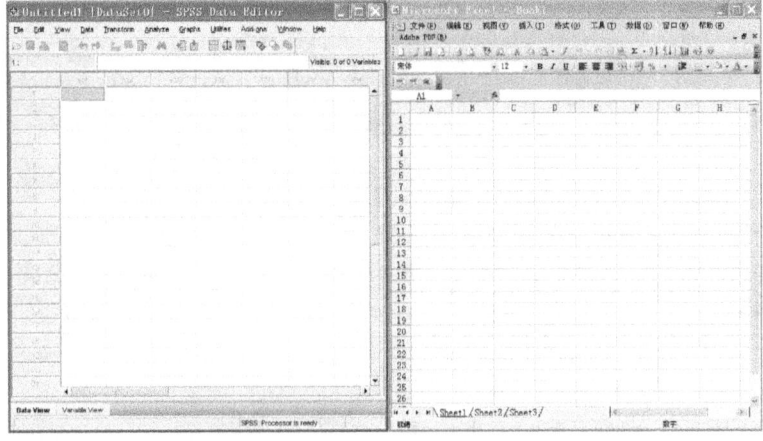

Figure 2−4　SPSS data input window A　　Figure 2−5　SPSS data input window B

Chapter 2 | Theory and Practice of Foreign Language Teaching

(b) Definition of variables (See Figure 2 −6), input of data (See Figure 2 −7), and output of results (See Figure 2 −8)

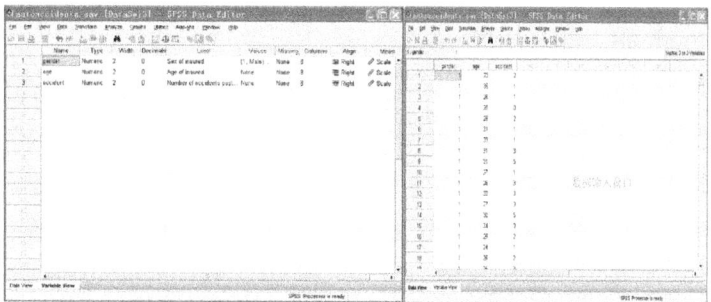

Figure 2 −6 Variable definition window

Figure 2 −7 Data input window

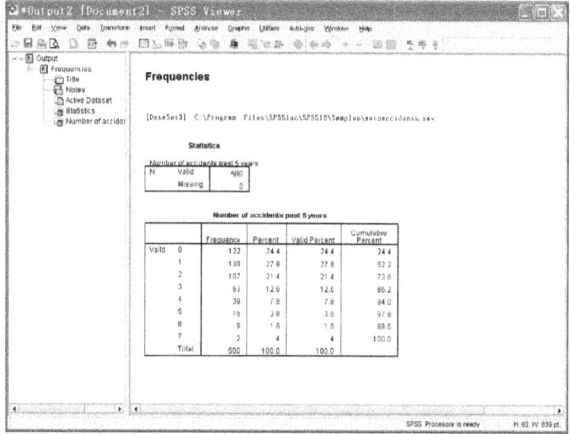

Figure 2 −8 Result output window

(c) Some editing commands and menus commonly used in data

• File: File management menu, related to the loading, storage, display and printing of files;

• Edit: Edit menu, select, copy, clip, find and replace text content;

• View: view;

• Data: data management menu, data variable definition, data format selection, observation object selection, sorting, weighting, data file conversion, connection, summary, etc.

• Transform: data conversion processing menu, calculation of values, re-assignment, replacement of missing values, etc.;

• Analyze: a statistical menu for the application of a range of statistical methods;

141

- Graphs: drawing menu, related to the production of charts and tables;
- Utilities: user options menu, related to command interpretation, font selection, file information, definition output title, window design, etc.
- Add-ons: SPSS plugin;
- Windows: window management menu, related to the arrangement, selection, display, etc. of the window;
- Help: Help menu, call, search, display, etc. of help files.

Variable types are: numeric, numeric with comma, numeric with comma as decimal point, scientific notation, date type, numeric with dollar sign, user-defined, string. The definition of the variable needs to be defined according to the type of data obtained or the statistical method to be applied. Generally, it is defined as a numerical variable without special needs (See Figure 2 −9, Figure 2 −10).

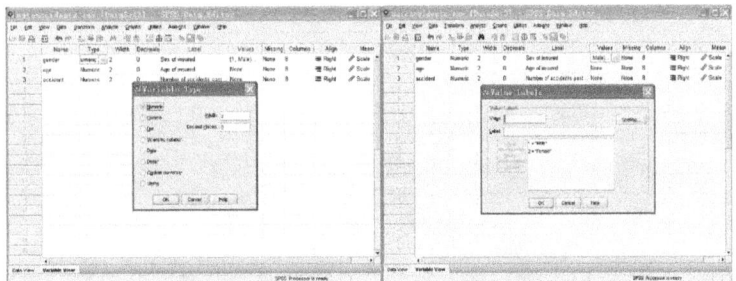

Figure 2 – 9 Define a numeric variable window

Figure 2 – 10 Define the variable window

After defining the variables, go to the data input window. At this point, we will see the three variables defined in the variable bar line: gender, age, accident. Then we can enter the data as we did excel (See Figure 2 −11).

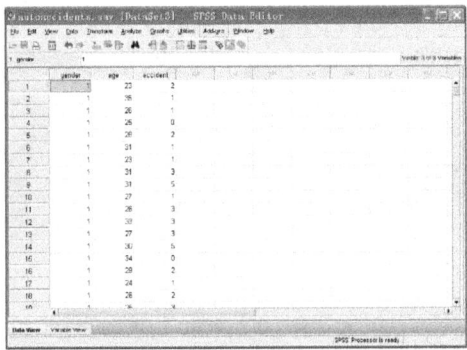

Figure 2 – 11 Enter the data window after defining the variable

The editing, sorting and other functions of data files are concentrated in the Data and Transform menu items (See Figure 2 −12A, Figure 2 −12B):

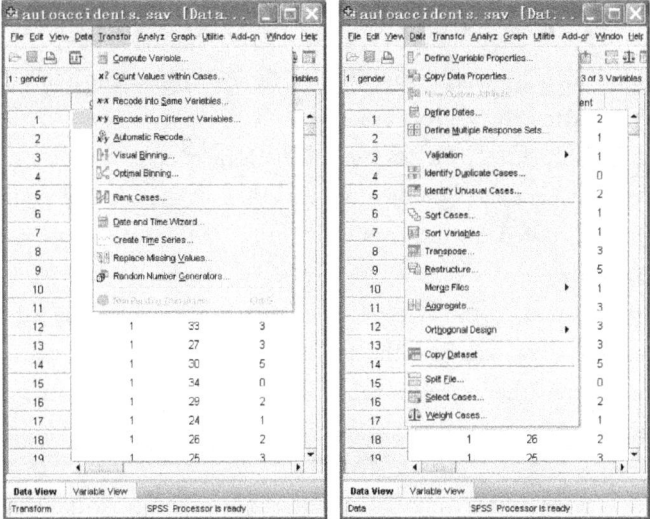

Figure 2 – 12 Data editing and finishing A

Figure 2 – 12 Data editing and finishing B

(d) Common statistical methods

Descriptive statistical analysis is the first step in statistical analysis. This first step is a prerequisite for correct statistical inference below. Descriptive analysis can be done on many SPSS modules, but several modules designed specifically for this purpose are concentrated in the Descriptive Statistics menu. The most common are the four processes listed first:

• The Frequencies process is characterized by the generation of a frequency table;

• The Descriptives process performs a general statistical description;

• The Explore process is used for exploratory analysis when the data profile is unclear;

• The Crosstabs process completes the statistical description of the count data and grade data and the general statistical test. Our commonly used X2 test is also completed.

There are many applications for correlation analysis. In data analysis, it is often encountered to analyze the relationship between two or more variables. Sometimes we want to know the intensity of the influence of one variable on another, and sometimes we need to understand the closeness of the relationship between variables. The former uses the next The chapter will be described in the regression analysis, and the latter will need to use the relevant analysis implementations described in this chapter. SPSS related analysis functions are concentrated in the Correlate submenu of the Analyze menu, which generally includes the following three processes:

- Bivariate process, which is used to perform parameter and nonparametric correlation analysis between two or more variables. If there are multiple variables, give two pairs of related analysis results. This is the most common one in the Correlate submenu.
- Partial process, if the two variables that need to be analyzed are affected by other variables, you can use the partial correlation analysis to control other variables, and output the correlation coefficient after controlling the influence of other variables. The covariance analysis is very similar. The Partial process is specifically for partial correlation analysis.
- Distances process, this process can be used to analyze the distance between the observation units within the same variable or the distance correlation between the different variables. The former can be used to detect the closeness of the observations, while the latter is often used to examine the predicted values to the actual values. goodness of fit. This process is used very rarely in practical applications.

Nonparametric statistics are an important part of statistical analysis. In SPSS, almost all nonparametric analysis methods are placed in the Nonparametric Tests menu, which are divided into the following categories:

- Chi-square test: to check whether the percentage of several values of the variable is statistically different from the expected ratio.
- Binomial Test: It is used to detect whether the given variable conforms to the binomial distribution. The variable can be divided into two categories, or it can be a continuous variable, and then cut off according to the given cut-off point.
- Runs Test: Used to check whether the value of a variable randomly fluctuates around a certain value. The value can be average, median, mode, or artificial. In general, if the test P value is statistically significant, then it is suggested that other variables have an effect on the value of the variable, or that the variable has an autocorrelation.
- The One-Sample Kolmogorov-Smirnov Test is used to analyze whether a

variable conforms to a distribution, normal distribution, uniform distribution, poission distribution or exponential distribution.

- Two-Independent-Samples Tests are non-parametric tests of two-sample mean comparisons in a group design.
- Tests for Several Independent Samples are non-parametric tests for the comparison of multiple samples of a group design. No two-two comparison methods are provided.
- Two-Related-Samples Tests are non-parametric tests of the two-sample mean of the paired design.
- Tests for Several Related Samples are non-parametric tests that are designed to match multiple sample means. No comparison is provided.

To analyze whether the experimental data is normal distribution data or non-normal distribution data, the data can be detected by the normality test, the variance analysis and the homogeneity test of variance. T-test—Statistical test of the mean of one or two sets of measurement data, including one-sample t-test, paired-t test, and t-test of two independent samples. The t test is the test used when the distribution of the sample mean is a t-distribution. The F test is the test used when the sample distribution is F-distributed. In addition to satisfying the basic conditions of analysis of variance, the covariance analysis also satisfies the linear relationship between the covariate and the dependent variable; there is no interaction between the covariate and the factor, that is, the regression slopes of each group are equal (the regression lines of each group are parallel). Therefore, before performing covariance analysis, it is first necessary to test whether it is suitable for covariance analysis. For the specific analysis method of data, refer to the teaching case study—"Study on the 'Trinity' teaching method in college public English teaching".

2.5 Expression of research results

2.5.1 Overview

The result of educational scientific research is the value-added knowledge of educational scientific research workers based on educational scientific research activities, combined with existing knowledge and experience, through text processing and theoretical analysis, which has certain academic value and social value. It must be based on educational scientific research activities, a re-creation result based on the re-creation process of word processing and theoretical analysis on the basis that educational scientific research activities have obtained certain information, and the results must be innovative. As a result, it is novel and value-added. Some of the educational scientific research results are educational and scientific research results based on educational facts, some scientific research results based on educational theory, and some comprehensive scientific research results. Educational and scientific research results are conducive to the promotion of researchers' research and research capabilities, while demonstrating research value, gaining social recognition and promoting academic exchanges.

2.5.2 Introduction to the method

The main methods include educational observation reports, educational investigation reports, educational experiment reports, academic papers, academic monographs, and dissertations. Although the various outcomes are presented in different forms and vary, they should generally include the five basic parts of the topic (title), preface, body, conclusion or discussion, citation notes or references.

2.5.2.1 Education survey report

The education survey report generally consists of five topics: title, preface, body, summary, and appendix.

(a) Topic: Reflect the main issues studied with clear and concise statements, supplemented with subtitles if necessary.

(b) Foreword: Briefly explain the purpose background, content, and value of the survey; summarize the time, place, object, scope, method, sampling method, etc. of the survey; simply analyze the favorable and unfavorable factors of the survey.

(c) Text: Through the narrative, survey charts, statistics and related literature, the main content is presented in a structured and accurate manner in the form of outlines, objectives, items or articles, chapters and sections.

(d) Conclusions and recommendations: On the basis of qualitative and quantitative analysis of the data, summarize the internal relations and laws of things, and propose new insights, new theories, find solutions to problems, and provide reference or reform plans.

(e) Appendix: Add a survey tool or part of the original material appendix to the report to provide a credible material basis for others. The appendix should not be too much and should be closely related to the theme.

2.5.2.2 Educational experiment research report

The experimental research report generally consists of topics, prefaces, methods, results, discussions, annotations, and appendices.

(a) Topic: Accurately and clearly present the problem to be studied, often using the name of the research topic directly, indicating the main variables studied.

(b) Foreword: including questioning, performance research purpose, subject selection basis, value meaning; current research status and trends at home and abroad; the main problems and theoretical framework that this topic will solve.

(c) Method: clarify the specific method and operation process of the experimental research, so that others can understand and verify the experimental research, including concept definition, subject selection, experimental design, experimental procedures, main tools and materials, analysis and processing of data, and experimental results. Hungry test methods, etc.

(d) Results: A brief description of the relationship between each result and the research hypothesis, presenting the research results as objective facts to the reader. The results should include both inductive analysis of qualitative data and statistical analysis of quantitative data; the results should be the actual results of experimental research, with objectivity and accuracy.

(e) Discussion: According to the factual materials in the results, combined with their own understanding, analyze the problems related to the experimental results, propose the theory or idea that should further explore the research, or put forward their own understanding, suggestions and ideas for the current educational theory or practice.

(f) Notes and references: At the end of the report, the source of the information directly mentioned or cited in the report should be indicated.

(g) Appendix: At the end of the experimental study report, the test tools or parts of the original materials used in the experiment may be attached as necessary.

2.5.2.3 Academic papers

The framework of an academic paper generally consists of six components: title, abstract and key words, introduction, body, conclusion, citation note or reference.

(a) Topic: Explain to the reader a high-level overview of the issues and implications of the research. The first requirement is to accurately summarize the content of the paper, which can reflect the research direction, scope and depth. Second, the text should be concise and novel, embodying the "beauty of the artistic conception" and the "beauty of the word".

(b) Signature: The signature should be serious. It not only symbolizes the recognition of scientific research results and the honor and intellectual property rights that researchers should enjoy, the more important significance is that it indicates that the signatory must bear the academic responsibility for the research results or even legal liability. The signature includes three main forms: collective signature, individual joint signature, and individual signature.

(c) Summary: The main content and method of scientific research with concise text. The results are summarized to help readers understand the full picture of the paper in the least amount of time to determine whether it is necessary to read the full text.

(d) Keywords (Subjects): A keyword is a word or academic phrase in a research report that best represents the subject of the article and expresses the important characteristics of its information elements. It helps readers to measure the value of the article and understand the focus of the article, as well as facilitate the storage and inspection of information.

(e) Foreword: Explain the purpose, intention and method of writing. First, clarify the background and motivation of the research, and put forward the problems that you want to study. Second, introduce the research direction and related means. Third, summarize the value of the research results.

(f) Text: The main body of the academic paper is the main part of the academic paper, including arguments, arguments, and arguments. It is the performance of the author's research results and plays a very important role in the whole paper.

(g) The connection between the arguments and the arguments in the text, the order of the arguments, and the hierarchical reasoning of the articles should be organized according to the inherent laws of the matter and considering the effect of the argument.

(h) Conclusion and discussion: The conclusion is the concluding remarks around the text, which is the end of the article. It mainly explains the significance of the research results in theory, summarizes the full text, deepens the theme, and carries out the precise summarization of the research results at a higher level. The discussion analyzes, interprets and evaluates the meaning and meaning of the research results theoretically.

(ⅰ) Citation comments and references: The significance of this part is that the first is to help readers understand the research history and achievements of the subject; the second is to respect the research results of others; the third is to provide clues for others to verify; Reflects the author's grasp of the history of the subject and the level of research, as well as the author's scientific attitude and realistic spirit. Mainly in the citations, the end of the page, the end of the article, the end of the article three forms. However, there are a few points to note when quoting: first, the method of annotation should be consistent throughout; second, the citation should be consistent with the order of comments; third, the comment should indicate the name, title or title of the translator, publication name or publisher name, publication time and edition, period, page number.

When carrying out the presentation of educational research results, we must first comprehensively plan the content and structure of the paper, so that the outline is clear and the structure is uniform and complete. Secondly, the discussion on the topic of the article center should be discussed. The expression and statement should be in a logical order. Again, the attitude should be objective. Based on factual material, the wording is based on neutrality, and there should be room for expression of intentional conclusions to avoid extremes. The expressions of nouns, numbers, symbols, etc. should be consistent with the standards of the authorities and the idioms of the authorities. Noun terms must be consistent in the same paper. When writing a thesis, stress is accurate, concise, and simple. Based on factual materials, we do not arbitrarily raise or devalue others' opinions, and do not arbitrarily vocalize, based on facts, to clarify opinions.

Chapter 3
Culture Teaching

3.1 Language and culture teaching

With the globalization of economy and the development of international communication, the world is becoming a global village, where people with different languages and cultures are living together. Cross-cultural interaction provides challenges and opportunities for all the peoples in the world. But it is unavoidable for them to involve some disagreements and conflicts due to the differences in the process of cross-cultural communication. English education should not only aim at a foreign language and its culture but also cross-cultural communication, because they are unseparated.

3.1.1 Language and culture

Language is a means of human thinking and communication. It has a phonetic symbol system which is used in human communication and has its arbitrariness. Each language came out and developed in a specific social and historical environment. As a symbol of people's cognition, thinking, communication and ex- pression, language participates in the concrete process of cultural formation. And it is a part of culture and also a special cultural phenomenon. Language is not only a cultural phenomenon, but also a carrier of culture and a container of cultural information.

As for culture, it is the whole way of life of a nation including patterns of faith, customs, goals, institutions, technology and language, which marks the life of the human community. The term used by Cicero, the Ancient Roman orator, is defined as a shared pattern of behaviors and interactions, cognitive constructs and affective understanding learned by people through a process of socialization. Culture is the human beings' production of living and social practice. Generally speaking, culture refers to the sum of all the material and spiritual wealth created by the people of a country or a nation, such as history, geography, customs, life style, values, literature and art, the code of conducts and the mode of thinking and so on, which include not only the outlook of the world and the philosophy in life, but also the non-ideological parts of natural science and technology and the languages. Culture covers a variety of aspects in human's life, the core of which is its spiritual product, and the essence of which is its dissemination. Culture is the total inherited ideas, beliefs, values, and knowledge, which constitute the shared social behaviors, the total range of activities and ideas of a social group with shared traditional customs and lifestyles. So it includes all aspects related to religion, food, style, language, marriage, music, morals and many other aspects that make up how people in a group act and interact each other.

Culture has an extensively social meaning. Its narrow meaning just focuses on language, literature, art and ideology of spiritual products. Generally speaking, it can be divided into three categories, such as material, spirit and language and text symbols. The mankind history is firstly a materiel one full of material production activities. When engaged in material production activities, people basically rely on their own bodies and hands for survival. Only when the first industrial revolution occurred, did people gradually free from the heavy manual labor. The spiritual goes second. As it is known, the second industrial revolution as the information technology is the human brain's liberation. The cultural problem of the contemporary world is actually the product of the era of information technology, because it makes people engaged in material production and more likely to manage more in spiritual activities. Actually, language and text symbols are part of culture and the spiritual activities of mankind. Now the world has entered the era of information technology, media culture has become dominant such as books, movies, television, Internet, mobile phones, which become the main carriers of contemporary culture.

3.1.2 The relationship between language and culture

Language and culture are accompanying with the history of mankind development. In a broad sense, all civilizations created by human beings can be referred to as culture; in a narrow sense, culture refers specifically to spiritual civilization, including philosophy, literature, customs and other concepts and ideological aspects. In fact, culture is the behavior pattern, cognitive structure and mutual understanding that people gradually form in the process of social development. Language and culture are essentially interdependent and have evolved together throughout the history. Language as well as culture is not innate but acquired. And they are influenced by the social development and constantly changing with the times. So they are inseparable.

Language is not just a set of signs, but is the main expressive means of culture. Language not only transmits but also shapes humankind's thinking, beliefs, and attitudes. In other words, language is a guide to culture. Some scholars argued that language merely reflects, rather than shapes people's thinking, beliefs and attitudes. In spite of their different opinions, all the scholars agree that a close relationship exists between language and culture.

Firstly, language is a material form of culture and also one of important culture carriers. The development and formation of culture cannot be separated from language, which is the most important means of storage. Human beings use language to communicate, record, preserve and inherit culture. That is to say, through language, culture is recorded and preserved with cultural achievements and labor experience, and it is also inherited and developed through a variety of communicative and disseminative forms. In the development of a culture, language cannot be ignored.

Secondly, language reflects the cultural psychology of a nation. And the language and characters are used to record the history and customs of a national development, which reflects the specific cultural features and psychological characteristics of different nationalities. Besides, the specific cultural and psychological characteristics of different nations have a counter-effect on the development of the language, which, to some extent, plays a restrictive role. There is no culture without language, and the two blend together.

Thirdly, language symbols are of society. Language learning is a cultural phenomenon of humankind's social activity and cognitive process. Language Learning is actually a learning of its culture when language is as a carrier of culture. Culture teaching undertakes the task of teaching a culture that exists in the form of language full of cultural elements of language, which is involved in its intrinsic language. Culture exists in the social communication rules and is an important content of cross-cultural education. Foreign language education not only aims at the teaching of the intrinsic language, but also the teaching of the external language. The purpose of learning language is in pursuit of good cooperation and connection in cross-cultural communication between different countries. Therefore, learning language is a means of communication and dissemination.

Fourthly, language teaching follows the step of the times. China's economy develops in the process of sustained and steady growth. With the promotion of "Belt and Road Initiative" strategy, China needs a large number of high-level talents in cross-cultural communication to promote the construction of projects and spread Chinese stories and culture. Therefore, English education should be quick to catch up with the pace of the times, take on the task of students' language and culture teaching at the same time, which is more conducive to the cultivation of students' cross-cultural communicative ability and better dissemination of Chinese culture.

The values of language and culture have not been emphasized enough in cross-cultural interaction for a long time. People used to take it for granted that they would communicate with the native freely just by mastering its language fluently, which turned out to be wrong in practice. The fact is that repeated mistakes will be made by the people from different backgrounds in the real cross-cultural communication. As a result, they were like bulls in a china shop once they stepped into a foreign country. Therefore, culture plays a very important role in the process of communication. It is of importance for communicators to combine the mastery of language itself with its culture.

A consciousness of cultural attitudes tends to be according to the hidden behaviors. People are superior to others in their own culture sometimes, because culture is ethnocentric. Ethnocentrism is a habitual disposition to judge foreigners with disfavor and a sense of inherent superiority, which should be avoided while communicating with foreigners. Only by doing so, people can know and interact each other freely.

3.1.3 Culture and English teaching

English teaching should not only make students master English language itself, but also understand its culture. Language is part of culture, and it carries its culture and the way of people's thinking. It is impossible to master only the language without understanding its culture. The former will lead to aphasia due to the cultural failure in cross-cultural communication. Therefore, cultural teaching should emphasize the cultivation of students' cultural literacy in English subject education. Cultural literacy is not innate but acquired on the basis of innate physiological characteristics to internalize the achievements of material and spiritual civilization of human development through the influence of environment and education, which is accumulated by individuals. The cultural literacy forms stably and solidly in physical and psychological attributes. And it is an embodiment of the humanism objective of language teaching and a part of the core accomplishment of students' English education.

English education has two requirements. One is the instrumental objective, and the other is the humanistic objective of language teaching. The former is the application of language, and the latter is the cultivation of students' language thinking quality, cultural consciousness and learning ability. Language as an implement of communication is he application of language and cultural literacy. English teaching should emphasize the dual functions of language teaching and focus on cultivating students' humanistic literacy. According to the requirements, English education, as a language subject, has its own educational rules and characteristics. Students should not only master the language but also understand its culture and the mode of thinking carried by the language. Therefore, both the foreign culture and Chinese culture cannot be ignored in teaching, especially focus on the integration of the two cultures in English education, which was underestimated by a lot of educators. In fact, it is the key to realize the unity of instrumentality and humanism in English language education.

Moreover, the instrumental and humanistic requirements of language are the whole of mutual influence and mutual promotion and the basic requirements of cultivating cross-national talents in English teaching. In China's English teaching, teachers teach the students the foreign language and culture, the Chinese culture, and the skills of cross-cultural communication in order to cultivate students' overall development guided by the Chinese socialist core values. The cross-cultural talents trained by the requirements are the ones who are needed for the economic and cultural development of our country. They have not only good language communication ability, international vision, extensive Chinese and foreign cultural knowledge, but also have national feelings with Chinese cultural background. In short, the cultivation of cross-cultural communicative competence is a realistic goal, while the cultivation of students' humanistic literacy is a long-term objective in English education.

3.2 Language Teaching and Cross-cultural Communication

Nowadays, the growth of interdependence of people and cultural communication in the global society in the twenty-first century pushes us to pay more attention to cross-cultural issues. As is known to us, the world is becoming a global village. The development of technology and transportation has enabled a constant flow of people to get a great deal of information and ideas across boundaries. Communication is faster and more available than ever. Demands for cross-cultural communication are increasing as more and more businesses go global. In order to live in this multicultural environment as effectively and meaningfully as possible, people must be competent in the cross-cultural communication. The competence of cross-cultural communication is of importance for cross-national talents as it examines how people come together to work and communicate with each other from different cultures, beliefs and religions. Without the help of cross-cultural communication skills, the students can unknowingly cause confusion and misunderstandings when communicating with foreigners. People will realize the barriers and limitations when entering a foreign territory. English education provides an opportunity to cultivate the competence of cross-cultural communication. It is vital for the students to fully understand the cultural differences that exist among the different cultures so as to prevent from damaging relations due to cross-cultural communication gaps.

3.2.1 Cross-cultural communication

The term communication can be defined in many ways. Myron W. Lustig and Jolene Koester (1996: 29) defined communication as a symbolic process in which people create shared meanings. In communication, everything is based on an interpretive processing. The words in this context are symbols that form the message of communication. Cross-cultural communication seeks to understand how people from different countries and cultures behave, communicate and perceive the world around them in an academic field of study and research. Communication is a dynamic process, and it changes, moves and develops all the time. All the communicative situations are unique in nature and the process can be seen as a sequence of distinct but interrelated steps (Lustig and Koester 1996:

30). Communication is interpretive in nature and people actively attempt to understand and organize their experiences with the shared information in the world. There are many researchers within the intercultural field, who naturally have different definitions of cross-cultural communication. As Samovar and Porter (1991) put it that communication is complete only when the intended behavior is observed by the intended receiver and that people respond to communication and are affected by others' behaviors. The definition of cross-cultural communication must also include strands of the field that contribute to the following such as anthropology, cultural studies, psychology and communication. It is also defined as the cross-personal interaction between members of different groups in respect of knowledge and symbolic behaviors. Cross-cultural communication refers to the communication between people from different cultures. According to Samovar and Porter (10: 1991) cross-cultural communication occurs whenever a message is produced by a member of one culture for consumption by a member of another culture, and the message must be understood. More definitions can be looked into the works of Edward T. Hall, Geert Hofstede, Harry C. Triandis and Shalom Schwartz, ect.

3.2.2 Cross-cultural education and research

Cross-cultural education generally refers to an education carried out between two cultures, which is also called cross-cultural education or trans-cultural education. All educational activities of human beings are based on a specific culture, and education is the carrier of cultural inheritance. In other words, everyone has a certain ethnic affiliation, and every kind of education is also inseparable from a specific national culture. Generally, language education can be further divided into two categories, single culture education and cross-cultural education. The single culture education means that the education received by the educated is basically limited to the culture of a nation and has a single national attribute, whereas the latter often takes place between two different cultures, which can be regarded as cross-cultural education such as English teaching in China.

The study of cross-cultural research has gradually formed a subject——cross-cultural communication since the 1950s, which integrates many disciplines such as anthropology, psychology, linguistics, philosophy and so on, and constructs a framework of the basic theory and research methods of cross-cultural communication. Some western scholars have carried out a lot of investigation and research on cross-cultural communication, integrating all aspects of culture, society and communication based on pragmatics of linguistic and nonverbal symbols as the core. Cross-cultural communication mainly studies the connotation, principles, strategies and the teaching mode of cross-cultural communication. Hall is known as the father of cross-cultural communication, and his book *Silent Language* (1958) is regarded as the foundation of the study of cross-cultural communication. In 1959, he first put forward the concept of cross-cultural communication, and made an in-depth analysis of verbal communication behavior. He divided culture into three levels such as explicit, implicit and technical. According to the internal structure, culture is divided into three categories as follows: elements, sets and patterns. He systematically explained the cultural change through the intuitive and practical *Culture Teaching Schematic Diagram*, and put forward the statement of "culture is com- munication", and advocated the concepts of "time language" and "space language". A large number of theoretical schools put forward their own views and ideas from different positions, purposes and disciplines. Today, cross-cultural education research has expanded from the United States, Britain, France, Germany to Canada, Australia, Japan, Southeast Asia, China and many other countries.

After more than half a century's development, cross-cultural communication has gradually formed an independent subject. Gudykunst's book *Theory of Cross-cultural Communication: Current Perspective* (1983) is regarded as a sign of the maturity of cross-cultural communication as a subject. He also divided the theory of cross-cultural communication into meaning construction, communication norms, cultural patterns, adjustment and adaptation, the formation and adjustment of identity, the psychological process of interpersonal communication and the group and network of communication. His theory not only systematically expounds the main theories of cross-cultural communication, but also makes a deep study on the uncertainty and anxiety of cross-cultural communication. His three criteria of evaluation theory make an outstanding contribution to the further development and innovation of cross-cultural communication. Porter et al. (1988) put forward the aspects of cross-cultural communication involving belief, attitude, values, world outlook and social organization factors in the process of communication, language and mode of thinking in the process of verbal communication and non-verbal behavior and the concept of time and space in the process of communication. Porter (1990) also listed eight factors that influence cross-cultural communication including attitude, social organization, mode of thinking, roles, role expectation, language, space, time and non-verbal expression, and pointed out that these eight factors do not exist independently in the process of cross-cultural communication, but affect each other. Porter et al. (2000) revised the above theory and summed up the previous three aspects and eight factors into four factors, and they are idea, speech, non-verbal and context. Ideas are the factors of how people perceive the material world involving beliefs, attitudes, values, world outlook and social groups.

  The achievements of foreign scholars in the study of cross-cultural communication also have some enlightening effect on Chinese scholars. The study of cross-cultural communication in China began in the 1980s. Since China's reform and opening up, cross-cultural communication between China and foreign countries has become more and more frequent, and the research on cross-cultural communication has become more and more necessary. Some achievements have been made. He Daokuan (1983), one of the first scholars who introduced the concept and theory of cross-cultural communication, proposed that cultural differences are the causes of cross-cultural communication failure, language failure and pragmatic failure. He also divided the cross-cultural communication errors from the perspective of the communicators into the following: the speaker error and the listener error; from the perspective of information coding, the cross-cultural communication error is divided into the information coding error and the information decoding error, which generally include the speaker coding correctly and the listener decoding error, and the speaker coding error and the listener decoding error coding. Wang Linhai (2006) divided the research methods of cross-cultural communication into three categories. Yao Chunyu (2008) studied the history, content and relationship between cross-cultural communication and foreign language teaching, and pointed out the gap of cross-cultural communication research at home and abroad. Jia Yuxin (2009) pointed out that globalization is a key factor in today's cross-cultural communication. In the context, people should dialogue with the concept of "harmony but difference", and the premise of dialogue is listening rather than persuasion. Gao Yongchen (2014) proposed the Evaluation Model of Cross-cultural Communication based on Chen Guoming's Thinking Model of Cross-cultural Communication, Byram's Model of Cross-cultural Communication Theory, and Deardorff's Pyramid Theory Model, which contains two sets of cross-cultural communication systems: knowledge system and performance system.

  In short, the research of Chinese scholars focuses on the translation and

Chapter 3 | Culture Teaching

introduction of foreign theories, the summary and classification of foreign studies, the evaluation of foreign theories and achievements and some practice and innovation on the basis of foreign achievements. Most domestic studies are based on foreign theoretical studies. With the continuous improvement of cross-cultural communication theory, the practice of cross-cultural communication teaching is also in full swing. The foreign language teaching has gone through the following four stages, such as teaching grammar knowledge, listening and speaking ability training, language comprehensive ability training and cross-cultural communication ability training. At present, the development of foreign language teaching is in the fourth stage, that is, the stage of cultivating cross-cultural communicative competence, which is developing towards the culture teaching as the core. Foreign language educators have also experienced different stages, from paying attention to reading ability to the cultivation of communicative ability, and from the cultivation of cross-cultural communicative ability to the development of cultural teaching. The ultimate goal of foreign language teaching is to communicate and spread ideas through the mastery of language and culture. Cultural teaching mainly refers to cultural information teaching and cultural process teaching, and there are four basic teaching modes like foreign cultural model, cross-cultural model, multicultural model and super-cultural model. In a word, cross-cultural communication is constantly improving, and many scholars draw lessons from the research findings of various disciplines, especially linguistics, sociology, psychology and so on. This research makes the subject mature day by day.

3.2.3 General introduction of research

There are many theories on the basis of cross-cultural communication, which have been brought up in many countries since the 1960s. The goal is to make the cross-cultural learning interactive so that both parties of communication can learn from each other. The theories help communicators iron out possible ripples of misunderstanding and provide a basic guideline on how to address situations and acculturate them into the major population of a nation. These guidelines are helpful to prevent clashes between different cultures caused by misperceptions. The basic skills are useful and fundamental in cross-cultural communication. They are universal and simple to make communicators take the cultural limitations into consideration and sort them out according to a series of strategies. And the theories developed by the researchers and academics have been applied to many fields especially in business. As Chinese businesses become more and more international, many international companies need to know how to communicate with their foreign customers best. Cross-cultural communication guided by these theories can give them an insight into the areas that they need to understand and learn. Therefore, English education should take on the responsibility to cultivate the talents' competence of cross-cultural communication in order to put it into real situation like how to create cultural synergy between people from different cultures within a business. Cross-cultural education is one of the hot spots of educational research in the today's world. As a new field of interdisciplinary research, it involves many subjects with regards to educational anthropology, comparative education, national psychology, sociology, ethnology, culture, communication and so on, thus forming many theories and schools related to the research. The following is a brief introduction on the theoretical schools that have great influence on the world, such as cultural change, cultural assimilation, cultural integration, cultural adaptation, cross-cultural communication and multiculturalism and so on.

3.2.4 The introduction of related theories

There are many influential schools of cross-cultural education and related theories. The following is to make a brief introduction for the theories of cross-cultural education.

3.2.4.1 The theory of cultural change

Cultural change refers to a slow changing process of cultural content and structure in quantity. It can be divided into two categories: natural change and planned change. Natural change is a process of natural development or an accumulation of unconscious culture, which is difficult to control. It refers to the phenomena of cultural environment, such as cultural characteristics, cultural patterns, the evolution of cultural style, etc. From the primitive society to the early capitalist society, the change of human cultural history belongs to this type. Planned change is a process of people consciously and systematically developing and reforming culture, such as social economic system reform, political system reform and educational system reform. It can be also referred to the phenomena of social environment, such as social relations, social groups and the evolution of social life. Cultural and social changes are different and related. Generally speaking, social change will cause cultural change; social change can be seen from cultural change, too.

The study of cultural change began in the early 20th century on the basis of the early theories of evolution, communication, function and history. In 1936, the American Anthropology Committee published a study entitled *The Memorandum of Study on Cultural Change*, which classifies the related existing research and has a great influence on the later research on cultural change. Acculturation is defined as the phenomenon of continuous and direct contact between different cultural groups, which changes the original culture or both of them. The research includes the index of the paper with reference value, the classification of data, and the method of analysis. The report has an analysis of cultural changes including the types of contact between nationalities, the status of cultural changes and the process of cultural changes. Another point is the psychological structure of cultural selection and integration in the process of cultural change including the role of the individual, the attitude of acceptance and rejection of different cultures, the personal characteristics of people, the differences of attitudes caused by gender and social status, belief, occupation, resistance and compromise in the initial stage of the process of cultural change and the mental anxiety caused by the abandonment of the inherent behaviors. The result of cultural change including acceptance, adjustment and rejection comes to a conclusion. Although this research cannot constitute a rigorous and complete theory, it provides a basic theoretical framework for the later cultural change theory and cross-cultural education research. The role and influence of cultural contact are often bidirectional. Moreover, the adjustment referred to therein actually points to the possibility of cultural integration and the creation of a new culture in addition to assimilation and refusal to assimilation. Besides, it correctly points out that attitudes towards different cultures can also vary according to individual personalities and specific circumstances. In 1954, the Committee added that the cultural change of immigrants and ethnic groups causes the negative cultural changes and positive side of creating a new culture in the United States. It put it like this that cultural change is a cultural change produced by the combination of two or more self-regulated cultural systems.

Taking culture as a system is very important to grasp the structure of cultural change. It helps to understand and judge the personalities of each cultural system in the process of change, showing an openness or closeness outside, rigidity or softness in the internal, and a systematical resilience in the cultural environment. In the process of cultural contact and change, the abandonment and loss of traditional culture is by no means a process leading to nothingness, which must be compensated by a new culture. Therefore, the active abandonment of traditional culture actually means the choice of new culture. In most cases, the introduction and integration of another self-regulated cultural system leads to the creation of a new culture. At times, when the threat of exclusion from other cultural groups is too high, there is a process of withdrawal contrary to assimilation, which creates a stronger sense of identity and reinforcement of various cultural forms in their own groups. This reverse adaptation is a backward adaptation; and fusion and assimilation are a forward adaptation. Fusion refers to the relationship between the two cultures, which is a bilateral process. Assimilation then in the opposite pole of integration is a unilateral process in which one group accepts the culture of another group. Fusion and Assimilation are, respectively, at the poles of a continuum. But both integration and assimilation result in the loss of the original culture of one or both sides. And neither integration nor assimilation, to a considerable extent, maintains the relative self-discipline of the various cultural systems to become the so-called stabilized pluralism.

3.2.4.2 The theory of psychological humanism

The psycho-humanism school developed after the World War II, which focuses more on the quantitative analysis of individual cognition, adaptation approach, behavior style and interpersonal relationship in the process of different cultural contact. Hallowell, as a representative figure, began to divide the process of cultural change into several stages in the 1950s, and used psychological measurement to determine the degree of cultural change. He classified the variant forms as the native, the native-modified, and the American-marginal in a changing continuum. Another scholar, Voget, argued that it is incorrect to treat cultural changes as homogeneous units. Bruner proposed Unacculturated Change Mode, Marginal Change Mode and Acculturated Change Mode. Immediately after that, the famous scholar, Spindler, used the method of psychological anthropology to sort out the different results after the process of adaptation to different cultures about the changes in the behavior of different people. He believed that the change is not fixed, which can be divided into conservative traditional tendency, part of the traditional faith-maintenance, transitional middle and the cultural change of the white culture. In the 1960s, Spradley further divided the different people into several types of behaviors including the one sticking to the traditional culture, the one rejecting traditional culture and western culture, the one creating a new type of belief and value system, the one rejecting traditional culture and the one being assimilated by the value system of western culture, the one standing in the middle of the two cultures and adapting creatively and effectively to the type of plural cultural environment, who are so-called double-cultural person.

3.2.4.3 Cultural assimilation theory

The most representative of cultural assimilation theory is the American Chicago academic school at the beginning of this century and in the end of World War II. The theory has a close relationship with the assimilationist thought on the ideological basis that has prevailed in the United States since the 19th century. That is, the so-called white American pioneers, who occupied the dominant position in the society, forced new immigrants and ethnic minorities to adopt the same language and culture as their own groups, that is, what is commonly referred to as Anglo-conformity or so-called Americanization. The assimilation of nations must go through a process of contact and contest, that is, to come into a cycle. This cycle generally consists of several phases of contact-competition-conflict-adjustment-assimilation, by which the immigrants eventually assimilate the culture of the dominant group. In the 1960s, the study of assimilation theory introduced by American scholars began to turn to the ethnic minorities and immigrants' consciousness of assimilation and the way of assimilation. Gorton's Seven-Phase Assimilation Theory (1964) stated that immigrants and ethnic groups show a tendency to move closer to the mainstream culture. They should establish close relationships with the mainstream members in work, study and entertainment to reduce prejudice against the mainstream, thus eliminating a sense of difference to abandon the power struggle with the mainstream. In the 1970s, American immigrant sociologist Greeley put forward the Six-stage Theory of Assimilation according to the analysis of the immigrants' inner world, who have the impact on mainstream culture with the group's emotional strengthening with the restoration of self-esteem and self-confidence caused by the impact of alien culture. Some began to face and absorb the culture of the mainstream people. others tried to eliminate the prejudice and differential consciousness of the group. However, the confrontational attitudes adopted by these people are often guarded and suppressed by the mainstream people, which often drive their prejudice and sense of difference to be strengthened again; and frustration and reflection have led them to deepening their understanding of both peoples and thinking about a third path that will enable them to live together and finally form a conceptual system that can be freely transformed in both worlds. That is to say, the result of assimilation is not necessarily along a straight line.

3.2.4.4 Cultural integration theory

It is also known as Melting-pot Theory. The representative figure is American historian called Henry J. Turner. In the heart of this doctrine of integration, amalgamationism does not completely exclude the religious and cultural background inheritance in the various ethnic minorities, while absorbing each other's excellent cultures including those of the mainstream ethnic groups, partially abandoning or amending their own culture and bringing them together to create a comprehensive and new culture. However, this ideal of integrationist has not been fulfilled. The Melting-pot Theory, in fact, also excludes the colored people out of the white European bloc.

3.2.4.5 Intercultural adaptation

It studies the psychological reaction and changing process in the adaptation of different cultures from the individual point of view, which includes many factors such as personal cultural attitude, mode of thinking, belief, motivation, national ownership consciousness, cultural friction, interpersonal relationship, cultural adjustment and cultural exchange ability and so on. The psychologist Berry divides people into four types in cross-cultural adaptation according to the sense of belonging to their own nation and their attitudes towards the mainstream nation. The cultural transfer type denies the sense of belonging to the nation. The rejection type has a strong sense of belonging, taking a negative attitude towards the mainstream ethnic groups. The balanced integration type holds a sense of national belonging while maintaining a positive relationship with the mainstream. The deculturation takes an attitude of rejection in the sense of belonging and the communication with the mainstream nationality. Another psychologist Adler proposed five stages based on the psychological process of adaptation to different cultures. First, there is a curiosity and an excitement about certain new features in the contact of the culture; second, there appears an estrangement, confusion, fatigue after their freshness disappears; third, the similarities and differences between the two cultures are evaluated objectively, and confusion gradually comes out; fourth, they understand the two cultures and give some new ideas to make them richer and more mature.

Atkinson focused on the study of the different cultural adaptation psychology of minorities in the environment of prejudice and discrimination against minorities by mainstream nationalities. His five stages of cross-cultural adaptation are as follows:

- Taking a positive attitude towards different cultures;

● Falling into confusion, vacillation and distress because of the differences between the two cultures in values and beliefs;

● Resisting different cultures and emphasizing the excellent points of their own culture driven by national self-esteem;

● Finding a balance between national self-esteem, national loyalty and reason;

● Coordinating the two cultures to handle the relationship between emotion and reason and taking a more flexible attitude towards problems.

Moreover, according to the process of cultural adaptation to foreign students, the Gullahorn summarized and put forward the Cross-cultural Adaptation Curve called W. This cross-cultural adaptation curve reflects a basic pattern that most people show when they come into contact with different cultures. Taking the cultural experience of young people studying abroad as an example, the curve is divided into seven stages: honeymoon period (feeling very fresh and friendly to the people around them, feeling powerless in the face of difficulties in daily life and work, and often wandering between struggle and escape), entanglement period (difficulties and problems which cannot be solved smoothly and make the situation worse), adaptation period (gradually adapting to local society and daily life), repetition period (self-righteously understanding different cultures, but still unable to grasp complex problems), early returning to the country (happy to look forward to returning to the country, uplifting, reluctant to give up) and the impact of return (contrary to expectations in life when contacting with people, there is a sense of alienation and cultural adaptation again).

3.2.4.6 Cross-cultural communication theory

The theory claims that there is a close relationship between culture and communication. One essential difference between man and other animals is that man holds culture. And culture is established and developed through communication. Therefore, communication is a unique function of culture. In a sense, it can even be said that culture is communication, and communication is culture. The so-called communication generally refers to people through speech and non-verbal media to convey the cross-cultural knowledge, feelings and meaning. But different disciplines have different interpretations of the meaning of cultural communication. For example, a Japanese encyclopedia has a definition of communication. The cross-cultural process mainly regards the interpersonal communication as the foundation which forms the interpersonal relationship and the social relations. People can interact through communication, which is a process of understanding each other and being understood by each other. In addition, cross-cultural communication is carried out between the information exporter of a certain culture and the information receiver of different cultures. In this sense, cross-cultural communication is a symbolic process of cross-culture between people from different cultural backgrounds through information transmission. Besides, similar concepts to cross-cultural communication include inter-state communication, international communication, inter-human communication, inter-national communication and so on. To sum up, there are three main types of cultural exchanges between different ethnic groups. The first is that the underdeveloped people learn from the developed nations and expect to introduce the advanced culture of the foreign nationalities into their own nationalities usually with the characteristics of civilization. The similarities and differences between self-national cultures and other national cultures can be viewed and understood more equally and objectively, that is, the so-called cultural relativism. What the world generally advocates today is the cultural exchanges of multicultural coexistence based on mutual respect.

3. 2. 4. 7 Cross-cultural understanding education

It is not a simple understanding and respect for each other's cultural differences, but as a complete and operable educational process, including all aspects of knowledge, emotion and meaning. First, it is necessary to understand the similarities and differences between cultures to increase the relevant knowledge and information through various kinds of learning, that is, the so-called cognitive process; second, the transformation of emotion and the establishment of correct values should learn to be broad-minded and equal to different cultures; and finally, it is important to put these knowledge and emotions into practice. The precondition of equal cross-cultural communication is cross-cultural understanding, while cultural prejudice is the biggest obstacle in cross-cultural understanding and cross-cultural communication. The social psychologist Brislin in his book *Prejudice in Cross-cultural Communication* divides prejudice into six types based on the red-neck racism. Judging a particular race as inferior by certain subjective criteria is a highly subjective bias, holding a symbolic-based nationalist bias against members of other cultures when they feel threatened by their symbolic racism and holding unconscious nominal bias against other cultural groups, although they are not conscious of tokenism and adopt an indefinite attitude according to the situation of other cultural members, which is called maintaining arms-length prejudice based on the familiar and unfamiliar. These prejudices, although to some degree, have a certain impact on cross-cultural communication. He also proposed six corresponding educational methods:

- Focus on information and facts, first of all, to enable the people concerned to acquire the necessary knowledge through lectures, discussions, photographs, discussions, photographs, videotapes and documents;
- Clarify the causes of these cultural phenomena from the perspective of local culture and point out different ways of conduct leading to misunderstandings especially from the evaluation and judgment of the self-cultural center;
- Establish a correct cultural and point out the people concerned with the characteristics of the values and behaviors of the self-culture; After that, these characteristics of local culture should be expounded so that they can understand the cultural differences that arise in the conduct of cultural exchanges;
- Revise the deviation of cognition and apply the principles of psychology to cross-cultural research such as the reward and punishment of psychological principles to make it easier for the parties to make appropriate amendments to the understanding of the local culture. The characteristics are to make the participants have cross-cultural experience with the help of the instructors and make the parties understand the cross-cultural characteristics through the simulation experience. Similar to experience learning, it requires action with people of local cultural origin and with extensive experience in the area to overcome uneasiness and unhappiness in direct interactions.

3.2.4.8 Multiculturalism and multicultural education

Culturalpluralism as early as 1915 was put forward by the American scholar Kalan. But the so-called right to equality and freedom had no guarantee in the social system under the historical conditions of the times, and the ideal could only stay in discussion. What is called multiculturalism today generally refers to the product of the black American civil right movement in the 1960s and 1970s. The sweeping whirlwind in the United States is not only a political movement against racial discrimination, distinction, demanding equality and civil rights, but also a cultural movement against assimilationism and integrationism. The wave soon spread to other minorities. It calls for a new understanding of ethnic minorities and their cultures, respect for the individual characteristics, the national feelings of all ethnic groups and the realization of the diversity of society as a basic concept of multiculturalism and multicultural education.

3.2.4.9 Multicultural education

Multicultural education generally refers to education carried out in multi-ethnic countries to guarantee equal educational opportunities for children with diverse ethnic cultural backgrounds especially ethnic minorities and immigrants and to ensure that their unique national culture. Its characteristics are duly respected. The representative speaker is American James A. Banks. He believes that the fundamental goal of multicultural education is to enable groups belonging to different cultural, ethnic, religious and social strata to learn how to maintain peace between each other and to coordinate to achieve symbiosis of the relationship. But multicultural education is not just an idea or a slogan. To become an operable educational activity, it must be carried out practical educational reform. The reform involves at least three aspects: firstly, the reform of the educational curriculum, which reflects the voices, achievements and struggles of ethnic groups, cultural groups and groups discriminated against in the curricula of all schools and universities; secondly, the full guarantee of the education right of all children, in particular, effective measures to enable children from low-income classes, non-white children, female students and adolescents with disabilities to receive and complete their education; and again, the establishment of a correct educational outlook with a positive attitude towards members of different ethnic and cultural groups. That is to say, it is a comprehensive educational reform movement from educational content, system to ideology. On that basis, he proposed eight basic characteristics for multicultural education schools:

- The teaching staff should have high positive attitude towards all students;
- The official textbooks of the school should correctly reflect the contributions, cultures and ideas of men and women and diverse cultural and ethnic groups;
- The teaching of teachers should be consistent with the students' learning, culture and motivation;
- The teaching staff should respect the students' mother tongue and dialect;
- The teaching materials used in the school should be based on a variety of cultures, classes and ethnic groups and impartial and objective in description.
- Students' evaluation and examination activities in schools should pay attention to cultural differences and proper mastery of standards;
- School culture and activities should reflect the diversity of cultures and classes;
- School development guidelines should be directed to all students of

different races, social classes and language groups with positive and progressive goals. He stressed that the education of multicultural education is not only for ethnic minorities and immigrants, but also for white teenagers in mainstream society and for all students. Moreover, multicultural education is not an independent subject and must be immersed in all relevant subjects. At the same time, James further divided the concept of culture into macro-culture and micro-culture. The so-called multicultural education is not intended to weaken or eliminate the macro-culture that represents the will of the whole people, such as equality, humanitarianism, free competition, etc. Its main purpose is to emphasize respect for small and weak nations and cultural groups so that children of all ethnic groups can be truly treated equally. The proposal of multicultural education has caused great repercussions in American society. Some people worry that the implementation of multicultural education is not conducive to the stability and unity of society and leads to the antagonism and even division between different nationalities and cultural groups in the end; others think that the idea of multicultural education is only an ideal, it is not easy to put into practice.

On the other hand, many civil society groups and governments at all levels and people from all walks of life have a positive and appreciative attitude towards multicultural education. A number of universities offer lectures and courses on multicultural education; some regions and schools begin serious experiments; and national organizations should be specialized such as the National Council for the Social Studies which covers formal guidelines. The New York City Education Commission also issued a formal statement on the introduction of multicultural education policies. It said that all students have the right to maximize their potential and access to quality education. People living and working in New York are from all over the world. Multicultural education is necessary in order to deepen understanding among different groups so that all young people can acquire the ability to play an outstanding role in the society. Multicultural education is not to eliminate cultural differences in schools or only to satisfy tolerance for cultural diversity, but to protect cultural diversity based on the spirit of multiculturalism, thus making it become a valuable resource. However, it should be noted that the understanding and interpretation of multicultural education in different countries and different people are not exactly the same. In particular, the pursuit of goals is sometimes far from each other because of the historical formation of various countries, ethnic characteristics and social reality of the various differences, although they are the same as multicultural education. Nine clear goals were set for the implementation of the multicultural education policy. For example, multicultural education in the United Kingdom is primarily directed at colored people; multicultural education in Germany is directed primarily at cultural frictions arising from immigrants such as those from the Eastern Europe in recent years; while multicultural education in Japan emphasizes respect for national cultures abroad and international understanding of education. Therefore, it is necessary to make a specific analysis of multicultural education policies in the different situations of various countries, and not to generalize. Different countries and different people do not have the same understanding and interpretation of multicultural education.

Students' learning, culture and motivation are consistent; teaching staff should respect their mother tongue and dialects; school materials should be based on a wide variety of cultures, classes and ethnic groups, which should be fairly and objectively documented; school student evaluation and examination activities should pay attention to cultural differences and appropriate standards; school culture and its activities should reflect cultural and class diversity; and school development guidelines should be directed towards all students of different ethnic, social and linguistic groups with a view of setting positive goals and helping them to achieve them. He stressed that the multicultural education is not only for ethnic minorities and immigrants, but also for white teenagers in mainstream society, and for all students. Moreover, multicultural education is not an independent subject and must be immersed in all relevant subjects. At the same time, he further divided the concept of culture into macro-culture and micro-culture. In short, the main purpose of communication is to earn respect from others including people, language and religion. Respect all cultures in the world is a key to culture teaching; and the favor is returned. Communication in the cross-cultural environment tends to listen to others without judging, repeat what you understand, confirm meanings, give suggestions and acknowledge a mutual understanding.

3.3 Cultural differences and identity between the West and the East

In college English teaching, it is helpful for students to understand the differences of the Western and Chinese cultures through cultural contrast. They are different due to the influence of various factors, such as history, living conditions, tradition and so on. The study of cultures is beneficial for students to deeply understand the historical roots of the Western and Chinese cultures and the different and similar ways of thinking to gain an objective understanding in the two cultures so as to establish the confidence of Chinese culture.

3.3.1　Differences of cultures between the West and the East

The awareness of cultural differences has certain practical significance for college English cross-cultural education, from which students can understand the Chinese and foreign cultures more comprehensively and objectively. It is conducive to cultivating students' sensitivity to cultural differences, tolerance and flexibility in dealing with cultural differences to adapt themselves to the changing international communication. Therefore, students learning a language and its culture should know the differences between the West and the East and the trend of cultural development.

A nation develops, so does its culture. What is a nation? It is a society with a particular culture, in which a group of people are involved in persistent social interaction sharing the same geographical or social territory, typically subject to the same political authority and dominant cultural expectations. With the cultural conflicts and integration in different nations and countries caused by economic globalization, cultural issues are becoming increasingly apparent and prominent in the contemporary world. In cross-cultural communication settings, it is easy to become trapped in some invisible barriers in communication, and they are not easy to perceive beyond one's imagination. The only way avoids making communication mistakes that come from them is that Students should know what the major barriers are and how to impede ineffective cross-cultural communication, fully understand the origins of the barriers, and then know how to overcome them. They are expected to find out the barriers from their own cross-cultural communication experience. It is very important for them to understand and appreciate the cross-cultural differences ultimately so as to break down barriers, builds trust, promote communication, strengthen relationships, open up their horizons and yield tangible results in terms of communicative success. There are two dominant cultural groups. There are many differences in culture in the following between the West and the East.

3.3.1.1　Difference in origins

Apart from geographical locations, the two cultures have differences in the way of life in general. The Western culture is mainly defined as the culture of European countries as well as those that have been heavily influenced by European immigration, such as the United States, Australia, New Zealand and Canada. The Western culture has its roots in the Classical Period of the Greco-Roman era and the rise of Christianity in the 14th century. The Eastern culture covers a wide swath of history in the East Asia, South Asia, the Middle East and North Africa as well. The Chinese culture is a part of the Eastern culture, and its social values are mostly derived from Confucianism, Buddhism and Taoism. Many countries are influenced by the Chinese culture throughout the world. Philosophy as the most popular and widest mode of thought can be totally and obviously different. Basically, the Western philosophy is considered to be the school of thought from the ancient Greek, which influences the greater part of the Western civilization and roots in Christianity. On the contrary, the Eastern philosophy is based mainly on Asian thoughts, more specifically, on the Chinese philosophy. The Eastern philosophy is rooted in Confucianism, Buddhism and Taoism. Actually, the Eastern philosophy is originated from Chinese thoughts, while the Western philosophy is more in its Latin root.

3.3.1.2 Difference in values

The commonly held standards of values in a community or a society are involved in what is acceptable or unacceptable, important or unimportant, right or wrong, workable or unworkable. Values of culture guide people's decision-making and balance the re- lationship between an individual and the society. Different peoples from different cultures are various in view of values. The distinct characteristics of values lie in individualism and collectivism between the West and the East. The Western values are more individualistic in pursuit of finding the meaning of life, which is self-centered as part of the divine. In contrast, the eastern values focus more on seeking an individual's life meaning as a member of the group, realizing his true "self-value" in relation to the group. The main principle of the eastern values is unity. The cosmological unity is the main point in life as it goes towards the eternal realities. Life is like a circle as "圆满" in Chinese, that is to say, everything should go smooth again and again at any point on the circle. Ethics is based on behaviors and depend on the external rules and internal moral constraints. In order to be liberated, the inner self must be freed first in accordance to the world around it. The Western phi- losophy, in contrast, is based on self-dedication to be of service to others. Life is service to God. Due to the Christian influence, there has to be a beginning and an ending for the meaning of life. Linear it seems to be, the Western philosophy is logical, scientific and rational compared with the Eastern eternal and recurring concepts.

The Eastern culture focuses on collectivism while the Western culture emphasizes individualism. In the East, people often seek the unity of meaning and values according to human behavior, thought, social collective value, and especially the cultural philosophy represented by China and integrate them to find a true "self". The oriental culture, represented by the Chinese culture, advocates the values of collectivism. People see family, group and social interests as center, and their individuals' behavior and decision must be consistent with the group's as the premise. Therefore, Chinese people would give up their own interests when there are conflicts between individual interests and collective interests. People first put it into consideration the interests of the whole group according to this mainstream oriental collectivist culture. And there is a strong tendency to cooperate with group members for the same goals, such as the idea of "Family's harmony goes first" and "Peace is the most precious" in the traditional Chinese culture, which reflect the harmonious values in the oriental philosophy and fully expresses the cultural value orientation of harmonious family and social system.

This collectivist value affects all aspects of Chinese daily life. It is actually an interdependent network under the influence of this traditional value orientation, communication and cooperation between people. Only by establishing and developing a harmonious relationship with the whole, can the individual be happier. On the contrary, the Western civilization based on individualism aims to discover the meaning and value of an individual. It believes that the power of the individual is given by God, the personal interests are above all, sacred and inviolable, and everything should ensure the personal interests and rights not to be violated. The main cultural difference between the East and the West lies in seeking truth in the Western ethics, while the Eastern culture focuses on the positive impact of individual behaviors on the whole. The difference of value orientation between collectivism and individualism is the result of the influence of different cultural traditions between the East and the West. In a word, the two cultures are influenced by their respective history, social customs and morals.

3.3.1.3 Differences in philosophy

Cultural differences lead to different thoughts in philosophy in the West and the East. Both the Western and Eastern philosophies come from people's production and life. The Eastern philosophy is more spiritual, while the Western philosophy is more practical. Although the Western philosophy is distinct from the Eastern one, it is sure to say that they are equal rather than one somehow superior to the other. They present peculiar modes of thinking based on different cultures.

  Cultural philosophy is to use philosophical viewpoints and methods to study cultural principles and form cultural views and cultural activities in a theoretical system. It mainly discusses the history and development of culture, the similarities and differences of culture, the conditions of cultural development and the role of cultural conflicts and blending. It is not a simple combination of culture and philosophy, but contains the important transformation and transition of theoretical paradigm in philosophy. In the view of cultural philosophy, all forms of cultural symbols such as language, philosophy, mythology, religion, science, art and so on, are the products of human spiritual activities, and the world has a richer meaning of cultural symbols through the continuous creation by human beings. In the process of continuous culture, human beings constantly confirm themselves, in fact, by self-creation of the world. It is helpful for the students to study the differences of the two cultural philosophies, further understand the two cultures and promote their cultural identity. Firstly, their cultural differences are mainly manifested by the two different views of the world and the ways of people's lifestyles in different cultural backgrounds. Of course, they recognize the outside world differently. The Western culture is represented by Aristotle's thinking mode, emphasizing logical thinking to carry out rational analysis to study causality of things through gradual reasoning, thus forming logical thinking mode with objective reason and reflecting objective facts. The philosophy originates from the rise of the city gangs in the Western society and the development of handicraft culture. The ancient Chinese philosophy originated from a kind of related thinking, describing abstract things with concrete images and perceptual knowledge to observe rules of the world. Chinese people analyzed them through association and reasoning and clearly expounded the essence of the world through language. The culture came from the development of self-sufficient agricultural economy in the ancient China, and the people paid more attention to the harmonious community in order to survive and reproduce continuously in the society. Therefore, both the unity of nature and man in Confucianism and Taoism are emphasized and understood by intuition, and the essence and the law of the world were expressed by intuition in the Chinese traditional culture. Confucius thought, starting from the intuition of human nature, points out the relationship between heaven (the highest criterion of all things) and absolute transcendence between people and the way of getting along——the concept of " the unity of nature and man", which is also the representative of oriental philosophy.

Culture is of uniqueness as the symbol of a nation. If the culture is neglected or looked down, even totally lost, the nation will disappear. So it is very important for Chinese nation to pay mere attention to understanding of different cultures, establish its own cultural confidence and achieve an equal communication in cross-cultural interaction based on respecting different cultures.

3.3.1.4 Difference in etiquette

The city-state society developed in the form of contract among the Western world, so it advocated free and equal trade. This tradition is conducive to the establishment of free and equal codes of conduct, which are observed by all. With regards to human nature, the westerners believe that it arises from individual relations, such as desire, reason, freedom, equality, fraternity and so on. In contrast, the social structure was based on the relationship of blood and marriage in ancient China. This kind of patriarchal system promoted the foundation of a social and political structure based on family and country isomorphism, and there was also a strict hierarchical system in the family and society such as the relations of between monarch and minister, between father and son, between male and female and between the elder and the young, which formed a hierarchical social order. Confucianism holds that man himself is not only the origin of benevolence, but also needs the enlightenment of transcendental relationships— the oriental philosophy of "the unity of nature and man". It is a process of human nature that it changes from spontaneity to consciousness by the inspiration of human nature.

3.3.1.5 Difference in the ways of thinking

The Western culture emphasizes more individual thinking, and it originated mainly from handicraft and navigation on the Greek peninsula. People paid more attention to the use of technology because of the developed handicraft industry and formed a scientific tradition through exploration of natural mysteries. Therefore, the Westerners have a rational thinking mode with logic based on objectivity. In modern times, the Western scientific experiment develops rapidly, the way of thinking also has the very strong positivism especially after the industrial revolution. Under the influence of organization, democracy and scientific thought, they tend to do business fairly, realistically and competitively. The core concern of the Western culture is the essence of the world, which aims to individual analysis and research on the essence of things.

In the Western philosophy, people use binary analysis to analyze the essence of things, emphasizing the conflict, contradiction and the internal differences of things. The analytical method divides the unified world into two completely opposite aspects, and studies the facade separately to reveal the multiple echelons and complexity of things. The Western philosophers insist on the dichotomy of the universe, that is, division of the world into two opposites including the subjective and the objective. This kind of thinking looks at the world from the point of view of decomposition, emphasizes the idea from one to more and decomposes the whole into parts, which is more conducive to solving specific problems. Its thinking way leads to a much more focus on objective facts and the essence of things.

On the contrary, the oriental culture, represented by Chinese culture, pays more attention to holistic thinking, which originated from the self-sufficient small peasant economy form in the ancient East. If people wanted to survive, they must live in harmony with their surroundings including human, nature and society. Therefore, the representative Chinese philosophy in the Eastern philosophy regards individual, nature and society as an organic whole. People grasped the essence of things and sought the natural harmony by "the integration of yin and yang" and "the unity of nature and man". This kind of value orientation has double results. One is to strengthen the dependence between people, and the other is to make the society stable. On the other hand, the Eastern way of thinking attaches importance to personal cultivation with regards to "self-cultivation" and "the root of life", relating personal interests with the group's interests with the concept of collectivism. Although this view will make some individual's interest lost sometimes, it preserves the overall interest of the community.

In addition, the difference in thinking mode is that the western thinking is linear, while the eastern thinking is circuitous. Handicraft industry development and commodity exchange are mainly contractual transactions in the process of the Western culture. They pursue free and equal transactions. Therefore, its way of thinking is also based on the way of exchange based on the expression of personal views and the linear way of thinking, that is, the Aristotle's logical way of thinking by taking logical empirical as a means, emphasizing the analysis of problems and the rational understanding of the essence of things. The Westerners believe that the world is unified. There are contradictory opposites of one or the other, which originate from the idea of dualism in the Western philosophy. They argue that a proposition is either right or wrong and that there is no other answer. The way of thinking makes them good at structural deconstruction of things they know, which dooms the Western philosophy full of strong logic and an integrated thought system. These advantages also promote the development of the Western science and technology. However, it also has its limitations. When the world's contradictions and conflicts escalate into difficult situations and even makes it fall into a stalemate, the idea of dualism cannot solve all these problems by the Western philosophy.

Different from the Western linear thinking, Chinese are better at roundabout thinking, as the saying goes "thinking as circle". For example, when a favorite girl is invited to see a movie, a British would say, "Would you like to see a film with me tomorrow", whereas a Chinese guy often expresses the same thing differently. He first talks about something else, and then invites the girl to see the movie at the closure of the conversation. Perhaps, it seems that the way is a waste of time, actually it does not. Through the communication, it makes them know each other better and enhances their feelings; on the other hand, he can observe the girl's attitude towards him, which decides his next timely offer of an invitation. The above chatting is actually to pave the way for the purpose of invitation. This is the Chinese roundabout philosophy of thinking.

3.3.2 Cultural identity between the West and the East

The Eastern and Western cultures constitute the two major mainstream cultures in today's world, and Chinese culture is the representative of oriental culture. As is known, the exchanges between the Chinese and Western cultures have always been interdependent and connected. In Chinese history, Zhang Qian was sent to the Western Regions (a Han Dynasty term for the area of Yumenguan including what is now Xinjiang and parts of Central Asia) to open up the Silk Road; the Roman Empire crossed the Silk Road and exchanged with the Eastern Han Dynasty, promoting the exchange and cooperation between the Chinese and Western cultures; and the Maritime Silk Road starts out from the coastal ports of China to the coastal countries of South Asia, Arabia and East Africa, reaching as far as the Red Sea, promoting the exchange and development of the Chinese and Western economy and culture. The exchanges of the Eastern and Western cultures can not only spread the Chinese civilization to many countries in the world but also promote the two-way exchange and common progress of the cultures. In particular, after the introduction of the four great inventions of China into Europe through Arab, the great impact of Chinese culture on Europe and the world is incalculable. In short, it is the exchange of cultures that speeds up the process of globalization.

In addition, there is an identity between the Chinese and Western cultures. Culture has its opposites and unity, which are also two aspects of contradictory relations in philosophy. The identity of culture refers to all parts of the ideology such as human's outlook on life and world, and non-ideological parts such as natural science, language and writing. They are the sum of the existence, inheritance, creation and development of the inner spirit of all. The contradiction refers to the mutually exclusive and separate struggle between the two sides. On the other side, the identity of contradiction is a struggle that the two sides of contradiction are interdependent and interlinked. Culture has its identity because culture is a unique phenomenon in human society and a civilization for human beings to survive and develop together, which is created and shared by human beings. At the same time, the cultures of different groups have their own unique features, so the multi-cultures of the world coexist, rich and colorful. They have identity and differences, depending on and connecting with each other.

Of course, culture is not static; it is dynamic. Peoples of different cultures play a certain role in the development and evolution of culture in communication, and different cultures are constantly changing while interacting and permeating each other. It is obvious that the values of life and world will also change with the change of culture in the process of cross-cultural communication. It will promote the integration of different cultures and even lead to the increasingly blurred boundaries of different cultures and cultural convergence. The interconnection between different cultures plays a great part in the development of human history. The constant exchange of cultures constitutes the richness of human civilization. However, it is important for us to maintain the subjectivity of Chinese culture in communication.

Speech refers to the influence of culture on the use of language. The study of cross-cultural communication is to study the use of language and the behavior of using language to communicate. Nonverbal is how to use nonverbal language to share thoughts and feelings, including body, behavior and time and space. Although people of different cultures use nonverbal communication, nonverbal behavior of different cultures usually represents different meanings.

Chapter 3 | Culture Teaching

3.4　Strategies of Cross-cultural Communication

With the development of economy and the progress of society in the world, the world gradually has a tendency of an integration and globalization. In this background of the common development of the world, the economic and cultural exchanges in many regions and countries have gradually increased, and cross-cultural communication is more frequent. The different cultures have an impact on people's behaviors, emotion and thought, which become the focuses of cross-cultural communication. The norms and values within a culture shape an individual's psychological make-up and how he/she interacts with his/her environment. The social structures, manners and values within a culture determine what type of experiences that a person has had. These experiences work to shape his/her perceptions, expectations as well as the sense of one's identity within the background of society. It is very important to learn how to adapt himself/herself to and maintain the thematic nature of culture in cross-cultural communication.

3.4.1　Significance of cross-cultural communication

In the era of economic globalization, mankind is faced with many problems that need to be solved, such as economic development and poverty, ecological environment protection and ecological destruction, peace and war, civilization and conflict. They are to be dealt with through communication, consultation and dialogue among different cultures. The purpose of this research is to make people aware of the growing conflicts due to cultural differences and rising global concerns in the world. Statistical data are compiled to determine how prevalent particular norms or customs perform within a culture. This helps with how influential particular customs are within the working of a society. Steps are addressed to bridge communication differences by understanding how customs develop and how they affect the behaviors within a society. Therefore, language is the key to communication between countries and the link of communication. The cultivation of communicative competence is the key to cross-cultural communication. Therefore, cross-cultural communicators should not only master the language of different cultures skillfully, but also understand the differences of each other's value orientation, social structure's roles, modes of thinking, behavior norms and so on, to explore the causes of cross-cultural barriers in practice and solve the problems by adopting corresponding strategies of cultural adaptation so as to comply with the development of the times.

3.4.2　Cultural adaptation of cross-cultural communication

In the context of globalization, the issue of cultural conflicts between countries and among peoples in the process of cultural exchanges and integration has become increasingly prominent. The research on cultural adaptation research and identity is very important, which can provide a certain theoretical reference for the practice of cross-cultural communication in the global perspective. Some people think that cross-cultural communicative competence just refers to language competence, which is obviously incorrect. The competence of cross-cultural communication includes many aspects. Communicators should not only master the language, but also understand its culture including history, politics, law, social customs, value orientation, mode of thinking and social norms. These cultural factors will narrow the cross-cultural communicators a certain psychological distance and cultural differences. The mastery of language and culture will cross cross-cultural barriers and avoided failures in the communication.

3.4.2.1　The theory of cultural adaptation

Bi Jiwan (2005: 66) mentioned that cross-cultural communicative competence is a comprehensive ability composed of linguistic communicative competence, non-verbal communicative competence, the ability to transform language rules and communicative rules, and the ability to adapt to culture in a cross-cultural communicative environment. Therefore, cultural adaptability is an important part of cross-cultural communicative competence. In cross-cultural communication, one or both sides of the original text will produce some changes to meet the need of cross-cultural communication in order to make cross-cultural communication successful. This change is actually a cultural adaptation to the environment. Culture is a unique phenomenon of human society and also a common feature of human society, which is a social phenomenon peculiar to human beings. Cultural adaptation is the basic concept that reflects cultural characteristics and cultural functions. Cultural adaptation refers to the integration, conformity and development of cultures in different environments and the mutual adaptation of various parts of culture. It is a basic concept of cultural characteristics and functions and a communicative implement for human beings to adapt themselves to the external environmental mechanism including the following three aspects, such as implement and technology adaptation, organizational adaptation and ideological adaptation. Redfiled's definition of cultural adaptation (1936) is that when there is continuous direct contact between different cultural groups and between individuals, the changes resulting from the original translation of one or both parties are called cultural adaptation. It mainly refers to the adaptation of culture to the environment and the mutual adaptation of various parts of culture. American cultural anthropologists stated that culture is a clear and specific mechanism used by specific animal organisms to adjust themselves to the external environment.

The study of cultural adaptation began in the 1930s. The study of cross-cultural adaptation is the intersection of research interests in many fields such as anthropology, sociology, psychology and cross-cultural communication and so on. The cross-cultural adaptation research in various disciplines has achieved fruitful results since the 1930s. The most interesting part is the theory of cultural adaptation, whose structural framework is called Berry's Theoretical Framework. Berry (1990) constructed cross-cultural adaptation models including assimilation, separation, integration and marginalization through research on the problem of immigration assimilation. He argued that the process of cultural adaptation actually has an impact on the two different cultures contacting with each other. There are some other representative theories besides the Berry's model, such as Gullahorn's W Curve Hypothesis, Gordon's Cultural Assimilation Model and Oberg's Culture Shock Model. Oberg (1960) divided the process of cultural shock into four stages, such as honeymoon period, depression period, adaptation period and stability period through the study of the lost feeling and anxiety of the sojourners in cultural adaptation. Ward (1994) proposed two new concepts, namely, one is Motional Psychological Adaptation, and the other Social Behavior Cultural Adaptation Process Model.

Chinese scholars have had some research on cultural adaptation. Zhang Weidong and Wu Qi (2015) created a three-part cross-cultural adaptation awareness, cross-cultural adaptation knowledge, cross-cultural adaptation behavior competence theory through the study of foreign cultural adaptation model. In addition, many domestic scholars put forward some new concepts, such as the Bidirectional Nature of Cultural Adaptation, Reverse Cultural Adaptation and Cross-cultural Success Theory. These theories have a certain guiding role for cross-cultural communicators in dealing with cultural barriers and differences in communicative practice.

  White divided the adaptation of culture to the environment into three types including implement and technology adaptation, organization adaptation and ideological adaptation. Implement and technology adaptation indicates that human beings need to overcome nature through labor in order to survive. In the early days of mankind, the condition of natural conditions determines the level of implement and techniques used in human labor by using axes to cut down trees, fishing with fishing nets, hunting with bows and arrows, axes and fishing nets and bows and arrows. The cultural elements are created by human beings to meet the needs of survival and adaptation of the natural environment. The concepts of human and nature on this basis are also based on the natural environment. Another one is an organizational adaptation. Social organization as a basic element of culture is produced to meet the needs of society. In the early civil society, primitive, tribal and clan organizations emerged as human beings living in groups for security and foraging needs. After the emergence of private ownership, the states and other social organizations came into being. With the development of social division of labor and the growth of human needs, human beings have to organize themselves more effectively to meet the needs of social life in all aspects. A large number of social organizations, including political, military, economic, cultural, religious, scientific, educational and recreational ones, have been established since the modern times. A large number of social organizations——including political, military, economic, cultural, religious, scientific, educational and recreational organizations——have been established. Each social organization is established for a specific purpose and operates around that purpose, which meets the needs of environmental change in organizational adaptations. Moreover, the ideas of adaptability are particularly obvious. Ideology is the reflection of material living condition, and it reacts to material living condition. The spirit of capitalism arises, only when the productive forces of society develop to turn labor products into commodities. When the capitalist system has been established and exposed all kinds of malpractice, it is possible for human beings to produce all kinds of socialist thoughts in order to extricate themselves from this predicament. Generally speaking, although the environment changes go first and the thought reflects later, the thought is most sensitive to the adaptation of the environment. Cultural adaptation reflects the changes of the environment, and the corresponding adjustment of culture may be progressive or retrogressive. From the development of the whole human history, the negative influence of

Chapter 3 | Culture Teaching

cultural adaptation is only temporary, and the general trend is progressive.

3.4.2.2 Cases in cross-cultural adaptation

Language reflects the essence and values of a culture, which best shows the differences between cultures. When carrying out international marketing activities, enterprises must pay full attention to the influence of the difference of language and characters on the customer's purchase behavior. Specifically, the influence of language and characters on customer purchase behavior is mainly manifested in two aspects, that is, one is information communication. All these require marketers to be able to master the customers' familiar language to communicate, otherwise interaction will appear obstacles. So some marketing activities are also necessary to achieve the goals of business, such as understanding the needs of customers, introducing enterprises and products to customers, understanding the customer's opinions, reactions to the enterprise or products and grasping the market dynamics and so on.

The second is the translation of brands and advertisements. Translation is actually the exchange of two cultures, and a little carelessness may make mistakes. There are also many examples of successful translation in the international marketing. For example, when Coca Cola in the United States first entered the Chinese market in the early 1920s, Coca Cola English pronunciation was translated into the Chinese brand "thirsty mouth wax". After the launch of the market, sales volume was extremely low. Because many people interpreted " thirsty mouth wax" as "drinking a mouthful of wax when thirsty" and would not like to buy it. After Coca Cola company discovered the situation, it immediately organized personnel to change the name of the product. On the basis of studying 40 000 Chinese characters, people finally identified the pronunciation of similar, pleasant pronunciation and subtle meaning of these four Chinese characters "可口可乐" for Coca-Cola. The success of the well-known case is also a successful example of foreign names in the international business. Like the "Red Bean" brand clothing in our country, it is not translated as "RED SEED", but "LOVE SEED" — "the seed of love", which contains the cultural meaning of red bean itself in Chinese, which makes the Red Bean brand popular abroad.

Some of the examples above show that it is necessary for us to understand the characteristics, taboos and metaphors of various languages and expressions in culture. We should use the language that can be understood and accepted to convey the information. When designing products and packaging, international marketers should pay attention to the differences of aesthetic concepts and values everywhere, and should not impose the aesthetic preferences and values of domestic consumers on the consumers in the target market so as not to create any obstacles in communication. More examples are as follows. In our country, green is a very flattering color, because it symbolizes peace, so many products take green as a popular color in the packaging of products. But if companies choose Malaysia as the target market, green is forbidden in the packaging of the product, because dark green is Malaysians' taboo, for they think of green as disease. Chinese people like lotus, which symbolizes high cleanness out of mud, so it is commonly used as a product packaging pattern or commodity brand. On the contrary, lotus means a memorial in Japan. Chinese people enjoy the Mid-Autumn Festival chrysanthemum, while Europeans do not decorate room with chrysanthemum on a happy day. Tortoise is Chinese taboo, while Japanese see tortoise as a symbol of longevity. In the eyes of the oriental, peacock is beautiful and auspicious, but it is regarded as a disastrous bird in France. Therefore, when determining the color of product packaging, we must pay attention to whether it represents a bad meaning in the target country and conforms to the aesthetic concept of local consumers in the cross-cultural interaction.

In addition, the design of products should be paid attention to whether to adapt to the values of local consumers, otherwise it may cause unsalable products. For example, some convenient foods, such as instant coffee, fast food and one-minute rice, are popular in some developed countries where people work hard and live fast, but they are not welcome in the underdeveloped countries with little emphasis on time, such as the countries in Latin America. Housewives there would rather buy coffee beans to make coffee themselves than instant coffee, because instant coffee is a sign of laziness in their eyes. Incorrect use of local culture often occurred in the process of advertising promotion.

Countries have different attitudes based on their cultural traditions and rules. In particular, those engaged in international trade must understand the culture in detail so as not to offend the local consumers by making mistakes. It is extremely difficult for any outsider to fully understand the social culture, customs and habits of different countries and regions. Listening to the opinions of the local's is very important to avoid mistakes. If this advice is to be heard by international companies, many mistakes would be avoided. For example, an American canned fish manufacturer made a serious advertising mistake in Quebec, Canada, where it adver- tised a woman in shorts playing golf with her husband. In a local newspaper, it says, "The woman and her husband went to play golf in the afternoon, and they didn't have time to make a big dinner, preparing for a canned fish in the evening". The advertisement made the local outrageous, because women never wear shorts and usually don't play golf with men according to the local custom. Moreover, no matter how short time is to prepare for dinner, the local women don't make dinner with a canned fish, especially for the main dish. Obviously, the company seems to know nothing about the local customs in result of making such a ridiculous advertisement.

Successful advertisements tend to take the local culture into account and integrate local culture as much as possible. The same advertisement cannot be applied to different countries, so it is not appropriate to use the same advertisement in many countries. One more example, a cosmetics factory in the United States employed some world-class models and attracted American women with various advertisements, saying that "if they use the cosmetics produced by the factory, they will be more beautiful and youthful". It gained great success. The same ads didn't work in France. French women cannot accept the ads, because they didn't believe that cosmetics would make them attractive. The French thought the company was not talking to all of them, but talking to a few.

In international exchanges, we must thoroughly study and analyze the customs of different countries so as to enter the country to ask for customs and follow the local customs, otherwise it may cause unnecessary misunderstanding. For example, people in the Middle East like to talk close to each other, if the marketers of enterprises do not understand the habit and are far away from talking to them, they will be considered impolite or not sincere, while Chinese think that distance is a kind of beauty. Japan is a ceremonial country, so the Japanese are never empty-handed when they visit others. They never give unpacked gifts, and the recipients never open gifts in front of the giver. American character is more straightforward, business negotiations with Americans should generally go straight to the subject. Communication with the Middle Eastern businessmen, negotiations are necessary before the formal business. The use of number should be taken care when communicating with foreigners. The Chinese don't like "4" very much, because "4" in China isn't a lucky number. On the con- trary, the Germen like it.

In addition to the various cultural factors cited above, religion has a great influence on cross-national communication. The religion of contemporary society is not only a belief and a culture, but also intertwines with the contemporary ethnic conflict, political conflict and economic conflict. Some people are causing trouble because they don't take into account the religions. In Asia, there are a large number of people who believe in Buddhism, and are influenced by Buddhism greatly. Some companies have caused public indignation because of the printing of Buddhist statue in advertisements, which aroused strong dissatisfaction because of the use of the religious symbol in advertisements. Another example, there was a sign on the advertising words intentionally or unintentionally pressed on the Buddha, the local people were even more disgusted. One company had adopted such a promotion, because it knew nothing about it. The event caused a great deal of trouble, and the company was almost burned to the ground by the angry believers. To communicate with the local people, they should respect the local religious beliefs, take the initiative to observe the local religious rules and respect its culture. So it is necessary to make some strategies and combine the local culture to open up to the cross-cultural road.

Different nations and countries have different cultural backgrounds, and the differences of these cultural backgrounds do bring many obstacles and difficulties to international communication. However, the existence of these different cultural backgrounds leads to different cultures in different countries. Successful communication provides international people with more opportunities and corporation. Only if international corporation successfully crosses the cultural differences of various countries, can people communicate successfully all over the world and remain invincible in the international competition of development.

3.4.2.3 Strategies for cross-cultural communication adaptation

Berry (1990) proposed a dual-dimensional model of cultural adaptation when studying the problems faced by individuals in the process of cultural adaptation, which summarizes the problems of minority groups in the process. There are two points: First, whether to maintain and develop the characteristics of the original culture; Second, whether to evaluate and establish a positive relationship through cross-ethnic communication with the dominant society. His theory directly aims at the core problems of globalization, interprets the process and results of cultural adaptation, analyzes the attitude and direction of cultural adaptation, clarifies the cultural adaptation group, and puts forward thought-provoking questions, such as how groups and individuals can position themselves in cultural exchanges and changes, how to correspond to the process of cultural adaptation, what kind of strategies are adopted, how to change their personal experiences and how to deal with the pressure to obtain the final cultural adaptation. He proposed a two-dimensional model of cultural adaptation, considering the process of cultural adaptation from two dimensions: the first is maintaining the tendency of traditional culture and identity; and the second is having the tendency of communication with other national cultural groups. He divided cultural adaptation into four categories including assimilation, separation, integration and marginalization. Assimilation means that individuals are unwilling to maintain their original culture but have frequent interactions with other cultural groups; separation means that individuals value their original culture and wish to avoid communicating with other groups; individuals in integration attach importance to maintaining traditional culture as well as daily interaction with other groups; and marginalization means that individuals can neither maintain their original culture nor accept other cultures. According to this classification, he also studied from the perspective of communication between mainstream culture and non-mainstream culture, and put forward the following cultural adaptation strategies: when mainstream culture implements melting pot strategy, non-mainstream groups adopt assimilation; when mainstream culture implements apartheid, non-mainstream groups adopt segregation; when mainstream culture implements exclusion strategy, non-mainstream groups adopt marginalization; when mainstream culture implements multiculturalism strategy, non-mainstream groups adopt integration strategy. From this model, it can be seen that the only possibility of homogenization shows four possible consequences: the homogenization of world culture will be from the gradual convergence of non-mainstream societies to mainstream societies; mutual change and globalization leads to the convergence of certain aspects of communication and the sharing of certain traits while retaining one's own uniqueness; mutual exclusion and non-mainstream groups resist and isolate the influence of mainstream groups and the inability of mainstream groups to interact with non-mainstream groups; A dominant and non-mainstream culture is destroyed and cannot be integrated into the mainstream culture, and its members lose their cultural ties. From the above strategic analysis, we know that the success of cross-cultural communication depends on how we change ourselves and integrate with different cultures.

Moreover, the ability of cross-cultural communication and cultural adaptation will be continuously improved through the improvement of theory and the grinding of practice. Cultural adaptability is stable once it is formed, but it is not static and changeable with the change of communicative situations and objects. For example, a Chinese staff member is sent to work in Washington, USA, who majors in international trade, capable of English, having worked in

London, England, for several years with successful experience in cross-cultural communication. Many people take it for granted that the man is suitable for the job because of his experience, but it is too early to think that it would certainly be the competent one. Regardless of his work, he can only easily cope with the work after a period of cultural adaptation from the single point of view of cross-cultural communication. The staff member's language ability of English as the target language has reached a certain level of communication, why does he need some time to adapt himself to the new environment after arriving in the United States? It is because that the ability of cross-cultural communication is not completely equivalent to cross-cultural ability, although Britain and the United States belong to the same language and culture system, the two cultures are actually different in thinking and customs. For example, the British are more conservative in work and more formal in language use, while the Americans are more direct and colloquial in language use. Therefore, the communicative person's language ability is only one aspect in the process of cross-cultural communication. Understanding and accepting the culture of a different nation, race or group is another thing. He will find a lot of differences in each other's cultures in communication. How to avoid the negative transfer of mother tongue culture to achieve the purpose of smooth communication is the critical issue.

3. 4. 3 Maintenance of cultural identity in cross-cultural communication

In the process of cross-cultural communication, cultural adaptation takes a certain amount of time, and different cultural groups have different communication rules and habits in the continuous learning and practice of continuous summary and reflection in order to better adapt to different cultures and communicative success. What should the cultural adaptation of globalization be addressed? We must balance the traditional culture and identity with the rest of the world's multiculturalism, without resisting, evading or attempting to dominate others.

Nowadays, globalization is the tendency of global development in the world, which has an effect on politics, economy, science and technology and ideology among different countries. Obviously, the cultural conflicts and integration are constantly impinging on the native cultures during the process of global development. The same goes with Chinese culture. So how to avoid the issue of cultural conflicts and maintain the characteristics and identity of Chinese culture in the process of massive interaction with different cultures is a subject worthy of study. The report of the 17th National Congress of the Communist Party of China put forward the idea of improving soft power of a nation, and the concept of cultural soft power is further generally recognized and deeply spread. In the constitution of national soft power, culture occupies the most important position in soft power because of its extensive permeability including social thought, political system and human behavior with the important characteristics of flexible power. Many scholars and politicians often refer to cultural soft power when describing the term. So how to inherit and develop the essence of Chinese cultural tradition in the context of globalization is a topic worthy of being studied.

3.4.3.1 The significance of maintaining cultural identity

With the rapid economic growth of China, Chinese culture is also booming and gradually going global, showing a colorful and dynamic image of our nation through different channels and carriers in the process of globalization. However, there is an inescapable fact that Chinese culture spread is still limited. Apart from some representative cultural elements such as Kung Fu, Chinese porcelain and Chinese Festival, the foreigners' understanding of Chinese culture is still not much. Chinese cultural spread throughout the world does not catch up with the step of Chinese political and economic development in the process of globalization. So it is imperative to protect, inherit and develop Chinese culture, especially Chinese traditional culture as the essence of our culture same as overall development of China.

Furthermore, Chinese culture going global has become the demand of the current times. And the development and inheritance of Chinese traditional culture is also an objective requirement of Chinese culture going out. As is known to us, globalization has an inevitable influence on Chinese culture in the process of globalization. On one hand, it promotes a recognition of the essence of Chinese cultural tradition and reflection of experience in the transformation of cultural spread in the world. On the other hand, the influence of western individualism, over-commercialization and cultural hegemony on Chinese culture should not to be neglected in the process of globalization cultural spread. Moreover, the effect is profound, long-lasting, and in particular, negative sometimes, which is worth paying close attention and taking into in-depth consideration the impact on Chinese culture while its going global.

The economic and cultural globalization leads to a series of challenges. There are some false concepts on the essence of Chinese traditional culture, which weaken Chinese culture identity and some misunderstanding of traditional culture among the young generation. Perhaps technology should be to blame, which causes the Chinese young men directly with the alienation of philosophical and social science while their solving many contemporary problems by implement. To be frank, Chinese traditional culture is the essence of our nation's wisdom as a part of philosophical and social science and is the crystallization of the working people's wisdom for more than 5,000 years. Chinese culture with great wisdom can resolve a lot of social problems that human beings face in the present world. Besides, the youths in China are lack of effective education of traditional culture. They as the carriers of traditional culture and emissaries of spreading Chinese culture should be well-educated especially in the essence of Chines culture. So it is very important for the educators to hand down the Chinese culture to the next generation through school education.

3.4.3.2　The essence of Chinese cultural tradition

Culture is the outcome of people's creation in spirit, the accumulation of a nation's civilization and a kind of social and historical phenomenon, which is unique in the human society. And it is also human beings' general production of living and social practice. Generally speaking, culture refers to the sum of all the material and spiritual wealth created by the people of a country or a nation, including history, geography, customs, life styles, values, literature and art, the code of conducts and the mode of thinking and so on, which covers not only the outlook of the world and the philosophy in life, but also the non-ideological part, natural science and technology and the languages inclusive. The culture has a variety of aspects in human's life, the core of which is spiritual product, and the essence of which is dissemination.

Traditional culture is different from cultural tradition. They are the completely different concepts. Cultural tradition is passed down from generation to generation by the way of thoughts, culture, morality, customs, art and behaviors. And traditional culture is a kind of national culture which reflects a national characteristics and features. It is an overall representation of its ideological, cultural and conceptual forms in the history of national development. Cultural tradition has an invisible influence on people's life and social behaviors. Tradition is the manifestation of the inheritance of historical development. In class society, tradition has its nature of classes and nationality. Positive tradition plays an important role in promoting social development, while conservative and backward tradition hinders the progress of a society. Therefore, people should distinguish between the good and the bad, then follow the good and ignore the bad when inheriting and developing cultural tradition.

The essence of Chinese cultural tradition is a profound force of Chinese cultural self-confidence, because and the Chinese nation developed it through the long-term historical inheritance, continuous revolution and social and economic construction in practice. Therefore, What is the essence of Chinese cultural tradition? It mainly consists of three parts:

- Chinese culture exists over 5 000 years and has been integrated into the blood of our nation, which becomes and civilization and soul of our nation. Chinese traditional culture is unique to China, different from other ethnic cultures in the world. Although the traditional culture of China has been interrupted in some short historical periods, it has not been separated as a whole, but inherited by from a generation to another. Chinese traditional culture is the culture with our nation's characteristics and the symbol of Chinese civilization. It is an overall representation of our nation's ideology and philosophy in the process of its historical development. It has formed its distinct characteristics with a broad and profound connotation in the long-term development, and the essence of Chinese cultural tradition is inherited and developed by our nation from generation to generation. The ideological basis of Chinese traditional culture is a national spirit of persistence and hard work, which is an internal driving force in the process of cultural development. There are some basic ideological dynamics of Chinese national culture in the continuous development, such as its strong and effective morality and the living concepts of harmony in a social community and so on. Chinese traditional culture is promoted by a special social productive relationship based on a self-sufficient and family-based economy with a consanguineous link. The whole nation forms a stable culture with the same social production relations, social system, social psychology and social consciousness in China. The culture is based on the consanguineous link with moral education different from the one in the western based on religion, the core of which is integration and freedom.

- The culture of the new democratic revolution. The new democratic revolution has been formed through the hard struggle of Chinese people for the national liberation, national independence and social progress. The Chinese Communist Party led Chinese people to struggle for success. The culture of the new democratic revolution embodies the essence of a great fighting spirit of our Chinese people in it. In particular, the War of Resistance against Japan demonstrates the great national core spirit of patriotism, the patriotic responsibility and the national tenacity. Chinese nation has created the great national spirits through long-term revolution including the patriotic responsibility, the grand virtues, and the spirit of national solidarity, self-improvement, perseverance and persistent struggle and so on, which are extensive and profound for Chinese nation so that we should keep inheriting and developing them in order to innovate Chinese culture in the new era.

- The culture of socialist construction. China has made remarkable achievements after taking the socialism way. Through decades of difficult and tortuous exploration and especially 40 years of reform and opening up, China is speeding up and follows the steps of developed countries. Our nation is gradually transforming from a closed and backward economic country to an open and a big economic power, becoming the second largest one in the world through 40-year economic development. This is also a transformation from unipolar traditional management to modern public service-oriented governance in the government of a country. Chinese governing system has its basic social functions of the framework including macro-control, market supervision, public service, social management and environmental protection as well as the Party Committee's leadership, government's responsibility, social coordin- ation, public participation, law guarantee and co-construction and so on. Moreover, a new model of modern public service system develops related to the change of urban and rural structure and the transformation from backward rural society to rich urban and rural integrated society. In the future, Chinese society will become a new urban-rural integrated society with interactive and harmonious development among different areas. The overall transformation of well-off society comes true firstly in the social people's livelihood, such as in food, clothing, residence and transport.

In addition, China's roles are gradually changing. We are already the followers, participants and contributors of the world development. China follows the equal foreign policy in diplomacy, that is, the overall layout of "Omni-directions, Multilevel and Three-dimensions". China devotes itself to the establishment of friendly partnership among different countries, which is the guiding principle of state-to-state interaction. Diplomatically, China creatively puts forward the idea of Human Common Community for the mankind throughout the world, which points out a new solution to the issues existing in the world. The idea of Human Common Community is a new theory based on the human history, the understanding of the real world and the exploration of future development, which is an important and innovative achievement created by Chinese nation in the interaction with different coun- tries. Through all-round economic, political, social and ecological reforms, our country will have more corporation and development opportunities for a broader communication with more countries, aiming to constantly improve people's livelihood, increase their income and make them live a better and better life continuously, sharing a common prosperity and civilization throughout the world.

3.4.3.3 The characteristics of the essence of Chinese culture

The essence of Chinese culture contains the traditional culture, revolutionary culture and socialist construction culture, which is still full of vitality and worthy of inheritance according to the above. Only when we keep and maintain its essence, do we stand among the nations of the world, because it is an inseparable part of Chinese nation. In order to do so, we must sort out some major points about its characteristics.

The independent development history of Chinese culture indicates that the subjectivity of its culture is very important. As is known to all of us, cultural subjectivity is becoming more and more prominent because of the trend of various ideological and cultural influences in the era of globalization. Although China attached great importance to the construction of cultural subjectivity in recent years, it still has some obstacles to maintain the cultural subjectivity due to various reasons including some historical reasons in the interaction with other countries. Our nation has many difficulties in it. On one hand, Chinese cultural subjectivity was lost in modern times, which resulted in the innate deficiency economically and politically; on the other hand, it is hard for our country to break through the western cognitive framework of the world. Therefore, China should strengthen " Four Self-confidences", develop socialist culture with Chinese characteristics, maintain the subjectivity of Chinese culture, actively have a talk with other countries fairly and equally and constantly spread and innovate Chinese culture while vigorously developing economy.

Chinese traditional culture has a long history and far-reaching influence throughout the world. There were a lot of examples about China's cultural dissemination and exchanges in the world, such as the Marco Polo's travel in China, the opening up of Silk Road and the western movement in China's modern times and so on. Globalization is the tendency of the world development with some basic features of the times. With the continuous progress of globalization, the mutual relations in the world among the countries are also constantly changing. At the same time, some of cultural exchanges and infiltration among various countries are also constantly deepening and strengthening, which has a great impact on the cultural development of countries. China, as the largest developing country, its traditional culture has also great challenge. Under the background of globalization, it is of great significance to inherit and develop Chinese traditional culture for building a modern country with Chinese characteristics. However, Chinese traditional culture itself is intermingled with essence and dross. If blindly respecting the traditional culture is not right, we should pick up the essence and give up the feudal decadent ideas. Therefore, we must dialectically look at Chinese traditional culture, adhere to the principles of taking its essence and removing its dross, treat Chinese cultural tradition correctly and scientifically distinguish the good from the bad in Chinese traditional culture so that Chinese culture can adapt itself to the rapid development of globalization. To follow the step of the times, Chinese culture should be innovated to promote the modernization of our country while keeping its features.

Although there are different views on the valuable spirits of Chinese nation, there is common one recognized by the public, that is, Chinese traditional virtues. It is very famous in China that the exalted moral can tolerate all. Tolerance is part of Chinese virtue. Looking back on Chinese history, Chinese nation is composed of many scattered and isolated ethnic units, which forms an inclusive pluralistic unity through contact and integrates gradually in a long time. There appeared a core of convergence and gradual integration of a number of ethnic groups along Yellow River watershed in the quite early period, which is the earliest Chinese civilization. People in different ethnics were attracted by each other's culture and integrated together, and finally formed a united nation known as Han Nationality. So the feature of national formation determines its tolerance of culture. Han Nationality also absorbs the cultural components of other ethnic groups to form a cultural network of cohesion and connection, which lays the foundation of the unity with many ethnic groups. Some major national characteristics include tolerance, collusiveness, strong assimilation and tenacious vitality. Like any kind of culture, Chinese culture has its important and special characteristics, one of which is inclusiveness. The features make China become one of the world four ancient civilized countries and the symbols of our nation existing up till now.

Any kind of national culture is a historic choice. Innovation is Chinese cultural vitality, which makes our culture develop further. Moreover, the rejuvenation of Chinese culture is part of the great rejuvenation of Chinese nation. So it is a historical choice for Chinese nation to be a well-off society and a modern socialist power in the future because of our great nation and rich civilization. In the process of cultural exchanges with other countries, some new cultural elements will come out, some may fade or even disappear. Culture is changing all the time following the step of the times, and it is also a rule of culture development. The Chinese culture going global must pay special attention to the following two points. One is to spread in physical space; the other is to spread at the psychological level, and the two should be combined together. That is to say, going out at the physical level refer to make an effort to increase the audiences, the cultural coverage of people. While the psychological level refers to the people who expose Chinese culture really appreciate it and become its followers. So what we need to do is to let more people know Chinese culture, accept it and love it. If we do not stick to the pioneering spirit of our ancestors all the time, we can't continue to develop the great socialist cause with Chinese characteristics. Therefore, if we want our culture to go global, innovation is the key. Reserving the essence of Chinese cultural tradition, we have innovation of Chinese culture on the basis of tradition.

To sum up, China's national tradition actually represents the Chinese spirits roughly summarized into the following four interrelated aspects. Rational spirit fully affirms the unity of between man and nature and between individual and society. The spirit of freedom manifests the struggle of the people against the rule of exploitative class and the oppression of foreign nationalities, which shows the ideological and cultural tradition of Chinese loving freedom. Chinese also emphasize implementation and respected fetishism in the seeking truth and advocate cause analysis of the Chinese realism. And Chinese have a tradition of innovation, such as the four major inventions. The world today is going through a great unprecedented change, and the metabolism and fierce competition brings out the new round of scientific and technological revolution. Chinese nation must actively seek some solutions to some challenges and issues in the new era by the innovation of Chinese culture to adapt itself to the world development.

3.4.3.4　Strategies for maintaining cultural identity

The profound humanistic core in Chinese culture is people-centered, people-oriented and people-owned. Then how to maintain the tradition of Chinese cultural essence, the following several points can be referred: First, we should distinguish the essence from the dregs, persist in the attitudes of sublimation and critical inheritance, take its essence and get rid of its dross, use the past lessons for the present reference and bring forth some new ideas. The essence of Chinese cultural tradition should be related to the present socialism values of mainstream culture widely shared and accepted by most Chinese people, which plays a leading role in our social life. It should note that some ideas that were thought to be correct in the past may not be correct with the changes of society or only partially correct at the moment. Second, we should avoid two extremes when adhering to the essence of Chinese tradition and follow the principle of "neither inferiority nor arrogance". One is that the cultural inferiority and cultural nihilism in China has led to the blind worship of the western culture and the total negation of our native culture under the historical background of poverty and weakness of the Chinese nation and being bullied by external forces since the late Qing Dynasty. The historical nihilism still permeates and affects the cultural development under the current situation of rapid development of globalization, which poses a threat to Chinese cultural self-confidence. The other is that the cultural conceit has emerged among some people because of the great achievements of reforms in the past 40 years. In order to cultivate a correct cultural psychology of the whole nation, we must strive to restore and strengthen Chinese cultural tradition of subjectivity, openness, inclusiveness and innovation instead of inferiority and arrogance. With the nourishment of this cultural psychology, Chinese will be sure of having self-confidence without any prejudice. And Chinese culture becomes part of colorful civilization in the world. Third, while adhering to the autonomy and subjectivity of Chinese cultural tradition, we should also be good at finding common ground in different cultures. Nowadays, China shares an important part in the world stage, but it is obvious that the world is still western-countries-centered. China is approaching the world center with Chinese plans and proposals to solve the exiting issues facing the world, and the idea of Human Common Community with a shared future for mankind is widely accepted. We call for a world full of equality and mutual development, which is also a lofty goal of the world. Common views among different countries help to understand more deeply each other in global governance, handle international affairs, resolve international disputes and create a good international environment. Therefore, it is necessary for Chinese to participate international affairs with different countries, seeking more extensive coordination. The idea of a common community for human beings reveals Chinese wisdom in our traditional culture, aiming at a new type of international relations and a common community with a shared future for mankind. Fourth, practice goes first. We should not only insist on the principle in practice. Chinese cultural inheritance and development has two tasks; one is to promote the productivity in economy in order to lead the people to a better life materially; the other is to strive for the popularity of Chinese culture in chin, spreading the essence of socialism core values with great efforts spiritually. Without the practice, the innovation develops both in economy and in spirit. To achieve the cultural heritage and prosperity, the key lies in practice.

Generally speaking, Chinese culture contains a great deal of philosophical wisdom, life wisdom, political wisdom, rich historical experience and the ideas of governing a country as well as Chinese spirits through a long-term development. These Chinese distinctive characteristics are the essence of Chinese cultural tradition, which are worthy of spread through the world, and our voice should be heard everywhere. In conclusion, there are some profound humanistic spirits in Chinese culture, such as people-centered, people-oriented and people-owned. The basic spirits of Chinese cultural tradition can be summarized as honoring the teachers, respecting teachings of ancestors, emphasizing the harmony of human relations and advocating good morals. The culture is rooted in people-oriented principle, for the Chinese history is created by the people, and the culture is also the crystallization of the collective wisdom of the people. In fact, the cultural tradition comes from the people and their life and is of the people. So Chinese culture originates from the people, is up to the people and services for the people. At the new historical moment, we firmly believe that the government led by the Party is of the people, the strength of the Party is from the people, the leading of the Party is for the people. The Party will rely on the Chinese people to promote enthusiasm and initiative creativity, following to the people-centered development principle, constantly adhering to the concept of all-round development to make all the people live better.

Chinese culture is the production of collective wisdom, so inheriting, carrying forward and reviving Chinese culture is the duty of Chinese people. It has not only the great wisdom of dealing with interpersonal relations, but also the extension of wisdom coping with state-to-state relations, which has been highly recognized by many countries and international organizations in the world. The wisdom of Chinese traditional culture is humanism. This humanism manifests in the following beliefs: avoiding isolating any man from a group, just living in a harmonious community together. The humanistic spirit has added brilliance to its cultural development of Chinese tradition. The wisdom is gradually spread to the world, but there are still some cultural obstacles to be broken through in order to set up a more harmonious community in the world by Chinese wisdom. By doing so, can we inherit, innovate and spread the essence of Chinese cultural tradition.

　　The essence of Chinese cultural tradition is our spiritual home. A nation lack of its natural home will be lost and eventually disappear because there is no place to live in. A nation lack of the spiritual home alike will also lose its way, for the spiritual soul has no space to belong to, and the ideal pursuit of culture will be lost in history. Therefore, we should strive to explore the difficulties and problems in the world on the basis of deeply understanding the profound connotation of Chinese traditional culture, properly inheriting and innovating Chinese traditional culture to find out the solutions to the problems. First of all, the cultural self-confidence and subjectivity are important in the spread of Chinese culture. So we should put into effect "the Overall Layout of the Five-in-One" under the guidance of Marxism, follow the theories of dialectical materialism and historical materialism, combine the current international situations with the domestic ones, strengthen the integration of localization and globalization and innovate the essence of Chinese cultural tradition. In English teaching, Teachers should teach students English and the cultures, especially to hand down the Chinese culture to them in order to make Chinese culture go global, which is also the real purpose of English teaching for cross-cultural communication and dissemination.

Appendices
Case Study

Appendix 1 Research on the "Trinity" Teaching Method in College English Teaching

Abstract: Based on the latest foreign language teaching method-communicative method, this paper tries to use the "three-in-one" teaching method in combination with Gagne's information processing theory. This teaching method is based on text teaching, and comprehensive listening, speaking, reading, writing, and translating methods to learn English. It uses the discourse (text) as the entry point and extends learning around the text. In the language teaching activities, comprehensive use of listening, speaking, reading, writing, translating five language learning skills, to develop students' comprehensive language skills. In the teaching process, the relationship between teachers and students is positively and equally interactive, which not only gives full play to the role of teachers, but also promotes students' enthusiasm for learning. Through experimental research and data analysis, it is proved that the implementation of the "Trinity" teaching method in the university public English teaching has incomparable advantages over the traditional teaching method.

Keywords: "Trinity" teaching method in College English Teaching
teacher and student positive and equal interaction relationship
language comprehensive application ability

1 introduction

As China's opening up process continues to deepen, international exchanges will also be further expanded, and people will have more opportunities to communicate with each other in English. The tremendous changes in the social environment have prompted the various sectors of society to increase the requirements for the English level and application ability of college students. Therefore, in the university public English teaching, it is necessary to strengthen the authenticity of "language input", improve the form of "language input", establish an open system of language teaching and a multi-latitude language teaching environment in a non-native language environment. Therefore, in the university public English teaching, it is absolutely necessary to seek an effective teaching method centered on text teaching.

2 statement of problem

2.1 Requirements for social development

With China's accession to the WTO, the social requirements of college students are getting higher and higher. The current employer not only requires students to be able to successfully handle foreign language letters and materials, but also requires them to have a strong ability to express English, rather than "dumb English". Therefore, in the university's public English teaching, it is imperative to cultivate the teaching reform of students' comprehensive use of language.

2.2 Requirements for the status quo of education

For many years, under the conditions of with many students and few resources, although the university public English educators have been seeking an ideal teaching method to achieve time-saving and efficient teaching effects, they still have not got rid of the shackles of traditional teaching methods. Students' ability to use language in a comprehensive manner is still weak. Moreover, the teaching staff has not established a systematic concept of foreign language teaching, which is one of the main problems that lead to the poor effect of public English teaching in universities. For example, the teacher can not really understand the connotation, principles and characteristics of communicative competence and the fundamental tasks and purposes of language teaching; does not understand the language output——the ability to speak and write, is the inevitable result of language learning, or the importance of the learning process. Components and other issues. As a result, the results of the reform failed to effectively guide teaching.

3 Theoretical basis

3.1 Based on the theory of communicative foreign language teaching

The Communicative Foreign Language Teaching Method, referred to as the Communicative Approach, can be summarized into two points. One is that "two understandings" means understanding the social meaning of the language and understanding the functional meaning of the language. Second, the " two sessions" are for students. The social and cultural environment and different language functions will use different language forms, and will accurately express their own ideas and achieve the purpose of communication. His communicative competence includes four aspects: Linguistic Competence, Discourse Competence, Strategic Competence, and Sociolinguistic Competence. It can be seen that in the communicative English teaching method, the cultivation of students' comprehensive ability to use language should be em- phasized.

3.2 Gagne's information processing theory

The basic model of the learning process of Gagne's information processing theory is shown as Figure 1:

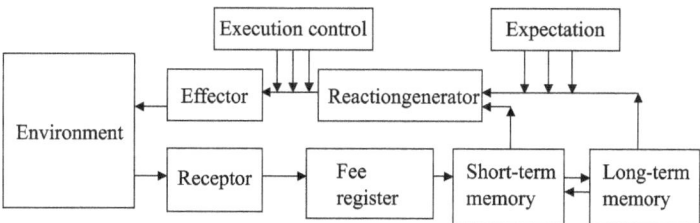

Figure 1 The basic model of the learning process of
Gagne's information processing theory

Gagne's learning model is proposed on the basis of learning viewpoints of behaviorism and cognitive science. It notes the characteristics of human learning and it is a relatively representative learning model. It alsohelpful in guiding college English teaching.

(a) Environmental factors play a leading role. This topic draws on and studies this learning model theory, trying to create a multi-latitude language learning environment for students, and promote students' language output and input, thus improving students' comprehensive language use ability.

(b) How to promote knowledge into long-term memory, it also needs a new teaching method, to establish a multi-latitude language learning environment to make students English input and output repeatedly, so that knowledge internalization. The environment is the external condition for providing language learning, and the language environment under the class is mainly based on the teacher's instructional design guidance. This teaching method also has a certain guiding role.

(c) Promote the learner's existing experience to positively migrate the current learning process and gain meaningful learning. Then act on the environment, this is the output of the language. This pedagogy study promotes this process through teacher guidance and inspiration.

4 Attempt of the "Trinity" teaching method

4.1 The Connotation of the "Trinity" Teaching Method

The communicative language view holds that language is not a simple and static formal system or a set of habits, but a communicative act or communication itself. It is a living, ongoing, and inseparable from the user. The "Trinity" teaching method takes text as an entry point, and through the use, use or reproduction of the context of the discourse, and on this basis, organizes students to listen, speak, read, write, translate and other teaching activities. Enable students to gain as many practical opportunities as possible in the learning process and develop students' comprehensive language skills. "Three" means: guided learning centered on textbooks, called Guided Practice; learning related to textbooks, and semi-instructive exercises based on individual students, also known as Semi-controlled Practice; the more free learning that is basically out of the textbook, also known as Free Practice. "One body" is to use the text as the entry point to organize students to listen, speak, read, write and translate various teaching activities, so as to improve the students' comprehensive use of language.

Its meaning can be expressed as Figure 2:

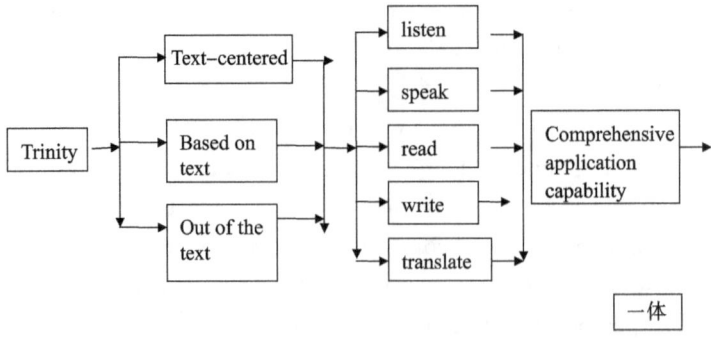

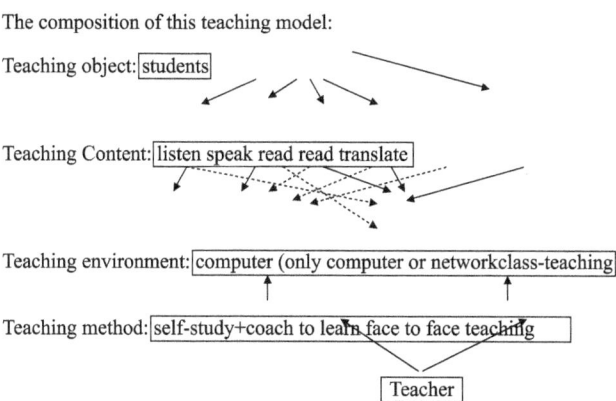

Figure 2 "Trinity" Teaching Method

The teaching management is done jointly by the Academic Affairs Office, teachers and computer management software management center. For example, Tianjin Normal University has built a digital network voice classroom, all of which can access the Internet and conduct online teaching. It includes CD image server, English online learning platform and other equipment, providing a software and hardware platform for teaching, and also has AOD (audio) and VOD (video) on-demand, which lays a good foundation for students to learn independently. In addition, a digital audio automatic broadcast system and a 21st century college English teaching network platform system are also deployed. And built a digital satellite receiving system, which can upload and download data, and can play audio and video data in real time. Moreover, with the radio transmission system widely used in our school, it provides a powerful material guarantee for modern foreign language teaching. The computer can store various audio-visual materials in various forms, such as enjoying English movies, music, etc. Students can enhance the English input and output by obsessing their favorite audio-visual programs, and realize implicit learning. Many forms such as online simulation classes are available for communication. Students can also find information, teacher-student interactions through the Internet. For example, through the use of English e-mail, complete the teacher's homework, answer que- stions, and practice English writing. In short, to create a better language learning environment for students to acquire language. Students should be independent in their own learning, and teachers should be the role of participants and consultants in the second English class.

4.2 Textbooks are a means of teaching, not an end.

The "Trinity" teaching method takes the discourse as the starting point, and does not emphasize the discourse as the center. It is to reflect that the teaching material is only a means of teaching, not a teaching concept of purpose. Students use textbooks and the Internet as a practical platform to cultivate language comprehensive learning ability through listening, speaking, reading, writing and translating.

5 Experimental research on the "Trinity" teaching method

5.1 Purpose of the experiment

Implement the "Trinity" teaching method in the university's public English teaching, create a good multi-latitude language learning environment for students, and improve their comprehensive language use ability. Through experimental research and data analysis, the "Trinity" teaching method is proved to be remarkable and superior in the university public English teaching.

5.2 Experimental hypothesis

The student test scores of the "Trinity" teaching method are significantly better than those of the traditional teaching method in listening, speaking, reading, writing and translating.

5.3 Experimental methods

Subjects: Students of two undergraduate classes at 08 Normal University of Tianjin Normal University.

Independent variables: The implementation of two different teaching methods - the experimental group A class uses the "three in one" teaching method, the control group B class uses the traditional teaching method, and the classroom explanation is the main method.

Covariate: Students take part in the English test results of the whole school when they enter the school.

Dependent variable: English test scores at the end of the third semester.

Control means:

- The correlation coefficient between English test scores and English scores of college entrance examinations is greater than 0.7.

- In the teaching process, the test methods and content are consistent, the students are not aware of the particularity of their own test, which avoids the impact of the experimental environment on the subjects, thus ensuring the reliability of the experimental results.

- Both classes are taught by myself, which eliminates the influence of teachers on the scores of the subjects due to different levels of teaching and experience.

● The experimental group A and the control group B use the same teaching materials, are "21st Century College English" (Shanghai Foreign Language Teaching Press), the same weekly class, the same teaching progress, the same amount of work inside and outside the class.

● Subjective topics, including the scoring of the essay and the oral test, were performed by two other teachers, and then the average scores given by the two teachers were taken. This avoids the negative impact of subjective awareness of the class teacher on the score.

5.4 Experimental Statistics and Analysis

This study used SPSS 12.0 software to statistically analyze the data obtained from the experiment. By using the covariance analysis method, the two results of the test group A and the control group B were compared. The experimental group A used the "three in one" teaching method for teaching, while the control group B used the traditional teaching method. The application of covariance analysis to evaluate the teaching effect must meet two application conditions, otherwise the results will be inaccurate. First, Whether the variance of the two groups of data is consistent (the homogeneity test of variance); Second, Whether there is a linear relationship between the two sets of data, that is, linear regression analysis.

Step 1: Whether the two groups of data variances are consistent (variance homogeneity test). Using covariance analysis, it is customary to use the variable to be compared with y, and the variable associated with it is represented by x and is called a covariate. For this experiment, the initial score is the covariate x, and the test score at the end of the third semester is the dependent variable y. Establish SPSS data statistics table. Using the SPSS covariance analysis statistics, the following data sheet is available. (See Table 1) The F values of the scores of the two groups of samples are 0.916, 0.136, 0.321, 3.000, 1.399, 1.058, 0.146, respectively, in the total scores of the standard scores, the total scores of the percentage system, and the scores of listening, speaking, reading, writing, and translation. The P values are 0.342, 0.714, 0.573, 0.088, 0.241, 0.307, 0.704, respectively, which are all greater than 0.05, indicating that the two groups of data are in variance.

Step 2: Analysis of the linear regression relationship between the two sets of data. Using the covariance analysis function of SPSS software, the following data can be obtained. (See Table 2) Table 2 shows the significance test of the public regression coefficient of each grade.

Table 2 shows the significance test of the public regression coefficient of each grade b_w (The table is expressed as B and needs to be unified. Subsequent figures are also different from the table, and the carry-in is not uniform. All is marked as b). It can be seen from the table that the common regression coefficients of standard score, percentile, listening, reading, speaking, translation and writing score are 1. 092, 1. 011 respectively. 0. 78, 0. 792, 0. 856, 0. 638, 0. 004, the difference is significant at the level $\alpha = 0.01$. It is proved that there is a linear regression relationship between the two sets of data.

Table 1   Levins's variance test

Parameter	Standard Scores	Centesimal Scores	Listening	Reading	Speaking	Translation	writing
F Value	.916	.136	.321	3.000	1.399	1.058	.146
Degree of freedom between groups (df1)	1	1	1	1	1	1	1
Intra-group degrees of freedom (df2)	72	72	72	72	72	72	72
P Value	.342	.714	.573	.088	.241	.307	.704

Table 2   Significance test of regression coefficients of various achievements

	Standard Scores	Centesimal Scores	Listening	Reading	Speaking	Translation	writing
Parameter estimation valueB	1.09	1.01	.78	.79	.86	.64	.004
P Value	.000	.000	.000	.000	.000	.000	.007

After satisfying the above two conditions, the covariance analysis proves that the difference between the two classes is significant. Similarly, using the SPSS covariance analysis function, we get the following analysis Table 3:

Table 3   Analysis table of results covariance

	Standard Scores	Centesimal Scores	Listening	Reading	Speaking	Translation	writing
F Value	236.79	243.41	18.54	22.12	32.18	11.98	5.63
P Value	.000	.000	.000	.000	.000	.001	.020

It can be seen from Table 3 that the covariance analysis data of the standard score total score, the percentage score total score, the listening score, the reading score, the spoken score, and the translation score show that F0.01(1,71) = 7.01 < 236.792, F0.01(1,71) =7.01 < 243.411, F0.01(1,71) =7.01 < 18.540, F0.01(1,71) =7.01 < 22.121, F0.01(1,71) =7.01 < 32.183, F0.01(1,71) = 7.01 < 11.977, so the difference is significant at the level $\alpha = 0.01$. That is, after eliminating the influence of the covariate (the score of the entrance examination), the standard scores of the final scores of the third semester of the two classes, the total scores of the percentage system, the listening scores, the reading scores, the oral scores, and the translation scores are significantly different. As can be seen from Table 15, the covariance analysis data of the written scores showed that the difference was significant at the level $\alpha = 0.05$ because F0.05 (1, 71) = 3.98 < 5.628. That is, after the influence of the covariate (initial bottoming score) is eliminated, the writing scores of the final exams of the third semester of the two classes are significantly different. Through the above analysis of the total scores of the standard points, the total score of the percentage system, and the covariance analysis of listening, reading, speaking, translation and writing scores, it is proved that the results are significantly different.

In order to compare the teaching efficiency of the two teaching methods, the average value needs to be corrected, thus deducting the influence of the initial score difference on the teaching evaluation. To do this, compare the mean ( ) of the dependent variable at the same covariate x level. Let x be the average value of the common covariate ( ), the average value of the corresponding dependent variable is ( ), and the average value of the corresponding covariate is ( ), which is the common regression coefficient. At this time, the average scores before and after the correction are obtained in Table 4:

Table 4   Average scores before and after correction

Average scores		Standard Scores	Centesimal Scores	Listening	Reading	Speaking	Translation	writing
Class A	Average score for the first semester $\bar{x_i}$	68.74	57.99	7.77	24.13	9.73	6.65	9.71
	Average score for the third semester $\bar{y_i}$	73.74	62.04	6.47	25.58	11.20	7.23	11.57
	The third semester average regression correction $\bar{y_i}'$	73.88	62.24	6.64	25.73	11.20	7.35	11.57

Continued

Class B	Average score for the first semester $\overline{x_i}$	69.00	58.41	8.23	24.51	9.73	7.05	8.89
	Average score for the third semester $\overline{y_i}$	66.87	55.38	5.61	23.03	9.94	6.20	10.60
	The third semester average regression correction $\overline{y_i}^\tau$	66.72	55.16	5.43	22.87	9.94	6.06	10.60
Overall average scores of the two classes	Average score for the first semester $\overline{x}$	68.86	58.19	7.99	24.31	9.73	6.84	9.32
	Average score for the third semester	70.49	58.89	6.07	24.37	10.60	6.74	11.11
	Public regression coefficient b_w	1.092	1.011	0.780	0.792	0.856	0.638	0.004

It can be seen from Table 4 that after the average scores of the third semester have been revised, the average scores of the revised Class A should be greater than the corresponding scores of the corresponding Class B. That is, the results of Class A are higher than those of Class B. Therefore, it can be concluded that in the public English teaching of universities, the use of the "three in one" teaching method is obviously superior to the traditional teaching method in cultivating students' comprehensive ability to use language.

5.5 Feasibility investigation of implementing the "Trinity" teaching method

After implementing the "Trinity" teaching method for three semesters, the author of this article has conducted a questionnaire survey. The author has taught 39 students in Chemistry Class A, and recovered 37 copies of the unnamed answer sheet. The statistical results are as Table 5:

Detailed rules	people	Percentage
Persons who believe that the teaching method is conducive to the understanding of the overall content of the text.	35	94.5%
Persons who believe that the teaching method is conducive to the memory of the main content and structure of the text.	32	86.5%
Persons who believe that the teaching method is conducive to the memory of the text and language of the text.	34	92%
Persons who believe that the teaching method can highly motivate students in the classroom.	33	89%
Persons who believe that this teaching method is conducive to cultivating students' ability to use language comprehensively.	37	100%

From the collected answer sheets, we can summarize the benefits and implications of some educational reform attempts. The implementation of the "Trinity" approach in the public English reading class at the university can help students better understand and memorize the texts they have learned. In addition, the implementation of this teaching method is more motivating than the traditional teaching method to motivate students to learn, and their ability to comprehensively use language has also been improved.

6 Conclusion and discussion

According to the above experimental research and questionnaire survey, the following conclusions can be drawn: In the public English teaching of universities, the test scores of students who implement the "Trinity" teaching method are significantly better than those of traditional teaching methods in listening, speaking, reading, writing and translating. Students test scores, and the implementation of the "three in one" teaching method is superior to the traditional teaching method, thus proving the experimental hypothesis. The "Trinity" teaching method is completely different from the traditional teaching method. It is more conducive to cultivating students' ability to use language comprehensively. It is more conducive to promoting the positive and equal interaction between teachers and students in teaching, giving full play to the guiding role of teachers and promoting students' learning. Enthusiasm. It is a teaching method worthy of promotion and further research in the teaching of public English in universities.

Of course, there are still many topics worthy of further study and discussion in the "Trinity" teaching method. For example, the implementation of this teaching method has special requirements for teachers and students; teachers will have more effective teaching design when implementing the "three in one" teaching method. When researchers further study it, there will be more control methods and experimental test methods. In short, the university's public English teaching should not be limited to the teaching of language knowledge, but should be continuously reformed, deepened and developed in terms of teaching content and teaching methods. The implementation of the "Trinity" teaching method in the university's public English teaching conforms to the trend of cognitive psychology development, and conforms to the trend of contemporary foreign language teaching "breaking through the barriers of sentence structure and entering the field of discourse analysis". For the extended learning of entry points, students can develop their comprehensive language skills and achieve the ultimate goal of language teaching.

Reference:

[1] Pariah, Steven, *English as a Foreign Language: History, Development and Methods of Teaching Norman*[M]. University of Oklahoma Press. 1972.

[2] Pariah, Steven, *English as a Foreign Language: History, Development and Methods of Teaching Norman*[M]. University of Oklahoma Press. 1972.

[3] Breen, M. P. and C. Candlin. *The Essentials of a Comm- unicative Curriculum in Language Teaching*[J]. Applied Linguistics. 1980. 1 (2): 89-112.

[4] Littlewood, *Communicative Language teaching*[M]. Cam- bridge University Press. 1981. pp78-132.

[5] Widdowson, *Teaching Language as Communication*[M]. Oxford University Press. 1978. pp78-189.

[6] Brumfit. *Communicative Methodology in Language Teaching* [M]. Cambridge University Press. 1984.

[7]国务院学位委员会办公室编.教育学学科综合水平全国统一考试大纲及指南[M].北京:高等教育出版社,1999:334-335.

[8]Howatt, A. P. R., *A History of English Language Teaching*[M]. Oxford University Press. 1984.

[9]戴曼纯.外语能力的界定及其应用[J].外语教学与研究,2002(6):5-8

[10]刘润清.外语教学研究的发展趋势[J].外语教学与研究,1999,117(1):7-12.

[11]吴一安等.中国英语本科学生素质调查报告[J].外语教学与研究,1993,20(1):12-17.

[12]徐锦芳.精读教学中的综合技能集成法——大学英语教学改革试验研究[J].外语教学与研究,2002,34(6):431-435.

[13]杨秀珍等.中学英语教学改革的误区[J].天津师范大学学报(自然科学版),2000,20(2):55-60.

Appendix 2 Investigation and Teaching Reflection on English Listening and Speaking Ability of Overseas Chinese Students

Abstract: What about the English listening and speaking ability of foreign students? Practice is the only criterion for testing. By means of questionnaires, this paper investigates the current situation of English listening and speaking ability of Chinese students abroad, and sets up questionnaires on their evaluation of College English teaching in China. Based on the results of the survey, descriptive statistical analysis of the data is carried out in an attempt to reflect on College English teaching in China from a new perspective.

Keywords: Listening and Speaking Ability; Overseas Chinese Students; Survey; College English Teaching

1 Research background

In recent years, teachers and researchers in Chinese universities have drawn lessons from some existing teaching theories and put forward many constructive teaching methods based on our teaching practice, which have been combined with teaching practice to improve students' comprehensive ability of using English. So, how about the students' listening and speaking ability? In this paper, the author makes a questionnaire survey on the current situation of Chinese students' English listening and speaking ability abroad, and tries to reflect on Chinese College English teaching from a new perspective by analyzing the problems existing in the process of students' communication.

2 Research method

2.1 Purpose of the survey

Mainly understand students 1) evaluation of English listening and speaking ability; 2) evaluation of English listening and speaking ability and evaluation of learning psychology; 3) evaluation of English listening and speaking teaching; 4) teaching of listening and speaking teaching materials evaluation of. Through the analysis of the results of the questionnaire survey, the analysis of the current situation of English communication ability of foreign students is triggered, which leads to the thinking of Chinese college English teaching.

2.2 Survey respondents

The subjects of the study are students who are pursuing a master's degree in an English-speaking country. Their main learning tasks are to overcome the English language, to supplement their professional knowledge, and to gradually adapt to English teaching. These students have completed the third year of undergraduate study in China, and all passed the University's Public English Test Band 4 and 6. The IELTS scores are all above 6.5. They are non-English majors in law, accounting, international relations, international finance, etc., totaling 48 people.

2.3 Form and content of the survey

The survey is conducted in the form of a questionnaire. The questions are mainly multi-choice questions. Each item has four options, and the best one is required. Topics include learning motivation, learning psychology, learning time and learning strategies, self-evaluation of English listening and speaking ability, evaluation of Chinese English listening and speaking teaching, and evaluation of Chinese English listening and speaking materials.

2.4 Implementation process

2.4.1 Questionnaire issuance

The questionnaire was distributed in mid-December 2009. The subjects were enrolled in September of the school year and have lived abroad for more than three months. Through this period of overseas study and life, students have an accurate understanding of their English listening and speaking skills. Pre-questionnaire explanation: It is only used as a reference for teaching research, and does not involve any personal information, so as to eliminate students' psychological concerns and faithfully reflect the real situation and opinions.

2.4.2 Questionnaire statistics

A total of 48 questionnaires were distributed and all were collected. There are 46 valid questionnaires, two of which give multiple options, so they are invalid. Descriptive statistics and quantitative analysis are then performed.

2.4.3 Survey results and analysis

(a) Evaluation of English listening and speaking ability. The results of the questionnaire show that 100% of students think that listening and speaking are very important in English application ability, but they think that their English listening and speaking level is not high, and there are some communication barriers. Only 10% of students believe that they are comfortable with their communication problems in life. About 30% of students believe that they can complete their life communication activities on their own; 60% of students need help to complete basic daily communication tasks. In learning, about 40% of students understand 60% of the slower speech; more than 90% of the students do not understand the faster speech. 100% of students think that their English listening and speaking ability needs to be improved. 100% of the students believe that in the three months of study abroad, English has improved rapidly, especially in English.

(b) Evaluation of English listening and speaking learning environment

• Class capacity and hours: the domestic class capacity is usually larger than that in other foreign countries, generally consists of 50—90 students. The teaching hours of listening and speaking classes are 1—2 sessions per week. There are few opportunities for speaking, and listening is the main method. The capacity of foreign classes is small, with 10—12 students in each class and 6 English listening and speaking classes per week. In addition, there are practical classes (Workshop), that is, games and shopping with native English speakers. Students with poor English can also apply for Tutor tutoring for 1—2 hours a week

• Opportunities for listening and speaking practice: College English listening and speaking teaching in China is a "temporary" teaching, mainly relying on some listening and speaking training in the classroom, with little practice after class. In foreign countries, there are always English input and output activities, and there is a good language environment for English acquisition.

• Multimedia use: Multimedia classrooms in China have a low utilization rate. They are often used for listening classes. There are too many students, and each student is separated by a desk baffle. It is difficult to operate oral practice. In foreign countries, the concept of multimedia is very extensive. Students have online learning addresses and can directly access the online learning system to view teaching courseware and related learning materials and information.

(c) Evaluation of English listening and speaking teaching in Chinese universities

90% of the students think that the domestic college English listening and speaking teaching mode is single, basically the listening teaching tape, CD, mp3 teaching, generally the listening-to-answer-listening mode. The teaching method is simple and mechanical, and students' interest in listening classes is not high.

(d) Evaluation of teaching materials

100% of students often have a sense of social frustration when applying

English language. They believe that most of the Chinese English textbooks are now out of the realities of life, with a single teaching content, lack of recreational English songs, humorous jokes or stories, news events, movie clips, etc. to alleviate the tension and fatigue of students and to activate the classroom atmosphere. Most listening materials focus on the correctness of the language, and standard communication terms are also used in the preparation of textbooks. However, in the context of real English language communication, people in different countries have different English accents, pronunciation habits, and use of proverbs. Many everyday language is not standardized English.

3   Reflections on Chinese College English Teaching

3.1   The language environment is the key to developing English listening and speaking skills

The results of the survey indicate that the language environment is the first element to improve English listening and speaking skills. Chinese students learn English in a single language environment, lacking input and output opportunities for English listening and speaking. Therefore, it is an important part of teaching to establish a multi-lingual learning environment that is conducive to cultivating students ' English listening and speaking ability in non-target language environment.

3.1.1   Reducing class capacity and grading teaching in listening and speaking classes is the first step in creating a multilingual learning environment

It is recommended that the maximum capacity of the class is no more than 30. In the case of a relatively small number of students and a small difference in English proficiency, students will reduce their learning pressure and increase their practical opportunities. Teachers establish corresponding teaching objectives according to different levels of teaching classes, emphasizing the use of intelligible language input materials for listening and speaking teaching. Slow classes use slower teaching materials and language, mainly to familiarize students with the pronunciation of English, continuous reading and how to correctly use the pronunciation of organs to send a standard English language and other language knowledge system. Playing a good voice foundation is an important guarantee for good oral English output. Classes with higher levels should use faster teaching materials and language of instruction. The teaching objectives are to improve students' ability to listen to different accents, and to guess words and grasp keywords according to context. It also takes into account the comprehensive development of the four skills of listening, speaking, reading and writing, and cultivates students' comprehensive English language skills.

3.1.2 Promote the application of multimedia technology and web-based autonomous learning

English learning requires environmental support. Language learning requires the participation of multiple senses. The rational use of multimedia-assisted teaching will fully mobilize the various sensory movements of learners. Based on online self-learning, regardless of time, space and content restrictions, students can enjoy the teaching of the world's top teachers through online virtual classrooms, choose the appropriate listening materials to learn, and enable students to access more new teaching methods and learning methods. The teaching in the teacher's class is only a guiding role, and the student's independent learning is the dominant. Advocating a network-based autonomous learning listening model is the development trend of future listening and speaking teaching.

3.1.3 Establish a second classroom for English study to improve students' listening and speaking skills

Establishing the second class of English learning is to solve the problem of insufficient input and output in the class, and is an important part of creating a multi-lingual acquisition environment in a non-English environment. In order to create a good language learning environment for students, teachers mainly play the role of organizers, can organize students to participate in the following activities: such as group activities, English corner, native film appreciation, English speech contest, self-edited drama, English dubbing, English songs Various kinds of English program performances such as singing competitions. These activities should be held regularly, and teachers should give guidance to encourage students to practice English listening and speaking in various forms. If there are conditions, students will have the opportunity to get in touch with the real way of communicating English. By communicating with them, they will increase their sense of achievement in English communication and their interest in learning English will continue to improve. Group activities are an ideal way to talk about teaching, not only to solve the problem of a large number of people, less exercise opportunities, but also to reduce students' anxiety in the process of English communication. It is not only conducive to the teaching of teachers in the class, but also beneficial to students learning under each class. The group is more suitable for groups of 4-6 people, which can guarantee the participation of each person and facilitate the dialogue between two people or other forms of group activities. Task-centered group activities are effective teaching models in listening and speaking. Teachers should design activities objectives, steps and tasks for students, and strive to be diverse, interesting, time-sensitive, communicative and expandable in the form of group activities. Teachers are the instructors and students are the centers.

3.2 Change teaching concepts and reduce the impact of examination-oriented education on English listening and speaking teaching.

In this questionnaire, the main reason why you think your English listening and speaking level is not high is that... More than 80% of the students are attributed to the examination-oriented education in China. In order for students to enter higher education and obtain various certificates, both teachers and students focus on answering questions and examination skills. Because many examinations do not involve oral ability, so the ability to speak is very little. Teachers neglect teaching strategies and methods, while students neglect learning strategies and methods. To change this situation, teachers should reform teaching methods, teach students learning strategies, cultivate students' correct learning outlook, clarify the purpose of English learning, so that students can be liberated from the traditional "practice-only" learning state in teaching and change to " learning".

3.3 The key to teaching is to change teaching methods, make use of strategy teaching and improve students' listening and speaking ability

3.3.1 Metacognitive strategy teaching

It is better to give fish to others than to fish. Learning strategies refer to the measures or methods adopted to complete learning activities. O. Malley and Chamot (1989) classify learning strategies into three categories: metacognitive strategies, cognitive strategies and social/affective strategies. Among them, metacognitive strategies are used to self-monitor and adjust language behavior, including a series of activities such as self-planning, selective attention, self-examination, self-adjustment and self-assessment. Metacognition is macroscopical and instructive, which controls the progress and effect of learners and other specific strategies. Metacognitive strategy teaching is of great help to improve learners' English listening and speaking learning efficiency. Because good English listening and speaking ability is not overnight, it requires students to have a plan, unremitting efforts to achieve. Therefore, students' self-adjustment and self-regulation are the most dynamic basis for the improvement of learning effect. Only on the basis of metacognitive strategies can the whole strategy learning activities operate successfully. Generally speaking, metacognitive strategies can be divided into three categories: 1) planning strategies. In other words, teachers should teach students to make a plan for language learning according to their own knowledge. In this process, teachers help students understand their English proficiency, put forward constructive suggestions, and let students make plans that are in line with their own language competence. 2) monitoring strategy. Students monitor their learning process, methods and effects at any time. Teachers' role is to teach students how to monitor their own learning methods and processes, give timely guidance and revision, and be the guidance of students' learning. 3) evaluation strategy. Students evaluate their learning process. Teachers provide some evaluation methods and means, and timely intervention in their learning process, teachers play a guiding role. In short, metacognitive strategy teaching can cultivate students to become effective learners and self-learning managers. Teachers teach students "fishing", not just "fish".

3.3.2 *Experience English teaching*

The philosophical basis of the experiential view of language understanding is Embodied Philosophy or Experientialism. Lakoff, the proponent of experiential philosophy, believes that "experience" can include all kinds of actual or potential experiences of individuals or communities, and it is the interaction between individuals with genetic structure and physics and society. Experiential philosophy holds that human categories, concepts, reasoning and psychology are formed on the basis of physical experience and are the result of the interaction between body and environment. The basic contents of experiential philosophy are: 1) mind is based on body; 2) thinking is mostly unconscious; 3) abstract concepts are mostly metaphorical. The language learning view of experiential philosophy demonstrates the importance of students' practice and their own experience in language acquisition from the origin of language and thought. It mainly includes three parts: 1) narrating language teaching methodology and listening, speaking, reading and writing skills; 2) studying language from the perspectives of pronunciation, vocabulary, grammar and discourse; 3) studying content-based instruction, computer-assisted learning, learning methods and strategies, autonomous learning in class and evaluation in class from the perspective of language learning process. On methodology. Teachers sometimes need to impart these theories directly to students. Through teaching practice, students can understand the purpose of teaching activities and arrange time reasonably, so as to improve their learning efficiency.

3.3.3 Knowledge system teaching

The main reasons for students' failure in English communication are the lack of vocabulary, pronunciation, grammar and cultural background knowledge. Teachers' effective teaching methods and strengthening students' knowledge system are effective means to improve students' comprehensive English ability. For example, in vocabulary teaching, using cognitive method to teach vocabulary can achieve twice the result with half the effort. In Second Language Teaching, the cognitive approach "identifies, analyses, stores and generates new languages with general cognitive factors", which is divided into global features, concepts, images, chunks, meanings, interests and deductions. For example, when teaching listening vocabulary by holistic approach, when we encounter the word weapon, we can list relevant vocabulary for review and learning. For example, when using chunk cognitive theory to teach grammar, when learning practice and adding gerund collocation, similar verbs are used. Teachers should consciously establish a complete knowledge system and a set of systematic learning methods for students through teaching, activate students' original cognition, establish new schemas, and experience the application of language in different contexts for many times, so as to deepen their understanding and memory of language and culture, and use self-knowledge in English communication. For example.

3.3.4 Use authentic corpus to teach and cultivate students' communicative competence

The process of listening, speaking and comprehension is a dynamic psychological process in which all kinds of knowledge and information input interact among listeners. Authentic corpus is a kind of linguistic material from the real English language communication scene, which integrates linguistic knowledge with linguistic functions or meanings. Authentic corpus such as English radio, TV news reports, interviews, discussions, debates, English songs and movies can be used as supplementary materials for listening and speaking textbooks. Appropriate use of these materials in listening and speaking teaching will help students to come into contact with various vocabulary and expressions in the real English language environment, and improve their language knowledge and communicative competence. Using authentic corpus to teach students to understand the natural spoken English and expression methods in real life is a prerequisite for improving their oral ability. Therefore, the introduction of authentic English corpus into college English listening and speaking teaching is an effective way to improve English listening and speaking ability. Teachers should guide students to make full use of multimedia and Internet platforms, select appropriate corpus, increase language input and output exercises, so that students can gradually adapt to the changes of English language, and acquire rapid response ability to English, thus forming acquisitional conditional reflex. In this way, in the process of listening training, students can gradually cultivate English thinking, listening comprehension speed will be greatly improved, thus promoting oral output.

4 Analysis and reflection

After a questionnaire survey of Chinese students studying abroad, we are soberly aware that:

- English listening and speaking ability is not isolated, it is only a higher embodiment of English comprehensive ability. Whether it is English listening and speaking teaching or literacy teaching, you should try to hear the leading teaching method, listen, speak, read and write, choose a variety of corpus and teaching methods, activate the classroom teaching atmosphere, and mobilize students. Enthusiasm to develop students' ability to use language comprehensively.

- Teaching and learning is a collaborative art. The teacher is the instructor, the student is the subject of learning, and has the autonomy of learning. English teachers should strengthen their own quality and re-train, not only to change teaching concepts, adjust teaching methods, but also to constantly update knowledge, expand horizons, and keep up with the requirements of the times. Students should clarify the purpose of learning, be down-to-earth, master the learning skills, arrange the study time reasonably, and listen, speak, read, and write. Because mastering a language and accomplishing things, you need good methods and efforts. Only on the basis of the combination of teachers and students can the task of teaching and learning be perfectly combined.

- College English teaching should be carried out for four years without interruption, and the university's public English specialization is imperative. Chinese colleges and universities generally offer English classes in the 1st—2th grade of the university. Many students have passed the English 4th and 6th grades. In the 3rd—4th grade, they have taken the English study to the forefront. As everyone knows, if language learning does not advance, then it will retreat, and even after passing college English level 6, it is still far from the level of proficiency. Faced with this situation, the author urges that college English should be taught for four years without interruption, providing students with continuous learning opportunities in English. It is recommended that colleges and universities set up basic English courses in grades 1—2, implement English professional courses, and speak and write. The courses are set separately, and the class time is increased; the English elective courses are added in the 3rd—4th grade, and the professional teaching of college English knowledge is implemented, that is, the English related to the major is opened, so that students with high English proficiency have the opportunity to contact academic English for further study. And lay the foundation for studying abroad. The topic of continuous English teaching in public English is worthy of further discussion and research by educators.

References:

[1] 桂诗春. 1993. 认知与外语学习[J]. 外语教学与研究(4)：2-9.

[2] 林琼. 2002. 第二语言听力理解不成功者的元认知研究[J]. 外语界(2)：40-44.

[3] 文秋芳. 1996. 英语学习策略论[M]. 上海：上海外语教育出版社.

[4] Harmer, J. 2000. How to teach English [M]. Beijing: Foreign Language Teaching and research Press: 99-109.

[5] Krashen, S. D. 1981. Second language acquisition and second language learning[M]. Oxford: Pergamon.

Appendix 3 Current Situation and Development Trend of Teachers' Professionalization in Primary and Secondary Schools in China

——*Based on the Research Papers Published in Important Chinese Periodicals in the Past Ten Years*

Abstract: Teacher specialization is the development trend of teachers. It is imperative to study the professional development of primary and secondary school teachers. This paper first summarizes the teacher specialization theory, including teacher professionalization definition, function, training paradigm, development stage, type and development orientation. Then, in the past ten years (2003-2012), the papers published in the important Chinese journals of China were searched, counted and analyzed, so as to summarize the research status of the professional development of primary and se- condary school teachers in China, and then prospect its deve- lopment trend.

Keywords: teacher education; teacher development; teacher professionalization; primary and secondary schools; retrieval

1 Preface

Since the 1960s, the research on teachers' professional development has become a strong ideological upsurge, with more and more research results. Teacher professionalization develops from ex- perientialization and randomization to teacher professionalization. Since the 1980s, teacher professionalization has become a world-wide trend, requiring high-quality teachers not only to have noble morality and solid profession, but also to become high-starting scholars and lifelong learners, not only specialists in disciplines, but also experts in education. Teachers' profession can not be replaced by professions like doctors and lawyers. In China, the pro-fessionalization of primary and secondary school teachers has gone through the same process, from the urgent need for teachers' quantity to the demand for teachers' quality. Moreover, the ex-pectation of education quality in our society is very high, and the attention to teachers' quality is very high.

Therefore, it is imperative to study the development of teachers, especially in primary and secondary schools.

2 Review on some theories

2.1 Teacher professionalization

From the existing research at home and abroad, researchers have put forward different views on the definition of teacher professionalization. Perry (P.) believes that the professional development of teachers means the growth of teachers' personal professional life, including the enhancement of confidence, skills, the continuous updating and deepening of teaching knowledge, and the enhancement of their awareness of the reasons why they do so in the classroom. Teachers should grow up to be artistic beyond the scope of their skills, to be a person who upgrades their work to a profession, and to transform their professional knowledge into authority. Hoyle (E.) believes that teachers' professional development refers to the process of mastering the knowledge and skills necessary for good professional practice at every stage of their teaching career. The book "The Theory and Practice of Teacher Professionalization" explains that teacher professionalization refers to that the teacher profession has its own unique professional requirements and conditions, and has a special training system and management system. Baidu Encyclopedia explains that teachers' professionalization refers to the process of professional growth of professional educators by means of professional training and lifelong learning, gradually acquiring knowledge and skills of education specialty and constantly improving their self-cultivation in the practice of education specialty. To sum up the above discussion, teacher professionalization includes the following aspects: teachers' professionalism includes both discipline and education professionalism; teachers' qualifications are required not only by academic qualifications, but also by necessary educational knowledge, educational ability and professional ethics; and teachers' specialized institutions and specialized education. Contents and measures; the system and management of teachers' qualifications and teachers' educational institutions; teachers' professional development is a continuous process, and education professionalization is also a concept of development and a deepening process.

2.2 Functions of Teachers' Professional Development:

2.2.1 Social function

Any profession has certain social functions, that is, it has the value of social existence and promotes social development. So does teacher professionalization. It is an important part of inheriting social civilization and an indispensable organism for the continued existence and development of social culture. It promotes the further development of teachers' profession. And promote the development of social material civilization and spiritual civilization.

2.2.2 Professional functions

As a profession, we must construct a relatively complete theoretical system, provide ideological guidance for specific professional activities, theoretically indicate the direction of professional development, define the framework of professional knowledge, define the object and scope of professional activities and professional knowledge needed for professional work. Teachers'professionalization in China generally requires that teachers should have both academic and teacher-training qualities. Academic emphasis is on the academic level of the subjects taught, while pedagogical emphasis is on morality and professional accomplishment of the subjects of education.

2.2.3 Achieve professional organization management and professional autonomy

The requirement of professional knowledge and skills determines that only after long-term professional training can practitioners master their working methods and practical abilities and be competent for professional work. Therefore, a high degree of professional autonomy and authority of professional organizations is the inherent requirement of professional practice and development. The management power of professional organizations mainly includes the examination, appraisal and registration of teachers' qualifications, the evaluation of curriculum, teaching methods and teaching level, the judgement of professional ethics level, teacher training, etc. These powers are basically exercised by educational management departments at all levels. However, all organizational management departments should be composed of authoritative departments and professionals in the professional field. Otherwise, it is difficult to realize teachers'professional autonomy.

2.3 Teachers' Professional Training Paradigm

At present, there have been some studies on Teacher Professionalization in primary and secondary schools in China. From the perspective of teacher training paradigm, the theory and practice of teacher professionalization can be summarized as follows:

- Knowledge paradigm: emphasizing teachers' knowledge reserve, teachers should attach importance to the imparting of cultural knowledge in teaching and the accumulation of teachers' knowledge in the process of teacher training. Teachers' specialization is knowledge-based.

- Competence paradigm: Starting in the 1960s, it is believed that teachers should not only have general knowledge, but also have comprehensive ability, teach students the ability to impart knowledge, communicate with students and deal with classroom affairs together. It requires teachers to have broad knowledge and profound ability.

- Emotional paradigm: After the 1960s, some researchers believe that teachers'knowledge and ability alone are not enough to be good teachers. When teachers'knowledge level reaches a certain level, affective factors affect teachers' teaching level and teaching quality. Therefore, this theory emphasizes such emotional factors as teachers'attention and concern for students in teaching.

- Constructivism paradigm: Influenced by constructivism philosophy, it is emphasized that teachers, as learners, should constantly construct their own knowledge structure to internalize knowledge, and then construct knowledge system through interaction between learners and teachers in the process of teaching.

- Criticism paradigm: It emphasizes that teachers should not only care about book knowledge, but also about the rationality of social, political, economic and cultural knowledge outside the discipline. Teachers should be concerned about the whole society outside the curriculum and the school system, and take the initiative to intervene in social life with a critical eye. In the development of teachers'specialty, it is advocated to cultivate teachers' independent thinking ability.

- Reflective paradigm: It advocates that teachers should cultivate " reflective" consciousness in the process of their growth, and constantly self-adjust and self-construct themselves by constantly reflecting on their own educational and teaching concepts and behaviors, so as to achieve sustainable professional growth.

In addition to the above teacher growth paradigms, with the development of educational technology and the wide application of network, there are also new teacher development paradigms such as distance education, online training, participatory training, cooperative learning, cooperative research community and "Teacher Professional Development School".

2.4 The stage of Teachers' Professional Development

It is generally believed that the growth of teachers needs to go through a certain stage of development[1]. Katz put forward four syllogism of teacher professional development, namely survival stage, consolidation stage, renewal stage and maturity stage; Burden and others put forward the theory of teacher career cycle development, which divides teacher professional development into survival stage, adjustment stage and maturity stage; Huberman divides teacher professional development into three stages: survival stage, adjustment stage and maturity stage; Huberman from teacher professional life From the perspective of natural aging, the five-syllogism of teachers' career development is put forward, that is, survival and discovery period, stability period, tasting new and doubting period, peace and accumulation period, free and idle period. Steffy's five stages include preparatory career stage, expert career stage, retreat career stage, renewal career stage and withdrawal career stage. He also focuses on the problems that teachers may be depressed, stagnated and re-entered the stage of development when they enter the mature stage. Berliner divides teacher professional development into "novice stage, progressive novice stage, competency stage, skilled stage and expert stage" according to the learning and mastery of teachers' teaching professional knowledge and skills; Benner puts forward the theory of teaching expertise development stage, which holds that teacher development generally goes through "novice stage, progressive novice stage, competency stage, skilled stage and expert stage". There are five stages: novice, senior novice, competent, skilled and expert. In short, teachers' professional development is the process of teachers' development from inexperienced to skilled and then to become experts.

2.5 Types of Teacher Development

Not every teacher will eventually become an expert, but will become a different type of teacher[2].

2.5.1 Skilled teachers

By comparing experts with novices, the researcher finds out the characteristics of expert teachers, and believes that these characteristics can be passed on to ordinary teachers, so that they can obtain professional development, and then become excellent teachers and skilled teachers.

2.5.2 Practitioners in science research

Stenhouse's theory that teachers become researchers points out that teachers constantly test, revise and improve their teaching theories through their own practical activities. Teachers are the masters of the classroom and have more opportunities to study teaching problems. Elliot's theory of "Teachers Become

Action Researchers" points out that teachers should change their original education methods to solve some practical problems, and constantly monitor and evaluate themselves in the process of solving problems, so as to revise, improve and improve their theories. He distinguishes between ways of changing practice: one is that teachers use the solutions proposed by researchers to solve practical problems in order to improve their teaching; the other is that teachers change their teaching methods in response to some practical problems, self-monitoring and self-evaluation in the process of solving problems. Teachers' initial understanding of problems is expected to be evaluated. The price process has been revised and improved. It also points out that the change of concept precedes the change of teaching strategy, that is, "thinking precedes action", and that the change of teaching strategy precedes the development of understanding, that is, "thinking through action". Kennis (S.) advocates that "teachers should be liberating action researchers". Teachers form their own research community with the help of "facilitators", i. e. foreign experts. Teachers' community guides them to constantly reflect on themselves and adjust their educational practice. He believes that "emancipatory action research" provides a way to test and improve teaching practice. Placing teaching practice on the basis of systematic theoretical knowledge and research will help to develop educators' critical self-reflection consciousness and expand teachers' professional autonomy.

2.5.3 *Reflective practitioners*

Schon (D.) on the study of "reflective practitioners", holds that the art of practitioners is embodied in the use of intuition, analogy, metaphor rather than universal rules to deal with the "mixed" teaching process, and advocates that practitioners should be practice-oriented. James Avis believes that only by introspective inquiry, beyond the limitations of tradition, can we hope to establish an education with potential changes and solutions to social problems. Osterman & Cottcamp argues that the process of teachers' educational reflection mainly includes four stages: concrete experience stage, observation and analysis stage, recapitulation stage and positive verification stage. Teachers' reflection on educational practice is a cyclical and rising process. In this process, teachers' educational practical ability has been continuously developed and the quality of education has been continuously improved.

2.6 Orientation of Teachers' Professional Development

Generally speaking, teachers' professional development can be divided into two main development orientations: one is "organizational development" stage, which pays attention to the improvement of teachers' overall quality, so as to improve the "trade unionism" orientation of professional social status and emphasize the high standard of "professionalism" orientation of teachers' entry[1]. Secondly, in the stage of "professional development", teachers' professional development pays attention to not only the rational value orientation of pre-service and post-service training, but also the subject knowledge and education knowledge, as well as the practice. It also pays attention to "reflection" on teaching practice, strengthens teachers' understanding of themselves, and forms the practice-reflective inquiry specialty. Industry development orientation.

In addition, research has also been done on the strategies and ways of teachers' professional development, such as using teaching logs, mutual help of teachers, teaching portfolios, case analysis, peer guidance, reflective teaching, action research, school research, blog forums and so on. There is also a cooperative development of teachers' cultural ecology through the cooperation of group teachers. In short, the development of teacher professionalization has been decades since the 1960s, and has established a certain theoretical basis and carried out a series of practical research.

3 Research on the Present Situation of Teachers' Professional Development in Primary and Secondary Schools in China

In order to further study the present situation of teachers' professionalization in primary and secondary schools in China, the researchers searched papers published in important Chinese journals from 2003 to 2012 on CNKI, studied the quantity and content of papers published, and then made statistical analysis of the retrieved documents. Then it summarizes the current situation of the development of teachers' professionalization in primary and secondary schools.

3.1 Overall Research Status of Teacher Professionalization in China

The development of teacher professionalization in China has experienced three stages: teacher education, teacher development and teacher professionalization. The research on this topic is mainly centered on these themes. Researchers retrieve keywords under the condition of "title" by using the retrieval entries of teacher education, teacher development and teacher professionalization respectively. The statistical results of Figure 1 below are obtained.

From Figure 1, we can see that more and more educators in China are studying this topic, showing an upward trend. The research on teacher education is the most, showing an upward trend. In the past ten years, 5,962 papers have been published, followed by teacher development, with a total of 4,380 papers. After 2007, the research on Teacher Education and teacher development has developed rapidly, with an obvious upward trend. The total number of research papers on teacher professionalization is 3,811, and the overall growth rate of research is slow, and after 2008, it shows a downward trend. The above data show that although there are some studies on teacher development in China, most teachers and researchers still stay at the level of teacher education and teacher development. They do not have enough understanding of the trend of teacher development towards teacher professionalization, and the research on teacher professionalization needs to be further strengthened (See Figure 1).

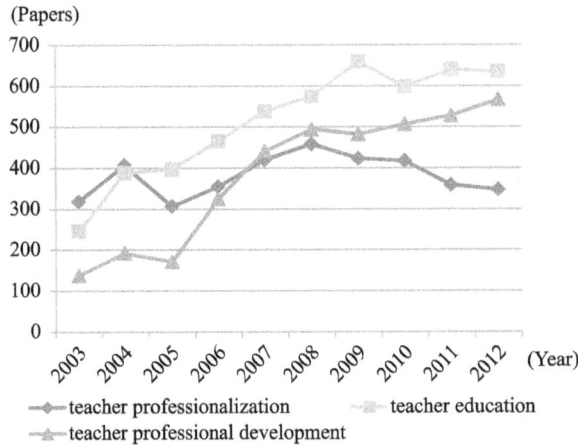

Figure 1 Statistics of the Number of Research Papers in Three Dimensions

According to the summary of the theory of teachers' professional development, we know that the content of teachers' professional development mainly includes the following aspects, such as teachers' knowledge level, ability composition, training, theory, strategy and educational technology. Therefore, on the basis of the above-mentioned retrieval, the researcher further searches, still under the condition of " title " retrieval, with three dimensions of teacher education, teacher development and teacher professionalization as the core, and then further searches from knowledge, ability, training, theory, strategy and educational technology, respectively, and data statistics can be obtained in the following Figure 2, Figure3 and Figure4:

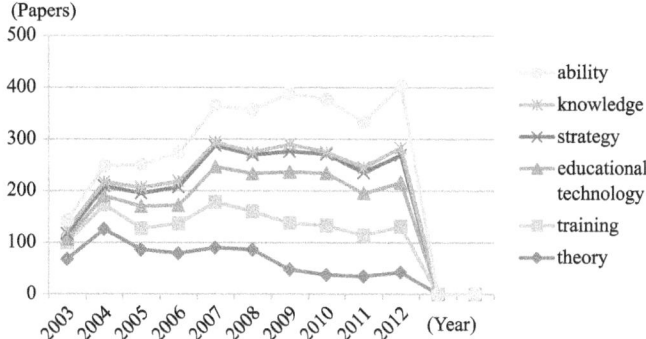

Figure 2 Statistics on the Number of Papers in Different Dimensions about Teachers' Education

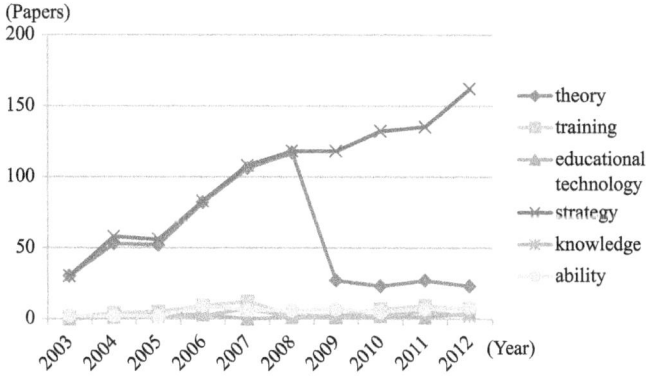

Figure 3 Statistics on the Number of Papers in Different Dimensions about Teachers' Development

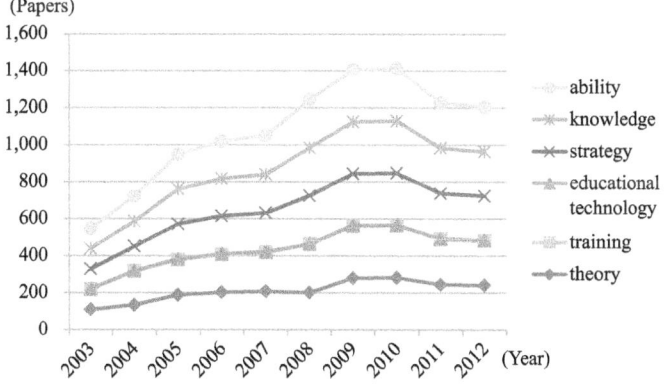

Figure 4 Statistics on the Number of Papers in Different Dimensions about Teachers' professional development

As can be seen from Figure 2, at the level of teacher education research, the research on teacher's ability ranks first, followed by knowledge, strategy, educational technology, training and theory. It shows that researchers have realized that besides professional knowledge, teachers' abilities are also important. However, the development of theoretical research is slow, and there is a gradual downward trend, indicating that the research is still in the primary stage of teacher education research, and the understanding of theoretical research is insufficient. From Figure 3, we can see that in the aspect of teacher development, the most studied aspect is teacher strategy, and the total number of papers is relatively large, with 1 000 research papers in ten years. Secondly, theoretical research, but after 2008, theoretical research declined sharply. There are few studies in other areas, and the growth is not significant. It shows that in the stage of teacher development, besides more research on strategies, there are less research on education and training, educational technology, educational theory, strategies, knowledge and ability. From Figure 4, we can see that at the research level of teachers' professional development, teachers' knowledge, ability, educational technology and other aspects have been studied, and the trend is on the rise. Among them, the research on teachers' competence is the most; the research on knowledge and strategy is more; education technology and training are in the middle; and the theoretical research is less, ranking last. It shows that at the level of teacher professional development, researchers have clearly recognized the various factors of teacher professional development, but there is still a lack of theoretical research.

From the above data statistics and analysis, we can see that the overall situation of the research on teachers' professional development by Chinese researchers is as follows:

(1) The total amount of research shows an increasing trend, which has its own characteristics in the stage of teacher education, educational development and teacher professionalization.

(2) The research on teacher professionalization development is less than that on Teacher Education and teacher development, which indicates that the theory and research of teacher professionalization should be further strengthened.

(3) Researchers can study different factors affecting teachers' professional development, including teachers' abilities, theories, knowledge and so on, but the research contents of each stage are not balanced. The research abilities of the first stage of teacher education and the third stage of teacher professional development are the most; the second stage of teacher development is the most. There are many

research strategies. But on the whole, there are few theoretical studies.

(4) From the content of the study, most of the theoretical studies are based on the research results of European and American countries, or introduce or practice their theories, lacking original theories. There are many strategies and abilities for teachers' development, and there are few theoretical studies at all stages.

3.2 Research Status of Teachers' Professional Development in Primary and Secondary Schools

In order to further study the research status of primary and secondary school teachers' professional development, the researcher conducted a further search, using " teacher education/primary and secondary school teachers' education, teacher development/primary and secondary school teachers' development, teacher professionalization/ primary and secondary school teachers' professionalization" as the search entries to retrieve keywords under the condition of "title" search. Chart 5 and 6 below are obtained.

As can be seen from Chart 5, in terms of the total amount, there are few and no obvious progress in the research of primary and secondary schools at all stages of teacher education, educational development and teacher professionalization compared with the total number of studies. In terms of three research directions, there are 598 studies on Teacher Education by primary and secondary school teachers, while few studies on teacher development and teacher professionalization. Researchers in primary and secondary schools have done a lot of research on teacher education. Researchers further make statistics from six aspects, such as theory and training, and get the statistical results of Chart 6 below. From the results, we can see that the main perspective of the research is educational technology, and the research results have steadily improved; there are also some studies on teachers' ability and training; and there are few studies on teachers' theory, strategy and knowledge.

Through searching and analyzing the research papers of primary and Secondary School researchers on this subject, we can see that:

1) The research on this topic by primary and secondary school teachers is generally less. According to the statistical data of the papers in the past ten years, the total number of papers on teacher education, teacher development and teacher professionalization is 14,153, and the research papers on teacher development in primary and secondary schools are 1,690, accounting for about 12% of the total papers in the past ten years. This indicates that the research on Teacher Professionalization in primary and secondary schools should be further deepened.

2) Among the three major research directions, there are relatively more studies on Teacher Education level, showing an upward trend, but the growth is not obvious. The number of research papers in past years is not more than 100, indicating that the research on teacher development in primary and secondary schools is still at the earliest stage of teacher education, at the initial stage, and the research on this topic has not been mentioned. It is as high as the awareness of teacher development and teacher professional development. There is a certain gap between theoretical research and practical research. Scholars in primary and secondary schools should improve their understanding on the level of theoretical and practical research and make efforts to develop teachers' professionalism.

3) The improvement of economic level promotes the improvement of educational technology. There are many studies on the development of teachers' educational technology by primary and secondary school researchers, which shows that primary and Secondary School researchers have realized that the improvement of educational technology is an important aspect of teachers' professional development. However, there are few studies on other aspects, including teachers' abilities and knowledge, which indicates that the research of primary and secondary school teachers only studies the development of teachers from the perspective of practical application, and does not look at the problem from the perspective of theoretical understanding and development, and studies the one-sided Mandarin. Therefore, it is urgent to strengthen the theoretical basis and practical research ability of primary and secondary school teachers and researchers (See Figure 5 and Figure 6).

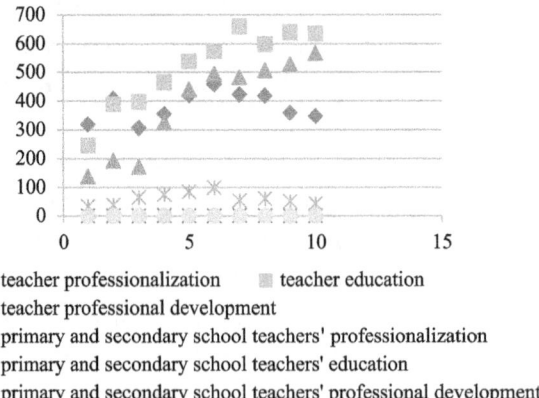

♦ teacher professionalization　　■ teacher education
▲ teacher professional development
✕ primary and secondary school teachers' professionalization
✕ primary and secondary school teachers' education
● primary and secondary school teachers' professional development

Figure 5　Proportion of Papers from Primary and Secondary Schools in Overall Research Papers

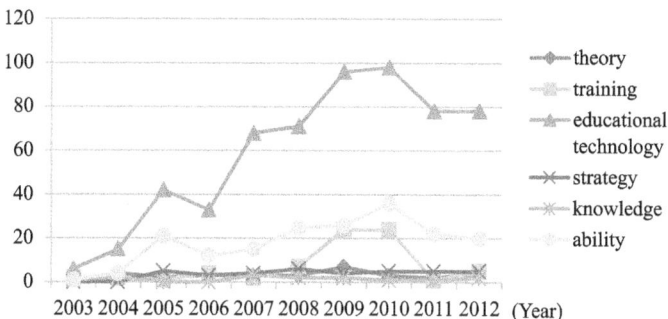

Figure 6   Statistics on the Number of Papers in Different Dimensions of Teacher Education in Primary and Secondary Schools

4 Prospects for the Development Trend of Teachers' Professionalization in Primary and Secondary Schools in China

Although the level of teachers' education and teaching in primary and secondary schools in China is constantly improving, there is still a certain gap in the degree of teachers' professionalization compared with developed countries. It is not difficult to find the general law of the development of teacher professionalization in our country from the above theoretical review and literature retrieval research: with the professionalization of teachers in our country, the reform of basic education will continue to deepen, and the overall teaching level of primary and secondary schools will inevitably improve. Specifically manifested in the following aspects:

1) The professional development and research of primary and secondary school teachers in our country started late and was very difficult, and the development of education in the central and western regions was unbalanced, which was still in the primary stage. With the deepening of education reform, it will develop further and become mature. In the mid-1960s, the demand for teachers' quantity was gradually replaced by the demand for teachers' quality in many countries. Therefore, the research on teacher professionalization emerges at the historic moment. Since the 1980s, teacher professionalization has become the trend of teacher development in the world. China began to pay attention to the development of teachers' professionalization in the 1980s. The development of teachers' level in China has gone through the process of teacher training, teacher education, teacher training and teacher professional development. The

Regulations on Teachers' qualification promulgated in 1995 and the Measures for Implementing the Regulations on Teachers' Qualification promulgated in 2000 marked the establishment of the teacher qualification system in China. In 2001, the work of teacher qualification recognition entered the practical stage. So far, the development of teachers in our country has embarked on the road of professional development of teachers, and there are clear regulations on teachers' standards and admission qualifications from the system. At present, there has been some progress in the study of teachers' professionalization in primary and secondary schools in China, but it is still at the initial stage. There is a great difference in the number, depth and breadth of the study. In addition to introducing foreign theories, researchers should also strengthen theoretical research suitable for China's educational level and national conditions, and combine theory with practice.

  2) Teachers' professionalization will continue to enhance the professional value of teachers, and the irreplaceability of teachers' profession will gradually emerge. With the development of teachers' profession from experientialization and randomization to specialization, teachers' professionalization has become inevitable. With the development of teachers' professionalization, teachers' qualification in primary and secondary schools will be more and more strict, and teachers' qualification will be standardized and standardized. Teacher training in primary and secondary schools in China has experienced from secondary normal school education to higher normal school education, from independent training of normal colleges to comprehensive university education, and has gradually formed the teacher education system of Bachelor of education, master of education and doctor of education. This change is not only the upgrading of the quality of primary and secondary school teachers' education, but also the upgrading of teachers' professional standards. Teacher professionalization promotes teacher professionalization. Teacher professionalization counteracts teacher professionalization. Only teachers' professionalization can make teachers' profession irreplaceable, teachers' professional value and social status will be improved, and the quality of education will be guaranteed. The key is to establish a high-standard teacher management guarantee system. The standards of primary and secondary school teachers' entry will be more and more strict, the level of knowledge and professional accomplishment will be higher and higher, and the salary and social status will be higher and higher.

  3) The role of teachers tends to be diversified. Our country has a cloud

since ancient times: "Teachers, professors and puzzlers also preach". However, with the development of teachers' professionalization, the role of teachers is not limited to this, but tends to be diversified. Teachers will become:

Integration of teaching, learning and research. Teachers are teachers, researchers and lifelong learners. As a teacher, teacher development has to undergo a process of changing the role of novice- Instructor - Researcher - expert. In this process, as a teacher and researcher, the role is clear at a glance, and throughout the whole career is the continuous learning process of teachers. It is a process in which teachers' professional ideals, professional ethics, professional emotions and social responsibility are constantly maturing, improving and innovating. Therefore, the traditional concept of teacher development emphasizes the function of teachers' imparting knowledge. With the development of teachers' professionalization, teachers should not be "candles" but "torches". Their energy should be constantly supplemented. Knowledge will never be exhausted. Lifelong learning runs through teachers' career. Influenced by the constructivist learning theory, it emphasizes the active construction, social interaction and situational nature of learning. The constructive characteristics of the new knowledge view require teachers to construct their own knowledge system by combining theoretical knowledge with practical knowledge based on their existing experience. This knowledge system includes not only subject knowledge, education and teaching knowledge, but also pedagogical subject research knowledge system, so as to accomplish the high-level task of teachers' practitioners, that is, as researchers, under the guidance of strong theoretical basis, to reflect on their work and cultivate the consciousness and product of reflection. The spirit of extreme exploration shifts from emphasizing the development of teachers' technical rationality and instrumental rationality to emphasizing the development of teachers' practical rationality and reflective rationality. In educational practice, teachers are encouraged to constantly reflect on teaching and to study the problems existing in teaching practice, so that teachers can gradually become researchers and school-based curriculum developers, and at the same time stimulate teachers' creativity.

Teaching-management-evaluation complex. Teachers are not only teachers but also managers, including managing themselves, students and teaching, but also evaluators, who evaluate their own teaching, students' academic level and school management level. As managers and evaluators, first of all, they should manage and evaluate themselves. Teachers' professional development requires that teachers must be lifelong learners, which requires teachers to plan their own career development, including career vision, professional development goals, autonomous learning, teaching practice and reflection. Teachers' professional development emphasizes teachers' professional growth in the process of their career, through teaching practice and learning, and in the process of interaction with situations. Secondly, the management and evaluation of students. In teaching practice, the "teacher-centered" classroom teaching management model is gradually replaced by the "teacher-led, student-centered" model. Teachers become organizers, instructors, supervisors and managers in the teaching process, and manage students' learning plans, contents, methods and effects. Thirdly, the management and evaluation of teaching. Teachers should not only manage students from the perspective of classroom teaching management and their own teaching progress and content, but also actively participate in school education management, participate in the formulation of educational policies and regulations, and carry out the function of supervision and evaluation, because front-line teachers have the best understanding of teaching practice and the most right to speak. The policy formulated is more conducive to promoting the improvement of teaching quality, thus realizing teachers' autonomy.

  Multivariate cooperation. Traditional teaching emphasizes too much on the professional characteristics of teachers as teaching craftsmen, and pays attention to the communication between teachers and students. Teachers' professional development emphasizes multi-cooperation, that is, cooperation between teachers and students, cooperation with colleagues, cooperation with teaching managers, and cooperation with society. Butler (D. L) pointed out that the process of teachers' teaching and knowledge construction is first of all a kind of social interaction and dialogue. Teachers do not construct knowledge in a vacuum. Their knowledge, beliefs, attitudes and skills are formed in a certain social and cultural context. Only when teachers get out of themselves, participate in multi-community dialogue and accept the influence of others, can they reflect on teaching according to others' attitudes towards themselves, and construct their own knowledge structure through "integration of horizons" in dialogue with others. Therefore, teachers should be good at communicating with students, understand students' needs, teach on the premise of students' development, and achieve mutual benefit. Teachers are good at cooperating with colleagues, and can make use of peer assistance, knowledge sharing, case study, professional community, cooperative action research and other organizational forms. Teachers are good at cooperating with society, participating in professional group activities, grasping the trend of professional development, strengthening links with families and communities, and grasping social needs and development trends. In a word, teachers' communicative development is a new requirement for teachers' professional development in primary and secondary schools from the perspective of teachers' sociality.

4) The common development orientation of "people-oriented" teachers and students. Teachers, students and teaching environment are three basic elements of education and teaching. The traditional teaching concept has refined the teaching concept of "people-oriented" into "student-oriented", emphasizing that education and teaching should be student-centered, pay attention to students' development needs, and require teachers to adopt effective teaching methods and means in teaching, so as to turn students into "I want to learn" students. However, as the main body of teaching, teachers have been neglected, leading to the neglect of teachers' development. There is a correlation between the various elements of education and teaching. In the practice of education, the development of teachers and students is mutually conditional and mutually reinforcing. Teachers' development is also a necessary condition to promote students' development. The so-called "teaching is mutually beneficial" should be interpreted as "students grow up in the development of teachers and teachers develop in the growth of students". Schools are places where teachers and students develop together. Therefore, the development of teachers' professionalization will surely lead to the study of "people-oriented" co-development between teachers and students. Teachers' professional development is to make both teachers and students develop in the process of education.

5) Emphasize the experience of teachers' subject. From Dilthey's "experience philosophy", that is, the most real thing can not be grasped only by rational knowledge, but by "experience", experience is actually the direct experience of life itself. Teachers' profession is a process in which teachers actively construct knowledge structure by combining their own experience with existing rational knowledge, and gradually cultivate lifelong learning habits. Teachers' professional development is the process of teachers' self-improvement and self-development. This kind of development lies in the exertion of teachers' subjectivity, the internal driving force and the exertion of teachers' subjectivity. In the practice of education, we advocate reflection and research, forming the movement of teachers' reflection and the movement of teachers becoming

researchers.

However, there are still some problems in primary and secondary schools in China, such as teachers' lower educational background, teachers' indifferent professional ethics consciousness, outdated educational concept, poor innovative consciousness, low level of teaching and research, backward teaching methods and means, etc. Education is the key to improve the quality of primary and secondary school teachers and to realize the professional development of primary and secondary school teachers. Necessary conditions for sustainable development of the level. The main ways to solve these problems are the extension of pre-service education system, the guarantee system of teachers' admission qualification, and the training of teachers in vocational schools.

Reference:

[1]蒋竞莹. 教师专业化及教师专业发展综述. 教育探索. 2004(04).

[2]教育部师范教育司.《教师专业化的理论与实践》. 人民教育出版社. 2003年第2版.

[3]王长纯. 教师专业化发展:对教师的重新发现. 教育研究. 2001(11).

[4]周成海,孙启林. 教师专业发展范式转移的基本范式.《中国教育学刊》. 2009(06).

Appendix 4   A Contrastive Study on Irish TY Education and Chinese Secondary Education

Abstract: The Republic of Ireland has developed rapidly since the early 1990s and is known as the "tiger" of the European economy. Education is one of the important driving factors. This paper begins with the education system of the Republic of Ireland, focusing on the Transition Year education in the secondary education stage, which is called TY education for short. It analyses its educational characteristics, educational objectives and curriculum settings, and interprets the characteristics and advantages of TY education in secondary schools in Ireland. Secondly, the differences between Ireland's TY education and China's first-year high school education in terms of education stage, objectives, curriculum, evaluation methods, teachers' roles and teaching methods are compared and analyzed. Finally, it points out the inspiration of Irish TY education to secondary education in our country from many aspects, that is, paying attention to quality education, emphasizing practical learning, emphasizing the cultivation of innovative consciousness, establishing a pluralistic evaluation system and attaching importance to career development and lifelong education.

Key words: Irish Education; Secondary Education; Transitional Year (TY) Education; Chinese Education

1 Introduction

As we all know, the Republic Ireland is a country with profound cultural connotations. It has always been known as the "Island of Saints and Scholars", and many excellent English writers have emerged, such as Yeats, James Joyce, Shaw Bernard, Wilde, Jonathan Swift and so on. Ireland has a long history and excellent education level recognized by the world. It is also one of the most educated countries in the world. 60% of students choose to enter higher education after graduation from high school. How did such a high level of education come about? As we all know, Ireland's educational system is deeply influenced by European educational system and educational thought, and it is a traditional British education. However, the difference is that in secondary education, transitional year education, or TY, is set up in the next year after students graduate from junior high school, which is rare in other countries' education system. Through the analysis of the educational purpose and curriculum of the transitional year in Ireland, the author tries to examine the uniqueness of Ireland's secondary school TY education and the impact of the transitional year on Ireland's high-quality education level, with a view to gaining some enlightenment beneficial to the development of education in our country.

2　An Introduction to Irish Education System and TY Education

2.1　Irish Education System

Ireland's school system developed gradually from the early dual-track education system in Europe. It mainly consists of eight years of primary education, including two years of pre-school education and six years of primary education. Students enter the pre-school class from the age of four. This shows that Irish education has partially incorporated early childhood education into the free education system. Secondary education generally lasts for five to six years, and three years of primary education is compulsory for the purpose of obtaining a secondary school diploma. When students graduate, there is no unified examination, which emphasizes the process evaluation and practical ability of students' level. The following year is Transition Year, or TY education, which is not part of high school education. It mainly focuses on students' interests and hobbies, and there are no formal examinations. The purpose of TY education is not to test, but to improve students'interpersonal skills, broaden their knowledge and broaden their horizons. Students can choose to enter the transitional year, or skip the transitional year, from junior high school to senior high school. Two years of high school education is for the purpose of entering a higher school. There are college entrance examinations, which are equivalent to the college entrance examination in China. They are mainly divided into three levels, and they can get the highest level certificate and enter the University for further study. Ireland's higher education system covers a wide range of universities, polytechnics, education institutes and private universities/colleges. The first three types of institutions of higher learning are funded by the government. Undergraduate education is generally 3—4 years, master education is 1 year, doctoral education is 3—5 years. In addition to disciplines in Institutions of higher learning, there is a sound system of Vocational and technical education and continuing education. Ireland's education system is built to achieve the goal of a "lifelong learning society". In recent years, Irish people have gradually formed the concept of "lifelong learning", and learning opportunities are everywhere.

2.2 The aims and objectives of Irish TY Education

The purpose of TY education is to enable junior high school graduates to gradually mature in their study and life, promote their individual development and accumulate social experience, and cultivate their ability to learn independently. Through TY learning, students can not only complete the transition from juvenile to adult growth, but also fully understand their own advantages and interest orientation through work practice and curriculum elections, laying the foundation for high school studies, which is very important for the development of higher education professional direction. Through the study of the core curriculum of TY school year, students learn independently, discover new fields of knowledge, cultivate interest and evaluate their progress, their abilities in various aspects have been improved, such as organizational ability, theoretical and practical ability, creative ability, team participation and cooperation ability, communication ability, school and home. Families and students themselves also participate in the process of evaluating academic performance.

2.3 TY Curriculum

In 1974, the Irish Ministry of Education and Science began to introduce the TY education system. After many years of practice, it was formally promoted in 1994. Its core courses include language (English, Irish, French, German, Italian, Spanish, Japanese, some schools have added Chinese); Natural Science (agricultural science, mathematics, physics, chemistry, biology); Applied Science (applied mathematics, construction, engineering, home economics, machinery). Cartography; Business (Business, Accounting, Economics); Humanities and Arts (Art Design, Geography, History, Music, Religious Education, Sports, Social Individuals and Health, Career Guidance, Information Technology), etc. In addition, there are some non-academic courses, such as first aid knowledge, cooking, typing, rock climbing, rowing, rugby, field adaptation training and tourism, which can be used as elective courses. In addition, work practice is an indispensable part of practical learning in TY education. The main forms are probation, job simulation, community service, entrepreneurial practice, etc. to help students accumulate work experience, establish entrepreneurship, break through the limitations of the classroom, and attach importance to the awareness of social contact.

3 Differences between TY Education and Secondary Education in China

The age of Irish transitional grade students is generally 14—15 years old, which is similar to that of Chinese senior high school students. They are all the first year of education after junior high school graduation. The age and period of education are basically at the same level. However, TY education is quite different from that of Chinese senior high school students in many aspects.

3.1 Different stages of Education

As a part of senior high school curriculum, the first grade teaching in senior high schools in China is an indispensable teaching period for obtaining senior high school diploma. It has strict credit requirements and can not issue senior high school diploma without completing credit. Ireland's TY education is not a high school education, it is a transitional school year between junior high school and senior high school. Students can choose the course of this academic year, or not, directly into high school, to obtain a high school diploma without any impact.

3.2 Different educational objectives

The purpose of TY education is to develop students' individual abilities and interests, and to acquire certain skills through learning at this stage, to cultivate students' future career development direction and goals, and to realize the transition from junior high school to senior high school. In the process of education, students' personality has been fully developed and gradually matured. TY education takes school education as the platform and practice as the basis to organically integrate theory with practice and carry out all-round quality education for teenagers. Focusing on cultivating students' innovative spirit and practical ability, emphasizing the combination of personal development and social development, respecting students' subjective status and initiative, and healthy development of personality, focusing on students' lifelong sustainable development is an important task of transitional grade. The first grade of senior high school in our country is a part of the stage of senior high school education, which is the preparatory stage for entering higher education. It emphasizes that academic achievement is the main factor, and basic knowledge of liberal arts and science is the main factor. The basic goal of senior high school curriculum reform is to transform exam-oriented education into quality-oriented education, and ultimately implement real quality-oriented education. However, in the present stage of high school education, academic examination is an important way of evaluation.

Under the pressure of entering school, high school education in China has the tendency of instrumentalism education. In the long run, high school education should go beyond its instrumentality to cultivate students' civic and personality qualities. It is better to learn from Irish TY education, where educators select the basic knowledge necessary for students' lifelong learning, and learn from the knowledge and technology of social progress and technological development; strengthen students' social ties and guide them. Innovation and practical awareness, broaden the horizon, and put into practice the evaluation method of combining students' academic achievements with their growth records.

3.3 Different curriculum settings

In the first year of senior high school in China, liberal arts and science courses are mainly set up. Physical education is compulsory, while other courses such as music and art are optional. Some schools even cancel these courses for college entrance examination. Ireland's TY education curriculum is very extensive, which covers liberal arts, science, business, sports and art and other disciplines, and some courses are also cross-disciplinary, cross-professional settings, which fully takes into account the improvement of students' interest and quality, taking into account the needs of students' future professional development. Secondly, the curriculum is very practical, such as tourism, internship and other projects completely divorced from book teaching, full practice, so that students can learn in practice. Thirdly, the curriculum has strong autonomy. Students can freely choose the courses listed by the National Curriculum and Assessment Commission (equivalent to the Education Commission of China) or the courses independently developed by schools. In a word, all courses which are beneficial to students' interest cultivation and skill development can be freely chosen.

3.4 Different evaluation methods

TY education emphasizes the diversification of evaluation forms and evaluators. Schools, families and students themselves can participate in the evaluation, and process evaluation is particularly valued. Teachers can give evaluation in the process of project guidance for students; parents can give evaluation in the support of financial and material resources needed for the project; students can evaluate the progress of the project and so on. There are many evaluation methods, such as report card, project progress evaluation, observation scale, reflective learning report, discussion and speech, etc. The content of evaluation is not only limited to academic achievement, but also students' organizational ability, self-presentation (dress, speech and manners, etc.), punctuality (not only refers to class, but also is a record of punctuality in various activities), independence, application ability, participation, initiative, cooperation spirit, leadership and problem-solving ability. Orientation evaluation. In this academic year, although there will be some written forms of evaluation, it mostly tests students' practical effects and abilities on the basis of projects. In the TY academic year, there is no unified quality evaluation mechanism and no final examination, so students can choose courses according to their interests and social development needs. To improve the overall quality of individuals, in order to adapt to the development of the future society. This is totally different from the evaluation system of the first grade of senior high school in China, which mainly focuses on the mid-term and final academic achievements.

3.5 Different teaching methods

The remarkable feature of TY teaching lies in the diversity of teaching methods. In active secondary school, education attaches importance to developing students' autonomous learning ability, focusing on discussion-based and practical learning, such as group discussion, simulated performance, field investigation, etc. It emphasizes the flexibility of learning forms and completes learning in the form of multimedia demonstration, lectures, seminars, study visits, field visits and community services. Task. For example, in business learning activities, students practice according to the theory they have learned from books. First, a group of students form a "public".

4 Enlightenment of TY Education to Secondary Education in China

After years of educational practice, the advantages of TY education have become obvious. More than 80% of Irish students choose to enter the TY stage after graduation, and TY education has been widely recognized. In addition, the research shows that after entering the stage of higher education, the self-learning ability and living ability of students who have carried out TY education are obviously higher than those who have not participated in TY education. Therefore, Ireland's high level of higher education has been widely recognized by European and American countries, and its graduates have a high employment rate in many countries, which is inseparable from the success of TY education. Of course, we will get some enlightenment when we study its educational system.

4.1 Pay attention to quality education

Ireland's TY education focuses on the development of multiple intelligences.

From the course offered, it covers language, natural science, applied science, business, humanities and art and practice. Students are free to choose courses according to their own wishes. Educational institutions offer courses in full accordance with students' personality development and social development needs. It aims at improving students' comprehensive quality in an all-round way, respects students' main body and initiative, pays attention to the development of human intelligence potential and cultivates students' sound personality. Students' cognitive ability, discovery ability, autonomous learning ability, life ability, development ability and creativity are paid attention to. This kind of education does not regard students as receivers of book knowledge, but as a platform for students to use and display. Quality education in our country has been advocated for many years, and some schools have also carried out some teaching reforms. However, throughout the country, it is still a situation of "quality education cries out brilliantly, exam-oriented education grasps firmly". Is there a Chinese school that dares to cancel the exam just like Ireland's TY grade, focusing entirely on students' quality education? In order to change the situation of examination-oriented education in China, we should start with the educational policy, carry out the reform of curriculum reform and teaching evaluation, attach importance to the value and migration of students' general development for future development, cultivate students' ability of self-development, enable them to learn to study independently and develop students' ability of lifelong learning. It is also giving students room for development.

4.2 Emphasizing practical learning

In TY education, a prominent feature is to emphasize learning from practice, learning from doing, and cultivating students' autonomous learning ability. Teaching breaks through the limitations of classroom, pays attention to the cultivation of students' own abilities, attaches importance to the connection with society, and pays attention to the theory of practical testing. Through various teaching activities, such as work practice, probation, work simulation, community service, entrepreneurship education, study visits and field visits, students' interest in learning, innovation spirit and theory can be cultivated. Practical learning methods. Mr. Tao Xingzhi has long discussed this issue. He once took farming as an example and pointed out that "if we want to do farming in the field, we must learn in the field and teach in the field". He emphasized the importance of practice. His teaching ideas of "life education", namely "life is education" "society is school" "teaching and doing in one", are also the essence of education which closely links education with life, society and practice. We may as well absorb more of its essence in teaching, resolutely oppose dead-end examination, and scientifically follow education and practice. The law of teaching is to establish a new education which closely combines with the reality of social life, so that students can really get "six liberations": liberating his mind, enabling him to think; liberating his hands, enabling him to be competent; liberating his eyes, enabling him to see; liberating his mouth, enabling him to talk; Liberate his space and enable him to acquire rich knowledge in nature and society; liberate his time and not fill his homework list, let him learn something he longs to learn.

4.3 Focus on cultivating innovative consciousness

Ireland has strengthened its educational reform since the early 1990s in order to cultivate students' innovative ability. The reform has been very successful with a high level of education, which has promoted the rapid development of its economy and made it the "economic tiger" of Europe, which is closely related to education. The value of life lies in exploiting and creating, and the value of education lies in teaching people how to exploit and create. This Innovation-centered educational reform focuses on increasing TY education. Students actively engage in learning and practice by choosing courses independently. This educational method gives students the opportunity to seek opportunities for personality development and to bring their potential into full play in the process of independently formulating project plans and implementing them, so as to cultivate them. Pioneering and innovative. In order to carry out educational reform and cultivate students' innovative ability, we must thoroughly emancipate the mind, let students use their own brains and hands, and really move.

4.4 Establish a multi-evaluation system

TY education establishes an evaluation system from two aspects. On the one hand, form diversity can be achieved. In addition to the form of written test to test students' academic performance, teachers can also evaluate students through comprehensive observation, student discussion and communication, practical operation, work display and other forms. On the other hand, there are many kinds of evaluation objects, such as teacher evaluation, student mutual evaluation, parent evaluation and student self-evaluation. A student who is recognized by teachers, students and parents is an excellent student. Such evaluation is more objective than written examination results. Therefore, in order to change the current situation of students' learning, we should first start with the means of evaluation, break the single evaluation model of written test scores, and adopt different academic evaluation methods according to the characteristics of the course content.

4.5 Emphasis on career development and lifelong education

TY Education offers courses in science, engineering, liberal arts, business and arts. These courses are basically seen in the curriculum of the university in China. Moreover, TY education emphasizes the extensive contact between students and society. Through the accumulation of experience in work placement, students can understand their own development direction, indirectly cultivate students' professional awareness, and pave the way for future career development. In addition, in TY education, students independently choose courses, design topics and conduct research, and reflect the diversity of characteristics in terms of learning content and methods, which is conducive to the cultivation of students' independent learning ability and the implementation of education democratization and lifelong learning. The educational philosophy to achieve lifelong education.

In short, due to the influence of traditional Chinese values and social and economic conditions, the development of education in China is still somewhat backward compared with some developed countries, which will not be conducive to meeting the urgent needs of China's social development and people's acceptance of advanced education. As a developed country, Ireland is a late starter, but it can be straightforward. The superiority of its education is worth learning and learning.

References:

[1] Benner, A. D. & Graham, S. 2009. The Transition to High School as a Developmental process among Multiethnic Urban Youth [J]. *Child Development*, 80(2):356—376.

[2] Isakson, K., & Jarvis, P. (1999). The Adjustment of Adolescents during the Transition into High School: A Short-term Longitudinal Study [J]. *Journal of Youth and Adolescence*. 28 (1):1—26.

[3]汪莲华. 从过渡年学习项目看教育职业化[J].《职教论坛》. 2010(8).

[4]赵萱. 爱尔兰小学跨文化教育研究[J].《外国中小学教育》. 2012(1).

Appendix 5 College English Oral Assessment Reform

Abstract: This paper starts from the evaluation of the communicative competence of College English in our university, combined with the summary and analysis of the reform results of the current colleges and universities in the test of oral English, it is proposed that the reform of the communicative competence of College English in our university should be further deepened, and the empirical research should be used. The method attempts to test the feasibility of the communicative competence test method combined with formative evaluation and summative evaluation, and proposes some constructive suggestions.

Key words: College English, oral assessment, reform, experiment

1 Introduction

In recent years, English communicative competence has become one of the important measures to measure students' English language competence. In recent years, there have been oral English examinations in our university, and oral English scores have been included in the final evaluation. This is a leap in English teaching and testing. It fully reflects the importance our school attaches to students' communicative competence in English. As we all know, the assessment of English communicative competence is still a bottleneck problem. Faced with a large number of College English (non-English major) students, how to carry out an effective, credible and practical large-scale oral test is a big topic worthy of serious study. It is not enough to simply test the students' oral English at the end of the semester, and it is also very difficult to test the students' real communicative competence in English. Therefore, the assessment of communicative competence of public English in our university needs to be reformed.

2 Research status

Canal and Swain summarize communicative competence into four aspects: linguistic competence, the ability to master vocabulary and grammatical rules, and sociolinguistic competence, which is the pragmatic aspect of how to use appropriate language. Discourse competence refers to the ability to master and organize coherent texts, not only the ability to isolate sentences; strategic competence, which refers to the use of linguistic and non-verbal means for effective communicative competence. However, college English teaching in China has been mainly carried out for improving the language ability of students (grammar, vocabulary, sentence pattern, sentence formation), ignoring the cultivation of the latter three abilities. The latter three abilities are related to language use and can be summarized as pragmatic competence, which can only be improved through practice. The following problems are common in the current college oral English teaching in our country: 1 limited time, limited participation of students. College English teachers must complete the teaching tasks according to the requirements of the syllabus. Classroom teaching is mostly a teacher-centered thorough reading or listening practice. It is difficult to take time out of class teaching to practice oral communication. 2 Spoken language is not subject to proper Value. These problems lead to high language ability, that is, grammatical ability, and the reading and writing skills are generally good, while the oral communication ability is poor. Therefore, college English oral teaching and evaluation reform is an urgent task.

The author of this paper has obtained some inspirations from the summary and analysis of the reform results of the current colleges and universities in the oral test, which provides some reference for the reform of the university's public English communication ability.

1) There are three main forms of oral English test: ① direct oral test (everyone's dialogue). Direct exams usually use reading aloud, group discussion, dialogue, short talk, and oral interview test. Commonly used direct oral exam questions are: imitation (read or play by the examiner, students follow), reading aloud (the candidate prepares for a few minutes, watching the text read aloud), dialogue (the candidate answers the questions raised by the examiner or the recorded short essay) The student is required to make a corresponding answer or response to the daily com-munication language spoken by the examiner or the recording. The candidate can also ask questions or dialogue with the language on the language materials, etc., and the monologue (the candidate can see the picture and speak in English and Chinese) Describe or narrate events, people and objects, discuss or argue (between candidates to discuss or debate based on the tips of the questions), interviews (interviews) through a variety of questioning techniques, multi-level and multi-angle observation of students' spoken language Ability, also allows students to ask questions to the examiner). Direct exam

validity is relatively high. However, due to the strong transient nature of the direct oral test, the level of examiner varies from person to person, the scoring standard is difficult to unify, and the reliability of the test will be affected. ② Inter-interface test form. The inter-interface test refers to an oral test in the form of a written test. Usually, the phonetic test is used to test the phonetic knowledge, intonation, accent, and other common communication terms. ③ Semi-direct form (human-machine dialogue). Candidates record by the tape prompts. The test method is similar to the direct form, but it is not possible to use the "discussion" or "debate" or "interview" to conduct the test directly. The semi-direct oral test questions are similar to the direct test questions, but do not use interviews and discussions. The advantages of semi-direct ex-amination are: a) can test many candidates in a short period of time, saving manpower and material resources; b) the performance of the candidate's oral level will not be affected by the examiner's mood or level difference; c) the score can be passed by The trained professionals are unified at the right time and in a comfortable place; d) The examiner can listen to the recording repeatedly, which is helpful to improve the accuracy of the score; e) It can avoid the examiner's clothing and instruments when the examiner scores. The impact of factors. The shortcomings of the semi-direct examination are: a) the examiner cannot understand the body language and facial expressions of the candidate; b) the examiner cannot intervene in a timely manner when the candidate is found to be unclear or too little; c) when the recording device is out When the problem or the tape is unclear, the scoring work is difficult. In the large-scale oral English test, the latter two forms are mainly used. At present, the college English test in China and the TOEFL test in the United States have adopted semi-direct examinations. The Cambridge Primary Certificate English oral exam is a direct exam.

2) The English oral test scoring method has the following three forms: not included in the total score, only as a reference score (can also not give scores, press a, b, c, d or excellent, good, pass and fail four Ratings). This scoring method can be used during the oral English test; the total score is included, accounting for about 10% to 20% of the total score. Oral questions generally have 3 to 4 questions, 5 points or 10 points for each question, and then score conversions are included in the total score; in addition to the total score of English listening and written test, the oral test score is added to indicate the participation in the oral test. Student incentives, this scoring method, is mostly used for independent examinations in schools.

3) The oral test scores are broadly divided into two categories: the overall score method and the analytical score method. The overall scoring method is based on the examiner's impression of the content and ability of the candidate's spoken language, giving a grade or score overall. The analytical scoring rule distinguishes the content of the candidate's oral test from the individual components of the ability and then scores separately. Both methods have their own advantages and disadvantages. It is best to use both standards at the same time to complement each other.

3 Theoretical basis

From the perspective of modern education evaluation, teaching evaluation can be understood as two levels of evaluation and evaluation. The evaluation is to measure and calculate the numerical value and obtain the data; the evaluation is to judge the value of the evaluation result. The main purpose of teaching evaluation is to check the learning effect of the students, so that teachers and students get timely feedback in order to strengthen or correct the teaching effect. Therefore, teaching evaluation has a guiding function, an adjustment function, an incentive function, and an authentication function. In the past, teaching evaluation overemphasized the function of screening and selection. The evaluation reform is to give full play to the function of evaluation to promote student development, teacher improvement and improvement of teaching practice. It is necessary to establish an evaluation system to promote the continuous development of students, teachers and courses. The development process of education evaluation science is the process of people's continuous understanding of the law of education, reflecting the footprint of education science progress. The development of education evaluation science is basically along the line from " focusing on the subjective needs of the evaluators" to " focusing on the evaluation. " The direction of the quality development of the people. In the implementation of developmental evaluation, the basis for value judgment is mainly "process orientation" and "subject orientation".

3.1 Process orientation

1) Incorporate all the situations of teachers and students in the teaching process into the evaluation scope, all activities with educational value should be valued by the evaluators;

2) emphasize the communication between the evaluators and the evaluators Emphasize the value of the process itself;

3) The methodological characteristics are the combination of quantification and qualitative, and are essentially dominated by practical rationality.

3.2 Subject orientation

1) The purpose of the evaluation is to make the evaluator agree, and the evaluator and the evaluation object jointly construct the meaning of the evaluation;

2) The human liberty and liberation as the fundamental purpose of the evaluation, emphasizing the evaluator and being evaluated Equal communication;

3) evaluation of objection, quality evaluation;

4) emphasis on self-evaluation of the person being evaluated.

4 problem solving

The author proposes a communicative competence test perspective that combines formative evaluation with summative evaluation, that is, a communicative competence test that emphasizes the process orientation of developmental evaluation. The results of formative evaluation should account for a certain percentage of the student's academic evaluation. Attention should be paid to the stimulating effect of formative evaluation on students' English language learning. At the same time, combined with the method of summative evaluation, the oral examinations at the end of the period and the end of the period should be evaluated. It is one of the important components of English teaching evaluation to examine students' oral English ability. The oral English test can play a good role in the English teaching, and promote the comprehensive development of students' listening, speaking, reading and writing skills.

In the second semester of 07—08, the author conducted a test of oral assessment reform for the two middle-class teaching classes that he taught. Among them, class A is in accordance with the traditional oral test method. At the end of the period, a speaking test is given to give some topics. After the lottery, students will give a speech. The teacher raised several related questions on the subject and gave results. Class B has 4—5 oral exams in the semester. The assessment principle is: the combination of examination and examination, combined with the mid-term, the end of the period and the usual, the combination of the assessment of the teacher and the unified test of the school. Teachers should evaluate the students' written homework, verbal answers, speeches, readings, and other in-class and other learning behaviors, learning activities, learning attitudes, participation levels, and cooperative spirits through examination, observation, and communication with student activities. As part of the semester oral test scores, plus the results of the final oral exam, students are given a comprehensive oral score. It also analyzes and summarizes several test results, makes correct judgments, and emphasizes the teaching-oriented function, adjustment function, incentive function and identification function of teaching evaluation.

Since both classes are middle shifts, they are all 57 people. The results of the placement at the time of admission are equivalent, which can be regarded as the initial scores of the two classes. Therefore, it is only necessary to compare the final test scores of the two classes to judge the success of the teaching reform. The final oral test was conducted by two non-class teachers, and the test format was the same. Grade A score is above 90 points, Grade B score is 80—89 points; Grade C grade is 70—79 points; Grade D grade is 60—69 points; Grade F grades are fail, 60 points or less. Table 1 is the statistics of the final oral test scores:

Table 1　　　　　　　Statistics of the final oral test scores

	A(excellent)	B(good)	C(medium)	D(pass)	F(fail)
Class A (number)	5	16	24	9	3
Class B (number)	13	22	17	4	1

From the table above, it can be seen that most of the students in Class A concentrate on medium and good grades, with only 5 excellent students. Yet the excellent students in Class B account for more than half of the class, which shows that the reform has been effective.

After one semester's oral test reform, the author conducted a questionnaire survey on students in Class B. Through the questionnaire survey, the author found that the students recognized the reform of oral test. It is believed that this oral test method is beneficial to (Table 2):

Table 2

Stimulate students' enthusiasm for oral expression	96%
Stimulate the enthusiasm of interaction with teachers in class	93%
Strengthen positivity of practicing oral English after class	93%
-Reflect the fairness and objectivity of oral test	100%
Improve English Comprehensive Ability	95%

5   Conclusions and Implications

In a word, the assessment of students' authentic communicative competence in English emphasizes the combination of formative assessment and summative assessment, and the analysis and evaluation of the test results from time to time in order to check the students' learning effect, so that teachers and students can get timely feedback in order to strengthen or correct teaching. However, there are still some shortcomings in using this test method, such as the choice of several test forms in the mid-term, the subjective con-trol of teachers in evaluation and the evaluation level of evaluators, which can not be ignored. Therefore, the evaluation must do:

First, understanding the characteristics of communicative testing and avoiding blind testing. Oral English activities have the following characteristics:

Interactiveness: a group-based form of activity, in most occasions, people need to communicate instantly to convey information through communication. It's hard to imagine the practical significance of oral activities without communicators.

- Purposefulness: People communicate orally in order to achieve a certain purpose. For example, make appointments for meetings, ask about train or airplane flights, describe past ex-periences, discuss travel plans, express your views on an event or person, and so on.
- Para-linguistic features: Sometimes the speaker expresses his intentions through changes in intonation, stress or volume. For example: I beg your pardon. apologize when you use the down key, but you don't understand when you use the up key. Please say it again.
- Non-linguistic features (NLPs) speakers sometimes convey information through body language. When using body language, we should pay attention to the unique body language of different nationalities.
- Listening is closely related to the inseparability of listening from speaking. When using language to communicate, listening and speaking are closely related. You need to understand before you can respond appropriately to what the other person says. The quality of listening will directly affect the quality of oral communication. Candidates with high scores in listening test will also get high scores in oral test.
- Decency of communication. Appropriateness of communi-cation includes two aspects: appropriateness of non-cultural com-munication and appropriateness

of cross-cultural communication.

Second, Grasp the principles of communicative testing and guarantee the fairness of testing. Language competence is mainly measured in the following aspects: the number of words understood in unit time, the complexity of language materials, the breadth of language skills, the speed of language communication, the flexibility of language use, the accuracy of language use, the appropriateness of language use, and the autonomy of language use. That is, the degree of reliance on cues from the communicating partner. There is no definite standard for these aspects, so the score is subjective. Therefore, teachers should grasp the principle of fairness in the process evaluation, and the final oral test can take the following measures to ensure the reliability of the score.

- First of all, we should formulate scientific, reasonable and feasible oral test scoring standards, which is the basis of ensuring reliability.
- To adopt a common scoring system for two or more evaluation teachers, teachers should avoid evaluating their students. This reduces the personal errors that may occur.

Evaluation of teachers is the key to ensure the reliability of oral tests. Some people take it for granted that teachers should be examiners. Do they need training? Of course, high-quality examiners are very important in oral English examination. In order to ensure the quality of the teachers presiding over the examination, the following tasks should be done well.

- Learning the theory of oral test;
- Selecting experimental classes for simulated test and making videos;
- Mastering the scoring criteria by watching videos and learning guides;
- Compiling relevant oral test syllabus and training materials.

Third, pay attention to the flexible use of communicative testing methods and avoid formalism.

- Combine testing with teaching. At present, the dominant method of English teaching in China is a comprehensive teaching method, which combines the explanation of language usage, the practice of language usage and the practice of language usage, and transits from cultivating micro-linguistic competence to macro-communicative competence. Therefore, testing should evaluate teaching, measure students' level, base on teaching, and measure students' macro communicative ability.
- The method and purpose are unified. Language competence is measured by the number of words understood and expressed in a unit of time, the

complexity of language materials, the breadth of language skills, the speed of language communication, the flexibility, accuracy, appropriateness and autonomy of language use, so the testing methods are different.

• Combining utilization with transformation. Improve the test type, implementation, scoring method, etc.

Forth, strengthen the construction of test questions bank for communicative testing and improve its standardization. The reliability, validity, difficulty and discrimination of the test are analyzed by computer sampling (or full sample). Then the suggestions for improving the test are put forward, and the question bank of the oral test is established.

Reference:

[1]张文中.国外第二语言流利性研究现状[J].外语教学与研究,1999,(2).

[2]杨庆萍.现状与对策:大学英语口试引发的思考[J].外语与外语教学,2001,(5).

[3]刘雪涛.英语口语教学中教师的主导地位[J].中国英语教学,2000,(3).

[4]周星,周韵.大学英语课堂教师话语的调查与分析[J].外语教学与研究,2002,(1).

Appendix 6 Analysis of Irish Innovation Education

Abstract: In recent years, the Republic of Ireland's economy has developed rapidly and is known as the "tiger" of the European economy, which has attracted the attention of the world. Ireland's "innovative education" is one of the important driving factors for economic development. This article begins with the Irish education system and elaborates on the Irish academic system, which is divided into primary education, secondary education and higher education. Then through the specific analysis of its academic system, it interprets the characteristics and advantages of Irish innovation education, and tries to get some inspiration from China's education reform, so that education can further promote the development of China's economy.

Key words: Irish education; academic system; analysis; inspiration

1 Introduction

As we all know, Ireland's long history and excellent education level are recognized by the world. It is also one of the most educated countries in the world. 81% of the citizens have received high school education, and more than 60% of secondary school graduates have entered higher education. How is such a high level of education created? Ireland has a profound cultural heritage. It has always been known as the "island of saints and scholars", and many literary masters such as Yeats and James Joyce have emerged. The Irish education system is also deeply influenced by European academic systems and educational thoughts, and is a traditional British education. This article takes the introduction of the Irish education system as a starting point and conducts further analysis to examine the uniqueness of its education in order to obtain some inspirations that are beneficial to the development of Chinese education.

2 Introduction to the Irish academic system

The Department of Education and Science is responsible for all aspects of education policy, including curriculum, syllabus and national exams. Full-time compulsory education is 6-15 years old. Free education ranges from four years old to undergraduate education. The Irish academic system evolved from the two-track academic system of early Europe and was divided into three levels, primary education, secondary education and higher education.

2.1 Primary education

Usually eight years of free education, the first two years of pre-school education, known as pre-school and senior infants (Junior and Senior Infants), students can voluntarily enter the school from the age of four. Then there is the six-year compulsory primary education phase, which is the 1—6 grade study. Primary education generally uses a student-centered approach to teaching that enables students to recognize their potential to develop their life skills. The course features a wide range of teaching and learning experiences. It generally includes language, mathematics, social and environmental sciences, art education, sports, social and personal physiology and health education. The purpose of education is to let children understand their potential and uniqueness to meet the challenges of the 21st century. At the same time, the course focuses on developing students' communication, problem solving, thinking, consulting, investigating, analyzing, and awareness of relationships and connections with society and others. At the same time emphasize the study of student literature and mathematical skills. There is no form of examination for elementary school graduation.

2.2 Secondary education

Generally, it is five to six years, mainly including secondary schools, vocational schools, community schools, and comprehensive schools. Most general secondary schools are managed by religious groups, and the Boards of Governors are managed by religious groups, local vocational education committees, and the Ministry of Education and Science. This management system is mainly derived from the Irish education tradition. 95% of teachers' salaries and allowances and 91% of scholarships are funded by the government. Students can choose to attend a boys' school, a girls' school or a mixed school for education. 33% of students enter vocational schools or community colleges after completing primary education. These schools are managed by the Vocational Education Committee of the Ministry of Education and Science, and focus on developing students' manual skills and business knowledge preparation. The comprehensive school covers academic and vocational skills courses, and students choose courses that are more flexible. The first three years of secondary education are compulsory education for the purpose of obtaining a high school diploma. It emphasizes the process evaluation and practical ability development of students' academic level. There is no uniform exam when students graduate. The following year is the

Transition Year, referred to as TY Education, and is not part of high school education. It mainly focuses on cultivating students' hobbies and interests, and there is no formal examination. The purpose of TY education is not to test scores, but to improve students' interpersonal skills, expand their knowledge and broaden their horizons. Students can voluntarily choose whether to accept the transition year education, or skip the transition year and go directly to high school. The two-year high school education is for the purpose of further education. The Post-Leaving Certificate Courses are used as a reference for further education in higher education. They are mainly divided into three grades. College further studies.

2.3 Higher education

The system of higher education in Ireland is very broad, including universities, polytechnics, colleges of education, and private universities/colleges. The first three types of institutions of higher learning are basically funded by the government. Undergraduate education is generally 3—4 years, postgraduate education is 1 year, and doctoral education is 3—5 years. In addition to higher education institutions, there is a comprehensive vocational and technical education and continuing education system. The Irish education system is built to achieve the goal of "lifelong learning society". In recent years, the Irish have gradually formed the concept of " lifelong learning", and learning opportunities are everywhere. In general, students can complete a two-year full-time course to obtain a high-level certificate; complete a three-year full-time course to earn a general bachelor's degree; receive an honours degree; complete one year (off-the-job) to two years (on-the-job) full-time Master's degree program, and obtain a master's degree through research papers; PhDs usually require at least three years of original research, writing a thesis, and obtaining a defense.

3 Irish education system analysis

3.1 The development of a two-track academic system to a monorail system

Due to its long-standing British colonial rule, Ireland is deeply influenced by British culture in terms of language and culture as well as education. Therefore, its academic system basically follows the early two-track academic system in the UK. One track is top-down education, from university to middle school; the other is bottom-up education, from elementary school to vocational school, this dual-track system It evolved from the medieval school system with obvious traces of hierarchical privilege. Since the 1970s, the Irish government has embarked on educational reforms. The reform aims to eliminate the inequality in the traditional academic system, promote the harmony between the two tracks, and give everyone more choices to ensure the fairness of education. It follows the reform of the monorail system represented by the United States and develops into a monorail system through the integration of high schools. Comprehensive secondary schools are an effective way to achieve integration. Therefore, we can see from the education system map that Ireland's transitional grades and comprehensive secondary schools have both academic and vocational skills courses for students to choose freely, indicating that Ireland's two-track academic system has been transformed into a monorail system.

3.2 Preschool education has been included in the free education system

At present, many countries have included early childhood education in the academic system. It is a symbol of the deep development of the academic system and an important indicator for the development of modern academic system in the direction of lifelong education. There are eight years of elementary education in Ireland. The first two years of pre-school education are called pre-school and senior infants. Students can enroll free of charge from the age of four. Mainly in English, Irish, math, nature, religion, art and physical education. It can be seen that Ireland has partially incorporated early childhood education into the free education system. Early childhood education is the foundation stage of lifelong education and an important stage for achieving lifelong education. Incorporating early childhood education into the free education system fully demonstrates the Irish government. Emphasis on education. At the same time, the high level of education is not only reflected in the degree and proportion of citizens' education, but also in the breadth and depth of free education and compulsory education.

3.3 Looking at Ireland's quality education from the transition year (TY) education

In 1974, the Irish Ministry of Education and Science began to introduce the TY education system. After years of practice, it was officially promoted in 1994. The transition grade students are generally 14—15 years old, which is basically the same as the age and education stage of the first year of Chinese high school students, but it is very different. The first year of high school in China is part of the high school education. It is an indispensable part of obtaining a high school diploma. It has strict credit requirements. Unfinished credits cannot be awarded for high school diplomas. The Irish middle school TY education is not a high school education, it is a transitional school year between junior high school and high school. Students can choose to study in the transition year independently and have no influence on obtaining a high school diploma.

The purpose of TY education is to enable students to gradually mature in their study and life, to promote individual student development and to accumulate social experience, and to cultivate the ability of independent learning. Its core courses include language (English, Irish, French, German, Italian, Spanish, Japanese, some schools have added Chinese); natural sciences (agricultural science, mathematics, physics, chemistry, biology); applied science Classes (Applied Mathematics, Construction, Engineering, Home Economics, Mechanical Drawing); Business (Business, Accounting, Economics); Humanities (Art Design, Geography, History, Music, Religious Education, Sports, Social Individuals and Health, career guidance, information technology, etc. In addition, there are non-academic courses such as first aid knowledge, cooking, typing, rock climbing, rowing, rugby, field adaptation training and tourism. In addition, work placement is an indispensable part of practical learning in TY education. The main forms include traineeship, job simulation, community service, entrepreneurial practice, etc. These activities break through the limitations of the classroom and attach importance to social contact. In the TY school year, there is no unified quality evaluation mechanism, and there is no unified examination. Therefore, students can choose courses according to their own interests and social development needs. It is based on school education, based on practice, aiming at cultivating students' innovative spirit and practical ability, emphasizing the combination of personal development and social development, respecting The student's main status and initiative spirit and personality develop healthily, focusing on the lifelong sustainable development of students and providing a comprehensive quality education for young people.

3.4 Strengthening of vocational education

Secondary education and higher education in Ireland highlight the importance of vocational education in Ireland. For example, in TY education, many professional courses are set up, with relevant career guidance, and students' work placements and trainees are emphasized, which strengthens professional knowledge and awareness. In addition to setting up academic and vocational courses for students to choose from, the comprehensive secondary school can prepare for both further studies and employment. After graduating from high school, students can get three kinds of certificates. One is a general high school diploma. At least five courses are required. The scores are divided into three grades. The highest grade A can get the opportunity to progress to higher education. One is occupation. Graduation certificate, there are two vocational and technical examination subjects in the five courses; the other is the application diploma. Students are required to take general education courses, vocational education courses and vocational and technical courses. The application diploma is not used for further study.

In higher education, the level of professionalism and practicality of universities is also high. Take Dublin University as an example. The school has signed student internship agreements with thousands of companies. The school is responsible for regularly recommending student internships to the internship unit. Students can also apply for internships. Almost all students have internship opportunities, and the internship period is usually about one year. Some schools, such as the Shannon Hotel Management School, offer students one year to one and a half years of paid internship opportunities. Dublin University of Technology attaches great importance to the professionalization of higher education. Most of the teachers in the school come from the industry and have rich experience in teaching. The teaching is also very practical. It is vital for students to gain valuable work experience during college. Once they graduate, they can make a career position and get into work quickly. The concept of vocational education in Ireland runs through the entire education process. Due to this professional education concept, Irish graduates not only have high comprehensive quality, but also have a high level of professionalism, and the employment rate in the world employment market is very high.

3.5　Higher Education, the Hot Land of Innovative Education

Ireland is a country dominated by agriculture and animal husbandry, but since the 1990s, Ireland's economy has developed rapidly, known as the "European economic tiger". Such achievements are closely related to its innovative ideas and policies for the transformation of innovative achievements.

First of all, we should advocate educational innovation. Since the early 1990s, the Irish government began to carry out the "innovation plan" reform. The government adjusted its development strategy and took innovation as the leading force. The innovation reform of higher education is also the most important part. First, the Ministry of Education and Science was set up to actively invest a large amount of money in support of education. Statistics show that 19% of Ireland's GDP is spent on education, which shows that the government attaches great importance to education.

Secondly, we should establish an innovative R&D system, which consists of universities, national R&D institutions and enterprises. 90% of basic research in Ireland is undertaken by universities. In the IMD International Competitiveness Assessment in 2005, Ireland ranked first in the indicator of "the education system meets the economic needs", which shows that there is a close relationship between education and economy.

Thirdly, we should promote the "Research Program for Educational Institutions", focusing on the integration of natural science and humanities. By 2005, 24 major research centers had been established, such as the University of Dublin and Trinity College of Dublin, which jointly established a union of research and innovation universities, located in the University of Dublin Science and Technology Innovation Park. The innovation plan stipulates that in the next five years, all Ph. D. students in both schools will be required to add an innovation and business course, aiming at increasing the awareness of Ph. D. students to participate in business operations. In addition to the curriculum, these students will also form groups in daily teaching, do some practical innovative projects, so that students can receive relevant training at school. It has changed the situation that doctoral students do pure and practical decoupled research and academic research in the past. This kind of research is difficult to apply for government funds, and it is also difficult to have commercial value. Doctoral graduates usually have to accumulate enough ability and capital to start a business after many years of work. Now, through the integration of industry, education and research, doctoral students can directly incubate companies through university incubation centers and facilities. To set up a University Alliance for scientific research and innovation is to shorten the distance between research and market and shorten the time from graduation to entrepreneurship.

Finally, we should promote the "Educational Research Program" and actively invest a large amount of funds for the infrastructure of higher education, the implementation of educational reform and the development of scientific research. To improve the overall level of international competitiveness of Irish universities.

4 The Enlightenment of Irish Education on Chinese Education

4.1 Reforming the education system and increasing government input are fundamental

System reform is a powerful driving force for the development of education. "Where is the channel clear, it is the source of living water. " If the results of education development are clear channels, education reform is the source of living water. The tremendous achievements brought about by the reform of the education system have effectively guaranteed the implementation of the strategic priority of education and have promoted the scientific development of education. The Irish "Innovation Plan" is implemented from the top down. It reforms from various aspects such as education system and educational concept, paying special attention to the universality, fairness, democracy, humanity and practicality of education. China's education reform has entered a critical period of institutional reform. Reforming existing institutional factors that lead to education unfairness requires effective public policies to promote the balanced development of compulsory education, and strive to narrow rather than artificially expand the various kinds of objective education. Gaps and social gaps. Through institutional innovation, decentralization and decentralization of management power, and the flexibility and diversification of the school-running system, education has once again become a vital undertaking for the whole society to participate. Carry forward the spirit of the Chinese nation's education and education, and the outstanding tradition of running a private school, further open up education and liberate the productivity of education. Education should be able to adapt to the needs of social development and economic life, meet the actual needs of adolescents' growth, and be able to effectively improve people's living conditions and improve their quality of life. In addition, government funding is also key. The Irish government invests 19% of GDP each year for education, while China's education in 2012 only accounts for 4% of GDP. Compared with other countries in the world, education investment is also low, still at a low level.

4.2 Incorporating early childhood education into the free education system to solve problems such as "difficulties in entering the park" and improving the breadth of education

From the perspective of the Irish education system, early childhood education before the age of four is still a paid education and is not included in its free education system. However, the education of 4—5 years old preschool is explicitly included in the free education system, but it is not compulsory. Parents are free to choose whether or not the child is enrolled. It can be seen that the Irish government has gradually integrated pre-school education into the free education system in stages, which is common in many developed countries in Europe and America. The breadth and depth of free education is a sign of education and education. In China, according to the Ministry of Education, at present, there are nearly 60 million preschool children of school age between 3 and 6 years old in China, and half of them are unable to receive kindergarten education because of the cost or quota. The number of public kindergartens cannot keep up with the speed of urban development and the needs of residents, and governments at all levels are not enough to support private kindergartens. The phased integration of pre-school education into the free education system is an educational initiative in many countries around the world. Let children receive civilized education earlier, especially in rural areas, to get into kindergartens and solve the problem of unequal access to education and unequal educational resources. We can emulate Irish education, partially integrate early childhood education into the education system, and at the same time not implement compulsory education, implement independent education, adopt educational courses that match the age characteristics of children, and especially oppose the advancement of primary school knowledge. Kindergarten education is an important part of implementing lifelong education and should be taken seriously.

4.3 Weakening the role of the baton of the college entrance examination, reform the education evaluation system, and develop students' independent learning ability and practical ability from the perspective of pragmatism

From TY education we can see that Ireland attaches importance to quality education. TY Education focuses on the development of multiple intelligences. From the courses offered, it covers languages, natural sciences, applied sciences, business, humanities and practice. Students can freely choose courses according to their own wishes. Educational institutions provide courses based on students' individuality development and social development needs. It is based on the overall purpose of improving students' comprehensive quality, respecting students' main body and initiative spirit, focusing on developing people's intellectual potential and cultivating students' sound personality. Students' cognitive, discovery, self-learning, life, development and creativity skills are valued. This kind of education does not regard students as the receiver of book knowledge, but a platform for students to use and display. China's quality education has been promoted for many years, and some schools have also carried out some teaching reforms. However, looking at the whole country, there is still a situation in which "quality education is shouting well and exam-oriented education is firmly grasped". To change the situation of China's "test-oriented education", we must start with the education policy, carry out the curriculum reform and the reform of the multi-teaching evaluation system, start with the evaluation method, break the single evaluation mode of the written test scores, and adopt different studies according to the characteristics of the course content. The evaluation method incorporates the process evaluation into the evaluation system. Pay attention to the value and migration of students' general development for future development, attach importance to cultivating students' self-development ability, enable students to learn independently, cultivate students' ability of lifelong learning, and truly give students space for development.

4.4 Strengthening vocational education, open up the channels of secondary school, gradually realize the con-vergence of the university and higher vocational and technical colleges, and improve the practicality of the majors to solve the problem of graduates' employment difficulties

The employment rate of Irish graduates in the international job market is high, mainly due to the emphasis on vocational education. First of all, from the perspective of secondary education, TY Education offers a variety of specialized courses in science and engineering, liberal arts, business and art, and encourages students to have extensive contacts with the society. Through work internships to accumulate experience, students can understand their own development direction, indirectly Cultivate students' professional awareness and pave the way for their future career development. The comprehensive middle school combines academic knowledge and professional knowledge to set the curriculum and gives students more choices. From the perspective of the professionalization process of higher education, with the need of college students for practical and vocational courses after the 1980s, higher education presents a dual-track trend, and the convergence of universities and higher vocational and technical colleges in the curriculum structure, However, the difference between the academic curriculum and the vocational curriculum still exists, which is often due to the continuation of the difference between the high school and the secondary school. The purpose of this reform is to improve the status of higher vocational education and to open up links between universities and higher vocational and technical colleges.

Promote the formation of a dual-track system for higher education by establishing short-term start-up degree programs at university institutions and increasing the proportion of vocational courses at universities. At the same time, through the cooperation and development of projects between universities and enterprises, strengthening the relationship between them will not only promote employment, but also realize knowledge transfer productivity faster.

4.5 Strengthening innovative education and cultivate innovative talents

In recent years, although the reform of education and teaching in China has been steadily advanced, the quality assurance system for higher education has also been continuously improved. With the expansion of the university, the number of graduates has increased year by year, which has led to a decline in the employment rate of graduates; on the other hand, it has led to job vacancies in the job market, students' ability to adapt to the requirements of the job market; more investment in education, less output, and expectations of parents A clear drop. It is time to reform higher education. Nowadays, Chinese universities are facing a shift from the direction of knowledge transfer to the cultivation of ability. The concept of education development will realize a strategic leap from expanding the scale of education to improving the quality of education. Therefore, we should learn from the Irish education system and give the university more autonomy in developing curriculum systems and teaching content to increase the flexibility of school teaching. Accelerate the curriculum reform, realize the gradual integration of undergraduate and vocational and technical colleges, enhance students' practical ability, and make it better suited to the employment market. Increase the research funding of higher education institutions, improve the scientific research level of higher education, and integrate organically with enterprises to transform science into productivity as soon as possible.

In short, Ireland, as a small country, is unknown, but it can be called the European "economic tiger" in just 20 years, and GDP ranks second in Europe. Its educational advantages deserve our research and study.

References

[1] Benner, A. D. & Graham, S. The Transition to High School as a Developmental Process among Multiethnic Urban Youth [J]. *Child Development.* 2009. 80(2): 356—376.

[2] Isakson, K. & Jarvis, P. The Adjustment of Adolescents during the

Transition into High School: A Short-term Longitudinal Study [J]. *Journal of Youth and Adolescence*. 1999. 28 (1):1—26.

[3]汪莲华. 2010. 从过渡年学习项目看教育职业化[J].《职教论坛》第8期.

[4]赵萱. 爱尔兰小学跨文化教育研究[J].《外国中小学教育》. 2012 (1).

[5] Haegeman. 1994. Introduction to Government and Binding Theory [M]. Blackwell Publishers.

[6] R. Ellis. 1985. Understanding Second Language Acquisition [M], Oxford University Press.

[7] Rod Ellis . 1985. Understanding Second Language Acquisition [M]. Oxford University Press.

[8] Stephen D. Krashen. 1981. Second Language Acquisition and Second Language Learning [M]. Pergamon Press.

[9] Diane Larsen-Freeman, Michael H. Long. 2000. An Introduction to Second Language Acquisition Research [M]. Foreign Language Teaching and Research Press (FLTRP).

[10] Vivian Cook. 2000. Linguistics and Second Language Acquisition [M]. Foreign Language Teaching and Research Press FLTRP.

[11] Jack C. Richards, John Platt and Heidi Platt. 1998. London Dictionary of Language Teaching and Applied Linguistics (English-Chinese Version) [M]. Foreign Language Teaching and Research Press (FLTRP).

[12] Cook, Vivian. 2000. Linguistics and Second Language Acquisition [M]. Beijing Foreign Language Teaching and Research Press.

[13] Ellis, Rod. 1994. The Study of Second Language Acquisition [M]. Shanghai Foreign Language Education Press.

[14] Polsky, Bernard, 2000. Conditions for Second Language Acquisition [M]. Shanghai Foreign Language Teachingand Research Press.

[15] Williams, Marion &Burden, Roberth. 2000. Psychology ofLanguage Teachers [M]. Beijing Foreign LanguageTeaching and Research Press.

[16]刘珣. 2000. 对外汉语教育学引论[M].北京语言大学出版社.

[17]王建勤主编. 1997. 汉语作为第二语言的习得研究[M].北京语言大学出版社.

[18]赵金铭主编. 2007. 对外汉语教学概论[M].商务印书馆.

[19]刘颂浩. 2007. 第二语言习得导论——对外汉语教学视角[M].世界图书出版公司.

［20］朱志平．2008．汉语第二语言教学理论概要［M］．北京大学出版社．

［21］吴旭东编著．2006．第二语言习得研究——方法与实践［M］．上海外语教育出版社．

［22］刘润清．1995．西方语言学流派［M］．外语教学与研究出版社．

［23］桂诗春．1985．心理语言学［M］．上海外语教育出版社．

［24］高霞．2002．第二语言习得的特性探讨——第二语言习得和母语习得的异同．楚雄师范学院学报［J］．第3期．

［25］李哲．2000．第一语言习得和第二语言习得比较研究．外语与外语教学［J］．第6期．

［26］贾冠杰,王跃洪,张冬梅．1999．第二语言学习与第一语言习得的异同．河南师范大学学报［J］．第3期．

［27］徐志明．《欧美语言学简史》．学林出版社．2005年．

［28］刘润清．《西方语言学流派》．外语教学与研究出版社．1995年．

［29］岑麒祥．《语言学史概要》．世界图书出版公司．2008年．

［30］罗宾斯．《简明语言学史》．中国社会科学出版社．1997年．

［31］封宗信．《现代语言学流派概论》．北京大学出版社．2006年．

［32］汪大昌．《普通语言学纲要》．北京大学出版社．2004年．

［33］赵世开．《美国语言学简史》．上海外语教育出版社．1989年．

［34］冯志伟．《现代语言学流派》．陕西人民出版社．1987年．

［35］伍铁平．《语言学是一门领先的科学》．北京语言学院出版社．1994年．

［36］李凤琴．《中国现代语法学研究论文精选》．上海外语教育出版社．1989年．

［37］顾钢．《乔姆斯基理论四十年发展概述．》．天津师大学报．1999．(4)．

［38］［英］库克．《乔姆斯基的普遍语法教程》．外语教学与研究出版社．2000年．

［39］石定栩．《乔姆斯基的句法形式——历时进程与最新理论》．北京语言文学大学出版社．2002年．

［40］程工．《chomsky新论:语言学理论最简方案》．外国语言学．1994年．

［41］刘宇红．《乔姆斯基语法的类典型分析》．外语与外语教学．2002年8月．

［42］徐志明．《欧美语言学简史》．学林出版社．2005年．

［43］刘润清．《西方语言学流派》．外语教学与研究出版社．1995年．

［44］汪大昌.《普通语言学纲要》.北京大学出版社.2004年.

［45］李凤琴.《中国现代语法学研究论文精选》.上海外语教育出版社.1989年.

［46］赵世开.《美国语言学简史》.上海外语教育出版社.1989年.

［47］冯志伟.《现代语言学流派》.陕西人民出版社.1987年.

［48］胡明扬.《西方语言学名著选读》.中国人民大学出版社.1988年.

［49］伍铁平.《语言学是一门领先的科学》.北京语言学院出版社.1994年.

［50］王钢.《普通语言学基础》.湖南教育出版社.2001年.

［51］李荣.《美国结构主义与转换生成语法之比较》.《伊犁师范学院学报》.2008（2）.

［52］王伟.《试论乔姆斯基的转换生成语法理论及其现实意义》.《辽宁教育学院学报》.1995（2）.

［53］赵永刚.《转换生成语言学的发展历程与研究走向》.《辽宁医学院学报》.2007（4）.

［54］李育林.《对乔氏语法发展轨迹的回顾》.《湖南科技学院学报》.2007（10）.

［55］何晓炜.《chomsky最简方案的新发展——最简方案之框架介绍》.外语教学与研究.2000（2）.

［56］徐烈炯.《生成语法理论》.上海外语教育出版社.1998年.

［57］诺姆.乔姆斯基著,宁春岩等译注.《乔姆斯基语言学文集》.湖南教育出版社.2006年.

［58］李延福.《国外语言学通观》.山东教育出版社.1996年.

［59］林玉山.《现代语言学的历史和现状》.河南人民出版社.2000年.

［60］［丹麦］威廉.汤姆逊著,黄振华译.《十九世纪末以前的语言学史》.科学出版社.1960年.

［61］陈友良.《乔姆斯基形式句法推导过程的变迁》.《外语教学》.2006（3）.

［62］徐烈炯.《生成语法纵横谈》.《上海外国语学院学报》.1986（3）.

［63］王鑫.《从结构主义到转换生成语言学》.《现代语文》.2006（10）.

［64］陆俭明.《乔姆斯基句法理论与汉语研究》.《外国语》.2002（4）.

［65］孔令强.《浅谈转换生成语法的独创性》.《陕西师范学院学报》.2006（7）.

［66］李红霞.《深层结构与表层结构》.《广东行政学院学报》.2004（6）.

［67］顾钢.《"乔姆斯基理论"四十年发展概述》.《天津师大学报》.1999（4）.

［68］潘怡.《从"深层结构"看乔姆斯基革命》.《吉林大学学报》1993（2）.

［69］陈友良.《乔姆斯基形式句法推导过程的变迁》.《外语教学》.2006（2）.

［70］孙继红.《生成语法的现阶段局限性》.《辽宁师范大学学报》.2009年.

［71］何晓炜.《最简方案新框架内的句法推导——chomsky(1998)〈语段推导评述〉》.现代外语.2000(3).

［72］王晓俊.英语写作教学新模式探索——中介语理论对英语写作教学模式的启示［J］.河南财政税务高等专科学校学报.2009年.

［73］陈慧琳.日本学生汉语语音偏误分析及教学对策［J］.山东师范大学硕士论文.2013年.

［74］周漫.藏族学生英语写作中的错误分析［J］.河西学院学报.2005年.

［75］田虎.中亚留学生汉语话题句习得研究［J］.新疆师范大学硕士论文.2014.

［76］黄飞龙.浅析大学生英语口语的石化现象［J］.考试周刊.2011.

［77］石进容.粤方言对英语语音学习的负迁移作用及应对策略［J］.华中师范大学硕士论文.2013年.

［78］张兰.试论英汉对比分析在高职英语教学中的应用［J］.成功（教育）.2007年.

［79］章铭.如何在外语学习中充分调动母语正迁移的作用［J］.上海师范大学硕士论文.2005年.

［80］李俏.二语习得和外语教学的认知心理学探讨［J］.课程.教材.教法.2005年.

［81］吴冬萍刘晓冰.从认知心理学角度浅析二语习得［J］.时代文学（下半月）.2010年.

［82］路云.英语精读课堂输入与输出的衔接［J］.泰安教育学院学报岱宗学刊.2008年.

［83］杨国顺.输出理论与高中英语写作教学［J］.南京师范大学硕士论文.2008年.

［84］张帆卢魁.基于输入输出假说的大学英语口语教学改革［J］.科技信息.2010年.

［85］吴宇.高职院校英语课堂提问有效性研究［J］.西南大学硕士论文

.2009年.

[86]张诚.语言输入假说对我国外语教学的启示[J].河北理工大学学报(社会科学版).2006年.

[87]陈静.论阅读教学中语法翻译法与交际法结合的必要性[J].华东师范大学硕士论文.2009年.

[88]王卓.浅谈第二语言习得在高职英语教学中的运用[J].长春理工大学学报(高教版).2009年.

[89]张曼.第二语言习得对英语教学的启发与指导[J].济宁师范专科学校学报.2007年.

[90]许冬梅.克拉申的输入假说在大学英语写作教学中的应用[J].湖北广播电视大学学报.2013年.

[91]邓跃平.可理解性输入对大学生英语词汇习得的作用[J].青海师范大学学报(哲学社会科学版).2007年.

[92]唐挺.语文学习中的习得与学得[J].读与写(教师教育).2008年.

[93]王文静.背诵在高职非英语专业英语教学中的应用[J].华中师范大学硕士论文.2008年.

[94]梁爱民."可理解性输入"与"最近发展区"概念支架类型研究[J].济南大学学报(社会科学版).2010年.

[95]穆晓岩.语言输入与输出模式在大学英语课堂中的运用[J].语文学刊(外语教育教学).2014年.

[96]张红王佳."可理解性输入"在"综合英语"教学中的应用[J].青春岁月.2012年.

References

[1] Argyle, Michael 1991: Intercultural Communication. In Larry A. Samovar and Richard E. Porter: Intercultural Com-munication: A Reader. Wadsworth, Inc., CA: USA.

[2] Lustig, M. W. and Koester, J. 1996. Intercultural Competence: Interpersonal Communication Across Cultures. Harper Collins College Publishers. NY, USA.

[3] Larry A. Samovar and Richard E. Porter 1991: Basic Principles of Intercultural Communication. In Larry A. Samovar and Richard E. Porter: Intercultural Communication: A Reader. Wadsworth, Inc., CA: USA.

[4] James A. Banks. 1996. An Introduction to Multicultural Education, SIMUL Press, p2.

[5] Barber, W., & Badre, A. (1998). Culturability: The merging of culture and usability. In Proceedings of the 4th Conference on Human Factors & the Web. Retrieved November 15, 2007, from http://research.microsoft.com/users/marycz/hfweb98/barber/

[6] Chen, S. J, & Ford, N. (1998). Modeling user navigation behaviors in a hypermedia-based learning system: An individual differences approach. International Journal of Knowledge Organization, 25(3), 67-78.

[7] Cowen, L., Ball, L. J., & Delin, J. (2002). An eye-movement analysis of web-page usability. In X. Faulkner, J. Finlay, & F. Détienne (Eds.), Proceedings of HCI 2002: People and Computers XVI—Memorable yet Invisible (pp. 317-335). London: Springer-Verlag.

[8] Salvucci, D. D. (1999). Mapping eye movements to cognitive processes. Unpublished doctoral dissertation, Carnegie Mellon University, Pittsburgh, PA.

[9] Faiola, A. (2005). Cross-culture cognition and online information design: Identifying cognitive styles among web designers of diverse national origin. Unpublished doctoral dissertation, Purdue University, West Lafayette,

IN.

[10] Ford, N., Wood, F., & Walsh, C. (1994). Cognitive styles and searching. Online & CD-ROM Review, 18(2), 79-86.

[11] Ford, N., Wilson, T. D., Foster. A., Ellis. D., & Spink. A. (2002). Information seeking and mediated searching: Part 4—cognitive styles in information seeking. Journal of the American Society for Information Science and Technology, 53(9). 728-735.

[12] Hall, E. T. (1959). The silent language. New York: Doubleday.

[13] Hall, E. T. (1976). Beyond culture. New York: Anchor Press.

[14] Hofstede, G. (1980). Culture's consequences: In-ternational differences in work-related value. Newbury Park, CA: Sage.

[15] Hofstede, G. (1991). Culture and organizations: Software of the mind. London: McGraw-Hill.

[16] Jacob, R. J. K., & Karn, K. S. (2003). Eye tracking in human-computer interaction and usability research: Ready to deliver the promises (section commentary). In J. Hyona, R. Radach, & H. Deubel (Eds.), Cognitive and applied aspects of eye movement research. Amsterdam: Elsevier Science, pp. 573-605.

[17] Kim, H., & Allen, B. 2002. Cognitive and Task Influence on Web Searching Behavior. Journal of the American Society for Information Science and Technology, 53(2), 109-119.

[18] Marcus, A., & Gould, E. W. (2000). Crosscurrents, cultural dimensions and global Web user-interface design. In-teractions, 7(4), 32-46.

[19] Masuda, T., & Nisbett, R. E. (2001). Attending holistically versus analytically: Comparing the context sensitivity of Japanese and Americans. Journal of Personality and Social Psychology, 81, 992-934.

[20] Nisbett, R. E. (2003). The geography of thought: How Asians and Westerners think differently—and why. New York: Free Press.

[21] Nisbett, R. E., & Norenzayan, A. (2002). Culture and cognition. In D. Medin & H. Pashler (Eds.), Stevens' handbook of experimental psychology (3rd ed.). New York: John Wiley & Sons. Retrieved May 15, 2007, from http://www-personal.umich.edu/~nisbett/cultcog2.pdf

[22] Nisbett, R. E., Peng, K., Choi, I., & Norenzayan, A. (2001). Culture and systems of thought: Holistic versus analytic cognition. Psychological Review, 108(2), 291-310.

[23] Singh, N., & Pereira, A. (2005). The culturally customized Web

site: Customizing Web sites for the global marketplace. Burlington, MA: Elsevier Butterworth-Heinemann.

[24] Poole, A., & Ball. L. J. (2005). Eye tracking in human-computer interaction and usability research: current status and future prospects. In C. Ghaoui (Ed.), Encyclopedia of Human-Computer Interaction. Hershey, PA: Idea Group Reference. (pp. 211-219)

[25] Riding, R., & Rayner, S. G. (1998). Cognitive styles and learning strategies: Understanding style differences in learning and behaviour. London: D. Fulton Publishers.

[26] Rubin, J. (1994). Handbook of usability testing: How to plan, design, and conduct effective tests (1st ed.). New York: Wiley.

[27] Virzi, R. A. (1990). Streamlining in the design process: Running fewer subjects. In Proceedings of the Human Factors Society 34th Annual Meeting. New York: Human Factors & Ergonomics Society. (pp. 291-294)

[28] Yuan, X., Liu, H., Xu, S., & Wang, Y. (2005). The impact of different cultures on e-business Web design-Comparison research of Chinese and Americans. In Proceedings of the 11th International Conference on Human-Computer Interac-tion [CD-ROM]. Las Vegas, NV: Mira Digital Publishing. References.

[29] He Hengheng, A Study on Chinese Culture Aphasia in College English Teaching, Overseas English, 2018, (6): 4-10.

[30] Hu Wenzhong, Foreign Language Teaching and Cultural Teaching, Changsha: Hunan Education Press, 1997.

[31] Zai Anran, and Cui Shuhui, Cultural Dialogue: Chinese Culture and Cross-cultural Communication. Beijing: Beijing University Press, 2010.

[32] Dai Xiaodong, An Analysis of the Evolution of Cross-cultural Communication from the European Center to the Multi-Center. Academic Research. 2011, (3): 137-145.

[33] Gao Yongchen, The Value and Culture of Empathy in Cross-Cultural Communication, Foreign Language and Foreign Language Teaching, 2005, (12):17-20.

[34] Gao Yongchen, An Appropriate Principle of Empathy in Cross-cultural Communication, Foreign Language and Foreign Language Teaching, 2003, (8): 32-36.

[35] Hu Genshen, International Exchange and Pragmatics from Practice to Theory, Beijing: Tsinghua University Press, 2004.

[36] Higher Education Department of the Ministry of Education, College English Curriculum Requirements, Beijing: Foreign Language Teaching and Research Press, 2007.

[37] Yu Jie, Wang Yunlong, Cultivation of College Students' Cultural Self-confidence in the New Age, Journal of Heilongjiang Institute of Technology, 2019(12):58-61.

www.ingramcontent.com/pod-product-compliance
Lightning Source LLC
Chambersburg PA
CBHW080408230426
43662CB00016B/2351